THE BIBLE DOCTRINE OF INSPIRATION

Basil Manly, Jr.

INTRODUCTION BY TIMOTHY GEORGE
TIMOTHY AND DENISE GEORGE, EDITORS

BROADMAN
& HOLMAN
PUBLISHERS

Nashville, Tennessee

4212-51
0-8054-1251-4

Dewey Decimal Classification: 286
Subject Heading: Bible—Inspiration
Library of Congress Card Catalog Number: 95-35293

Unless otherwise noted all Scripture quotations are from the King James Version
or the author's own translation.

Interior design by Leslie Joslin
Cover design by Steve Diggs & Friends

Library of Congress Cataloging-in-Publication Data
Manly Jr., Basil, 1825–1892
    The Bible Doctrine of Inspiration/ Basil Manly, Jr.; Timothy
George, editor; Denise George, editor.
        p. cm.—(Library of Baptist Classics, vol. 1)
    Originally published: New York: A.C. Armstrong, 1888.
    ISBN 0-8054-1251-4
    1.Bible—Inspiration. 2. Southern Baptist Convention—Doc-
trines.
    I. George, Timothy. II. George, Denise. III. Title. IV. Series.
BS480.M32   1995
220.1'3—dc20   95-35293
                                                   CIP
1 2 3 4 5 6 00 99 98 97 96 95

Contents

Part III: Objections to Inspiration

General Editors' Introduction

The Baptist movement as we know it today began as a small persecuted sect in pre-Revolutionary England. One critic labeled them as "miscreants begat in rebellion, born in sedition, and nursed in faction." Excluded by law from the English universities, Baptists developed their own structures for pastoral training. They also wrote hymns, preached sermons, published confessions, and defended their beliefs against skeptics, detractors, and rival religious groups of all kinds. From the popular works of John Bunyan and Benjamin Keach to the learned theology of John Gill and Andrew Fuller, Baptists wrote with a passion and with a purpose. In time a large body of Baptist literature was developed, writings that both reflected and contributed to the emerging sense of Baptist identity.

The Southern Baptist Convention was organized in 1845 for the purpose of "eliciting, combining, and directing the energies of the whole denomination in one sacred effort, for the propagation of the Gospel." This was an ambitious undertaking for the 293 "delegates," as they were then called, who gathered in Augusta, Georgia, and embraced this far-reaching vision at the founding meeting of the convention. Through the years the SBC has suffered numerous setbacks and distractions—the Civil War, Reconstruction, the Great Depression, social unrest, denominational strife, and much more. Yet through it all God has graciously blessed Southern Baptists in ways that future historians will surely record as remarkable. By the end of the twentieth century, Southern Baptists had grown into America's largest Protestant denomination, a fellowship of some fifteen million members in nearly forty thousand congregations supporting more than nine thousand missionaries.

Drawing on this rich heritage, the Library of Baptist Classics presents a series of books reflecting the faith and vision of Southern Baptists over the past 150 years. We are republishing in fresh editions and with new introductions a collection of seminal writings. These works have proven their worth as classics among Southern Baptists in the past and still speak powerfully to Baptists and other evangelical Christians today.

The Library of Baptist Classics includes writings of pastors, theologians, missionary statesmen, and denominational leaders from the past. Some of them are popular, others scholarly in form. They include sermons, doctrinal treatises, missionary biographies, and an anthology of Baptist confessions, covenants, and catechisms. Most of these writings have been long out of print. We present them now in the fervent hope that the Lord will see fit to use them again, as He has in the past, not only to remind us of the great legacy we have received, but also to inspire us to be faithful shapers of the future under the lordship of Jesus Christ.

Timothy George and Denise George,
General Editors

Introduction

TIMOTHY GEORGE

Basil Manly's *The Bible Doctrine of Inspiration* was written for one reason: to present a clear, comprehensive account of the historic Christian belief in the Bible as the divinely inspired Word of God. When the book was first published in 1888, it was acclaimed as "the best monograph on inspiration that has been produced by an American scholar."[1] From England the famous British preacher, Alexander Maclaren, wrote to the author praising his lucid, well-considered treatment of such a vital topic and commending his "unflinching contention for the authority of the Bible, which so many of our would-be theological instructors now-a-days ignore."[2]

Significantly, Manly did not call his book the "Baptist Doctrine of Inspiration." It was the "Bible Doctrine" he sought to expound. Manly was loyal to his denomination, but on this issue he realized that Baptists stood shoulder-to-shoulder with all evangelical, Bible-believing Christians as champions of the Reformation principle of *sola Scriptura*, "Scripture alone." For this reason his book appealed not only to Baptist believers in America but to earnest seekers throughout the Christian world.

All the same, Manly's book did have a direct influence within his own denomination, the Southern Baptist Convention. Indeed, as we shall see, it was precipitated by a crisis within the very seminary Manly had helped to establish some thirty years before. In a sense, Manly spoke not only for himself in this book but also for the founding of the Southern Baptist Theological Seminary and, even more broadly, for the vast majority of Baptist folk—pastors and lay persons alike—who would have heartily agreed with Roger Williams when he declared that "every word, syllable and tittle in that Scripture of writing is the word, or immediate revealed will of God."[3]

The Bible Doctrine of Inspiration is a classic exposition of this fundamental Baptist commitment to the authority of Holy Scripture. More than one hundred years after its first publication, it remains a timely and powerful book. The topic with which it deals is still at the heart of Baptist theology and church life today. For this reason we have chosen it for inclusion in the Library of Baptist Classics. To place this important work in its proper context, we shall review the life and ministry of its author, examine the circumstances of its writing, and discuss its relevance for the life and faith of the church today.

Basil Manly, Jr. (1825–1892)

Basil Manly, Jr., was born on December 19, 1825, in Edgefield, South Carolina. He came from a noble line of descent. His paternal grandfather, also named Basil, had served as a captain during the American Revolution. His father, Basil Manly, Sr., was one of the leading Baptist ministers in the South.[4] While Basil, Jr., was still a nursing infant his father became pastor of the historic First Baptist Church of Charleston. When he was twelve the family moved to Tuscaloosa, Alabama, where Manly,

Sr., served as the second president of the University of Alabama. In 1840, Manly, Jr., enrolled as a student in this school where he excelled in all of his studies.

Under the godly influence of his parents, Manly, Jr., was brought up in the nurture and admonition of the Lord. At age fourteen, while reading a biography of Jonathan Edwards, he came under deep personal conviction of sin.

"I was brought to such a loathing of myself, for the ingratitude, and neglect, and meanness, as it seemed to me, of disregarding the Savior, and to such an admiration of holiness that I came deliberately and solemnly to the conclusion, that I would try to become a Christian."[5]

Manly publicly shared his experience in Christ with the Baptist congregation in Tuscaloosa, and was baptized the following week by his father in the Black Warrior River. "The afternoon was very agreeable for the purpose," his father recalled, "the sun overshadowed, dry ground, scene tranquil, and multitudes of people present. I committed him to God, so far as belongs to me, wholly and unreservedly hoping the Lord may like him and use him for His glory."[6]

In May, 1844, Manly was licensed to preach the gospel. Later that year he began his theological studies at the Newton Theological Institute in Massachusetts, the first seminary founded by Baptists in America. In the course of his studies at Newton, the Baptist denomination, along with the entire country, became embroiled in a fierce debate over slavery and abolitionism. Two days after the Southern Baptist Convention was organized in Augusta, Georgia, Manly transferred to Princeton Theological Seminary. Here he completed his ministerial preparation under such notable teachers as Charles Hodge, Archibald Alexander, and Samuel Miller.

On May 17, 1847, Manly received his diploma indicating that he had successfully completed the required course of study. Two years later another southerner, James P. Boyce, also enrolled at Princeton. He and Manly, together with John A. Broadus and William Williams, would be linked as partners in the founding of the Southern Baptist Theological Seminary. Boyce, like

Manly, drank deeply from the wells of his great Reformed teachers at Princeton. In two important respects Princeton became a model for the first Baptist seminary in the South: first, the commitment to historic Christian orthodoxy expressed in a confession of faith conscientiously subscribed to by every member of the faculty; and, secondly, a desire to hold in balance academic excellence and genuine piety, to model the ideal of godly learning.[7]

Following his studies at Princeton, Manly was ordained to the gospel ministry and called to the Providence Baptist Church in Sumter County, Alabama. In September, 1850, Manly, only twenty-four years of age, moved to Richmond, Virginia, to begin his pastoral labors at the First Baptist Church in that city. Four years later he resigned to become the founding principal of Richmond Female Institute. During these years he was involved in many activities which had a far-reaching impact on the life of the church: the establishment of Sunday schools in local congregations, the publication (with his father) of the first Baptist hymnal, the distribution of the Scriptures, the promotion of missionary and benevolence programs, along with numerous writing, preaching, and evangelistic activities.[8]

When Southern Seminary opened its doors in Greenville, South Carolina in October, 1859, Manly was one of the four founding faculty members. His official title was Professor of Biblical Introduction and Old Testament, although he fulfilled many other roles as well in his long association with that institution. One of his first assignments had been to draft a confessional statement, the "Abstract of Principles," for the new school. Boyce, in setting forth the plan for the seminary, had stressed the importance of a solid theological foundation.

"The doctrinal sentiments of the faculty are of greater importance than the proper investment and expenditure of its funds; and the trust devolved upon those who watch over its interests should in that respect, if in any, be sacredly guarded."[9]

Drawing upon earlier Baptist confessional standards such as the First (1644) and Second (1689) London Confessions, Manly proposed an Abstract of Principles which consisted of twenty articles ranging from the Scriptures to the Last Judgment. These articles of faith were included in the fundamental laws of the seminary. Every professor was expected to teach in accordance with and not contrary to these articles. Failure to do so would be considered grounds for his resignation or removal by the trustees.

Manly shared fully in the labors of the young seminary as it struggled to survive amidst the convulsions of the American Civil War, Reconstruction, denominational strife, and economic duress. On one occasion the four original founders gathered at the Boyce home in Greenville to join in prayer and a deep seeking of the will of God. At the end of the day Broadus said, "Suppose we quietly agree that the seminary may die, but we will die first."[10] All heads were silently bowed and the matter was decided.

From the beginning Manly was greatly beloved by his students for his judicious and reverent handling of the Scriptures. For him the Bible was never merely a book of ancient history or great literature. He led his students to apply the meaning of the biblical text to their own spiritual walk. John R. Sampey, who sat in Manly's classes, described the approach of his mentor:

"He knew how to unfold the deep spiritual content of the Psalms with rare delight and sympathy. Having himself been chastened by bereavement and affliction, he could put the student into closest sympathy with Job and Jeremiah and other suffering saints. He taught men reverence and resignation and faith."[11]

Manly's reverent approach to teaching the Bible reflected a disciplined life of devotion and prayer. The coherence of piety and intellect was at the heart of his pedagogical method and made a lasting impression on his students. One of them later recalled the powerful impact of Manly's classroom prayers.

> It was the custom at the seminary, then, as now, to spend a few moments in prayer before each lecture. We have forgotten a great many things in the lectures of Dr. Manly, but we shall carry the memory of his prayers through all eternity. Sometimes he seemed to forget his surroundings and quietly to soar aloft on the wings of

prayer—and he carried his student hearers with him near to the throne. When prayer was done we all felt that after all the first and best things was piety, and yet this very connection quickened our interest in the study of God's Word. Not unfrequently, when the "amen" was said, we had to brush away the tears before we could see our notebooks. After an experience of many years in all sorts of meetings I can deliberately say that nowhere at any time have I felt heaven on earth so sweetly and so powerfully as in Dr. Manly's lecture room.[12]

Manly's tenure as a professor at Southern Seminary was interrupted by an eight-year stint (1871–79) as president of Georgetown College in Georgetown, Kentucky. Manly had a measure of success in this post although the difficulty of imposing discipline on rowdy undergraduates ("If only I can manage to reduce to order the boisterous boys," he lamented), and the never-ending task of raising enough funds to keep the institution afloat, took their toll.[13]

During his years as president of Georgetown, Manly remained vitally interested in the progress of Southern Seminary. In 1877, the seminary was moved from Greenville to Louisville. Two years later Manly returned to the seminary to fill the position vacated by Crawford Howell Toy. We turn now to the circumstances which led to this decision as it had a direct bearing on the origin of Manly's *The Bible Doctrine of Inspiration*.

The Toy Controversy

One of the most painful episodes in the history of Southern Baptists was the controversy over Crawford H. Toy, who had joined the faculty of Southern Seminary in 1869. At that time, Toy's commitment to the total truthfulness of Holy Scripture was explicitly stated in his impressive inaugural address: "The Bible, its real assertions being known, is in every iota of its substance absolutely and infallibly true."[14]

Over the years, however, Toy gradually moved away from this position as he came more and more under the influence of Darwinian evolutionism and the theory of Pentateuchal criticism advanced by the German scholars Kuenen and Wellhausen.

Enamored by the heady theories of "progressive" scholarship, Toy came to deny that many of the events recorded in the Old Testament had actually occurred. Moreover, he also questioned the christological implications of many messianic prophecies, including Genesis 49:10 which the New Testament (Rev. 5:5) specifically applies to Christ. In 1876, Boyce wrote Toy a "gentle remonstrance and earnest entreaty" concerning his views on inspiration.[15] During the 1878–79 academic year, Toy's teaching became a matter of concern to the seminary trustees, chaired at that time by the venerable Baptist leader, J. B. Jeter. Boyce requested Toy to refrain from espousing his radical critical views in the classroom. The latter agreed, but found that he could not do so. In the spring of 1879, Toy, under considerable pressure, tendered his resignation, acknowledging that it had "become apparent to me that my views of inspiration differ considerably from those of the body of my brethren."[16]

Broadus spoke for Boyce, the faculty, and the trustees (with the exception of two dissenting members) when he characterized the painful necessity of Toy's removal from the seminary community: "Duty to the founders of the institution and to all who had given money for its support and endowment, duty to the Baptist churches from whom its students must come, required [Boyce] to see to it that such teaching should not continue." Boyce took no joy in the departure of Toy. In a poignant scene at the railway station, Boyce embraced Toy and, lifting his right arm, exclaimed: "Oh, Toy, I would freely give that arm to be cut off if you could be where you were five years ago, and stay there."[17] Toy subsequently became a professor at Harvard University where he affiliated with the Unitarian church and embraced even more radically critical views on the inspiration and authority of the Bible.

At the time the Toy Controversy broke loose, Manly was serving as a member of the seminary's board of trustees. He was an active participant in the negotiations which led to Toy's resignation. Both the faculty and the board felt that only Manly could fill the vacancy. No one else commanded sufficient respect, or possessed adequate scholarly acumen, to restore the damaged credibility of the seminary. With some apprehension, but sensing clearly the leading of divine providence, Manly accepted the new assignment, hoping, as he said, "that this move will be my last one."[18]

It is important to note that Manly, no less than Boyce and Broadus, was grieved personally over the forced departure of Toy. There was never any thought of a personal vendetta or witch-hunt. Manly was deeply concerned for Toy's spiritual welfare. He hoped that the shock of the experience might lead his brilliant friend and former student to realize "the extent to which he has drifted from the moorings of his own older position." Regrettably, such was not to be the case. In 1881, Manly reflected on certain writings of Toy which had come to his attention:

"I read them . . . with professed sadness, and a despair of the return to truth for a man for whom I have so high a respect, and so sincere an affection. He has breathed an atmosphere of doubt, till it has become his ritual air, and is as firmly convinced of the speculations as others are of the most unequivocal realities."[19]

Still, on a personal level, the two men remained friends to the end. When Manly died in 1892, Toy wrote a moving eulogy for his former teacher whom he always held in high esteem.

What was at stake in the Toy Controversy was not merely the deviant views of a single professor but rather the theological integrity of the seminary itself. No one saw this more clearly than Manly who, after all, had originally drafted the Abstract of Principles, including the first article on the Scriptures:

"The Scriptures of the Old and New Testaments were given by inspiration of God, and are the only sufficient, certain and authoritative rule of all saving knowledge, faith and obedience."

Toy believed that his views had not violated the confessional commitment of the seminary despite the wide variance between his teaching and that of his colleagues. However, with reference to the Abstract, Manly insisted:

"This language must be understood in accordance with the well-known convictions and views of the founders of the seminary, and of the Baptist denomination generally. While I am accustomed to insist on no *theory* of the manner in which inspiration was effected, I hold and teach the fact that the Scriptures are so inspired as to possess infallibility and divine authority."[20]

Doubtless, the departure of Toy contributed to the conservative reputation which Southern Seminary enjoyed within the denomination and beyond. Once on a trip for the seminary, Boyce heard about certain students from Crozier Theological School who were trying to dissuade young preachers from coming to Southern because of the "antediluvian theology taught at Louisville." To which Boyce replied, "If my theology were not older than the days of Noah, it wouldn't be worth teaching!"[21]

On October 1, 1888, just two months before he died, Boyce wrote to his colleague, Basil Manly, Jr. With an eye to the Toy Controversy which was just beginning to subside, he said:

"I greatly rejoice in the certain triumph of the truth. I feel that nothing but our own folly can prevent the success of the seminary. If we keep things orthodox and correct within and avoid injudicious compromises while we patiently submit and laboriously labor, we shall find continuous blessing. So much do I feel this that I look back on my life's work without any apprehension of future disaster."[22]

The Bible Doctrine of Inspiration

On September 1, 1879, Manly delivered his introductory lecture as Professor of Old Testament at Southern Seminary. His topic was "When and How to Study the Bible." Everyone was anxious to hear what the man elected to replace Toy would say in the highly-charged atmosphere of the crisis which still loomed over the school.

Manly began by expressing renewed confidence in and affection for the seminary community. Even though "the years have tinged our locks with gray," he urged his colleagues to march on together as "tried soldiers in the conflicts and successes that await us," in the certain knowledge that the work in which they were engaged was not their own but God's.

He then set forth his philosophy of theological education, the primary purpose of which was to provide "a practical knowledge of the Scriptures."

> "Every school and department of the seminary is mainly valuable as it promotes the elucidation of the Word of God, and the practical application of its teachings. Nor do we fear being charged with bibliolatry in giving the Bible the central, dominant place in our system and in our affections. From the doubt of denial of God's book, the road is short to doubt or denial of God;—and after that come *the abyss*, where all knowledge is not only lost but scoffed at, except that which the brute might enjoy as well."[23]

In this same address he made clear that confidence in the centrality and total truthfulness of the Scriptures in no way lessened the importance of careful, exacting scholarship, including the mastery of the original biblical languages of Hebrew and Greek. Hebrew, of course, was his own specialty and he referred to it as "the earliest tongue which God saw fit to consecrate, by using it for His written communication to man." He concluded his lecture by asserting, "If we are to be mighty in God's work, we must be mighty in God's Word."[24]

Manly's *The Bible Doctrine of Inspiration* grew out of his seminary lectures on this topic. Because of the lingering suspicions from the Toy affair, it was necessary to issue a clear affirmation of the seminary's position on this controversial subject. Manly also hoped to address the wider implications of the assault on the authority of Scripture which stemmed from the acceptance of higher critical theories throughout the Protestant world.

In the summer of 1881, Manly had studied in Germany under Franz Delitzch at the University at Leipzig. He was well acquainted with the current trends in biblical scholarship. He also knew that the dangers posed by destructive criticism of the Bible were not limited to his own fellowship. Among English Baptists Charles Haddon Spurgeon and others were seeking to stave off "the boiling mudshowers of modern heresy" which resulted in the Downgrade Controversy.[25] In 1890, two years after Manly's book was published, Charles A. Briggs condemned "the dogma of verbal inspiration" in his inaugural lecture at

Union Theological Seminary in New York City. Although he was suspended from the ministry by the Presbyterian Church, he continued to teach at Union Seminary.

In the face of these developments, Manly drafted his *The Bible Doctrine of Inspiration* as a deliberate restatement of the historic Protestant doctrine of Scripture. Without naming Toy, he reviewed the impact of the so-called "higher criticism" on biblical studies and made the following conclusion which has lost none of its relevance in the intervening century: "We have no need nor disposition to undervalue either the legitimate method or the fairly established results of modern critical research . . . a true 'higher criticism' may be just as valuable as a false and misguided attempt at it may be dangerous and delusive."

In December, 1886, Manly was assaulted and severely beaten by two robbers as he walked home from the seminary in the evening. For some time he was unable to meet his classes and the following summer was spent in convalescence in Coopers, North Carolina. During this time he completed the manuscript for *The Bible Doctrine of Inspiration*. The book was published by A. C. Armstrong and Son of New York in April, 1888.

Taken as a whole the work is a classic defense of verbal, plenary inspiration of the Bible which he defined thus: "It is that the Bible as a whole is the Word of God, so that in every part of Scripture there is both infallible truth and divine authority." Manly divides his book into three parts in which he first carefully explains the doctrine, then offers proof for it, and then defends it against objections. Manly understood inspiration as that divine influence that secures the accurate transference of truth into human language by a speaker or writer in order to communicate the will and purpose of God to others.

Manly specifically refutes the dictation theory of inspiration and allows fully for both the divine and human element in the process of inspiration. "The Bible is God's Word to man throughout; yet at the same time it is really and thoroughly man's composition. . . . The Word is not *of* man as to its source, nor depending *on* man as to its authority. It is *by* and *through* man as its medium; yet not simply as its channel along which it runs, like water through a lifeless pipe, but *through* and *by* man as the agent voluntarily active and intelligent in its communication. . . . It is all by singular and accumulated evidence declared to be the Word of God; all written by man, all inspired by God."

Manly's Legacy Today

Basil Manly, Jr., died on January 31, 1892, in his 68th year. At his funeral, John A. Broadus remarked: "He was the most versatile man I ever met. I never saw him try to do anything that he did not do it well. The worth of such a man only God can measure."[26] Manly's legacy lives on today in the institutions he served, in the agencies he helped to establish, in the churches he strengthened, above all, perhaps, in the widening influence of the students he taught through whose ministries the gospel of Jesus Christ has been carried throughout the world. In 1933, the Sunday School Board of the Southern Baptist Convention honored the memory of both Broadus and Manly by blending the first syllables of their names into "Broadman Press."

The Bible Doctrine of Inspiration was Manly's major literary contribution. At the time of its publication, it was highly esteemed by leading evangelical scholars such as Benjamin B. Warfield at Princeton and Charles Rufus Brown at Newton. Its purpose, as one historian has put it, "was to forestall any trend on the part of the younger generation of ministers towards the denial of the supernatural element in the Bible. It served as an able work in resolving the conflict that clouded the minds of many truth-seeking Southern Baptist ministers."[27]

In retrospect, we can see how the strong theological foundation laid by Manly and others served Southern Baptists well in the generation which followed them. In the first three decades of the twentieth century nearly every major Protestant denomination in America was wracked by the Fundamentalist-Modernist Controversy. Many theological seminaries founded by godly men to train young ministers in the truth of God's Word succumbed to the alluring tenets of liberalism and the destructively critical study of the Bible. During this period Southern Baptists remained overwhelmingly committed to a high doctrine of Holy

Scripture. This view, which Manly had summarized so ably, was set forth with clarity in 1900 by James M. Frost in a book dedicated "to the Baptists of the world in their contending for the faith once for all delivered to the saints":

"We accept the Scriptures as an all-sufficient and infallible rule of faith and practice, and insist upon the absolute inerrancy and sole authority of the Word of God. We recognize at this point no room for division, either of practice or belief, or even sentiment. More and more we must come to feel as the deepest and mightiest power of our conviction that a 'thus saith the Lord' is the end of all controversy."[28]

Notes

1. Henry C. Vedder, review of *The Bible Doctrine of Inspiration*, in *Baptist Quarter Review* 11 (1889): 253.

2. Letter of Alexander Maclaren to Basil Manly Jr., June 5, 1888.

3. *The Complete Writings of Roger Williams* (New York: Russell and Russell, 1963), 5:387.

4. Timothy George, "Faithful Shepherd, Beloved Minister: The Life and Legacy of Basil Manly, Sr.," *The Alabama Baptist Historian* 27 (1991).

5. Letter of Basil Manly, Jr., to Charles Manly, October 8, 1869.

6. *Diary of Basil Manly, Sr.* (1834–1846), 202.

7. This spirit is expressed in the following statement of Samuel Miller who taught both Manly and Boyce: "Resolved, that I will endeavor, by the grace of God, to set such an example for the candidates for the ministry committed to my care as shall convince them that, though I esteem theological knowledge and all its auxiliary branches of science very highly, I esteem genuine and deep piety as a still more vital and important qualification." William L. McEwan, "Princeton in the Work of the Pastorate," *The Centennial Celebration of the Theological Seminary of the Presbyterian Church in the United States of America* (Princeton, N.J.: The Theological Seminary, 1912): 404–5.

8. On Manly's contribution to Southern Baptist hymnody, see Paul A. Richardson, "Basil Manly, Jr.: Hymnist and Hymnologist," Founders' Day Address, February 4, 1992, at The Southern Baptist Theological Seminary.

9. Boyce's inaugural address, "Three Changes in Theological Institutions," delivered before the Board of Trustees of Furman University, July 31, 1856. See Timothy George, ed., *James Petigru Boyce: Selected Writings* (Nashville: Broadman Press, 1988), 52.

10. John A. Broadus, *Memoir of J. P. Boyce* (New York: A. C. Armstrong and Son, 1893), 200.

11. John R. Sampey, "B. Manly, Jr." *Review and Expositor* 5 (1908): 414–15.

12. William H. Williams, "An Old Student's Reminiscences," *The Seminary Magazine* 5 (April 1892): 390–91.

13. Letter of Basil Manly, Jr., to Sarah M. Manly, October 9, 1871.

14. C. H. Toy, *The Claims of Biblical Interpretation on Baptists* (New York: Lange and Hillman, 1869), 13.

15. A. T. Robertson, *The Life and Letters of John A. Broadus* (Philadelphia: American Baptist Publication Society, 1901), 301.

16. Quoted, L. Russ Bush and Tom J. Nettles, *Baptists and the Bible* (Chicago: Moody Press, 1980), 233.

17. Broadus, *Memoir*, 263–64.

18. Letter of Basil Manly, Jr., to Charles Manly, May 15, 1879.

19. Letter of Basil Manly, Jr., to Charles Manly, December 24, 1881.

20. Letter of Basil Manly, Jr., to Norman Fax, January 4, 1882.

21. George, *Boyce*, 23.

22. Ibid.

23. Basil Manly, Jr., "Why and How to Study the Bible," *Manly Pamphlets*, September 1, 1879, 1–5.

24. Ibid., 12–13.

25. Charles Haddon Spurgeon, *Autobiography* (London: Passmore and Alabaster, 1900), 4:261–62.

26. Robertson, *Life and Letters*, 398.

27. Cox, *Manly, Jr.*, 344.

28. James M. Frost, ed., *Baptist Why and Why Not* (Nashville: Sunday School Board, 1900), 12.

1888 Preface

BASIL MANLY JR.

For more than a quarter of a century it has been my privilege and duty, in giving theological instruction, to discuss the subject of inspiration. As each year I have studied it afresh, my sense of its importance has increased. In examining the accumulating literature on the topic in books, reviews, and newspapers, I have felt moved to get closer to the original sources. I have determined to ask the attention of the public to a study of it specially from a biblical standpoint.

It is easy to present theories. But the question is one of fact, and not of theory. The Bible statements and the Bible phenomena are the decisive considerations in the case. And recognizing this, I have attempted a frank and thorough discussion of the Bible doctrine of inspiration.

At the same time, I have not failed to read anything that seemed to promise to shed light on the subject. I have been desirous to examine all sides of the question, and to seek for truth whether old or new; resolved neither to cling slavishly to confessional or traditional statements, nor to search for original and startling ideas. Originality on a subject like this, which has been under discussion for centuries, would surely be error. But there may be, after all, honest independence of inquiry, a careful sifting of opinions, a fair recasting of views in the mold of one's own thinking, and a subordination of the whole simply to the controlling authority of God's Word. This is all at which I have aimed.

I have freely used whatever I have found in the writings of the able men who have discussed this and kindred themes, without a studied effort either to avoid their phraseology or to conform to their ideas or expressions.

To the candid, faithful examination of those in all Christian denominations who love and honor God's blessed Word, this brief work is offered, whether they are disposed to accept or reject the views advocated. And may the blessing of God rest on this humble attempt to serve Him!

PART I

THE DOCTRINE
OF INSPIRATION

CHAPTER ONE

Preliminary

The Importance of the Subject

The importance of the doctrine of inspiration needs scarcely any elaborate comment or proof. The theological atmosphere is full of discussion on the subject, either directly or indirectly.

Christianity is the religion of the Book. It is not an external organization, nor a system of ceremonies, nor a philosophy. It is not a vague inquiry and aspiration, nor a human invention for man's own convenience or advantage. It is a definite system divinely given, consisting primarily of:

1. *facts*, occurring both on earth and in heaven;

2. *doctrines* in connection with those facts;

3. *commands* growing out of both these; and

4. *promises* based upon them.

The history is so interwoven with the doctrinal teachings, the precepts so combined with the promises, as to be inseparable. The whole is contained in the volume or collection of writings which we call the Bible.

The question, therefore, "Is the Bible the Word of God?" is of the highest importance to us as Christians, as theological students, as ministers, for all our work and life, in our present and in our future labors.

Evangelical Christians generally have recognized this as a vital question. "The Bible, the Bible only, the religion of Protestants," has resounded through many a hall of discussion as the watchword of victory. It has been re-echoed from many a pulpit as the battle cry of freedom from ecclesiastical domination.

While not ignoring the noble and animating history of our Christian forefathers, or forgetting the testimony of all the witnesses for Jesus who have lived and died, we do not base our own confidence, or ground our appeals to others, on conformity to any other standard than the Word of God. Historical associations, ancient confessions, compacts and compromises, the opinions of good and great men within or without the ranks of the denomination to which we belong, can have no decisive weight with us. We must go for guidance, not to the Fathers, but to those who were earlier and greater than the Fathers. We must go to the apostles, and above all to the Lord Jesus Christ Himself.

Deficiencies of an Uninspired Bible

The difference between an inspired and uninspired Bible is of a momentous character. It is closely connected with the question whether we are following God or men, whether our religion is of divine or of human origin. An uninspired Bible, whatever its excellences might be, would have three serious defects.

First, it would furnish no infallible standard of truth. It would leave us liable to all the mistakes incident to failure of the writers, to their errors in judgment, or their defective expressions of correct thought. It would furnish no principle of accurate discrimination between the true and the false, the divine and the human.[1]

Second, it would present no authoritative rule for obedience, and no ground for confident and everlasting hope. It would contain advice instead of commands, suggestions instead of instructions, surmises of good men (perhaps not even of good men) instead of promises of the faithful God. It would give no firm ground on which to base our convictions, to build our hopes, or to order our life.

Third, it would offer no suitable means for testing and cultivating the docile spirit, for drawing man's soul trustfully and lovingly upward to its heavenly Father. It would minister to the pride of reason, instead of to the culture of faith. It would generate perplexity instead of repose, conflict instead of submission, resistance instead of reverence.[2]

Yet we must guard against extravagance of statement, even here. Inspiration is not essential, as it seems sometimes to have been stated or implied, to the historical credibility of Scripture. The facts there recorded would be true and immensely important, even though the record of them were not inspired. The facts given are amply established on historical grounds, and are sufficient, if admitted, to condemn those who reject the Bible. Those facts are necessary logically to furnish a starting point from which to lead them, step by step, into the higher truths.[3] "If you know anything, tell me that," said a great philosopher. "Keep your doubts to yourself. I have enough of my own."

Some Sources of Misapprehension

All professed Christians agree on acknowledging in general that the Bible is "from God," and that it is inspired in some sense, and to some degree. But it cannot be concealed that great differences of opinion often take refuge under this ambiguous phraseology. It is of extreme importance, especially for ministers and teachers of God's Word, to have clear views and correct views of this subject. Inspiration has become the central topic of some of the great and burning controversies of the age. Doubts concerning it are widely felt, and are apparently spreading. These doubts originate, I will not say altogether, but certainly in large measure, in the following sources:

a. In *misconceptions*, either of the doctrine itself as generally held by Evangelical Christians, or of the evidences and arguments by which it is supported;

b. In *presuppositions* and *assumptions* hostile to any supernatural fact, and therefore to any personal, divine communication;

c. In *faulty interpretation* of particular passages of the Bible, bearing on the question.

An unwary advocate, with more zeal than knowledge, may honestly assume an indefensible position. When driven from that, in his panic he may find no secure stopping-place. Or, on the other hand, a kind-hearted, liberal man, in striving to propitiate opponents, and to gain them over by making a specially mild and unobjectionable statement of truth, may unconsciously surrender the very citadel to the enemy.

CHAPTER TWO

Distinctions to Be Noticed

Inspiration Distinguished from Kindred Topics

The question before us is simply: In what sense is the Bible the Word of God? Is it strictly *theopneustos* (divinely breathed) or not? And if so, what does that expression imply?

The subject of inspiration needs to be distinguished from certain kindred topics of great importance. It has complexity and extent enough of its own without borrowing burdens from correlated subjects of investigation. But many students of the subject are unwarily misled by writers who create confusion in a bewildering display of their own learning. They blend in inextricable disorder topics, each of which demands separate and elaborate study. The attempt is sometimes made to embrace at one view, in a brief discussion, all the manifold questions which arise in the study of the Canon, of text criticism, higher criticism, hermeneutics, biblical history, and its connection with secular history. One hurried glance is given at all these subjects. The only result is either the confidence of a shallow dogmatism, which experience shows may be found in the blind following of some rationalist, as well as in adhering to tradition; or else there is a vague impression of extreme mistiness and uncertainty.

Let us name some of these subjects which demand and deserve distinct study, though often confounded with other topics, so as to complicate the discussion as to inspiration.

a. *The Genuineness of the Scriptures*. In this the question is one of authorship; whether the various books that make up the Bible were composed by the men claimed to be their authors. Or, in those cases where no particular author is named, whether they originated at the time and in the circumstances alleged.

b. *Text Criticism*, or *Integrity of the Scriptures*. The question is whether the books that we have are the same as the original. Whether they have been correctly transcribed and faithfully preserved without material addition or diminution.

c. *Higher Criticism*. This is the name given of late to inquiries depending on style, on the mode of thought and expression of different writers, on the vocabulary and tone employed, and various internal peculiarities, by which the age and circumstances and method of composition may be discovered. Of course, these conclusions bear more or less directly on the authorship. They are connected with the topic first named—genuineness—but may extend beyond that question.

d. *Authenticity of the Scriptures* (credibility), or the historical verity of the facts recorded. In that part of the subject the inquiry is: Did those events really occur? Were those discourses delivered? Were those miracles performed as stated? Is the Bible narrative a collection of myths, or legends, or deliberate fictions? Or is it mainly history, with some intermixture of exaggerations and fables? Or is it throughout a statement of facts?

e. *The Canon of Scripture* (what books constitute the inspired volume). On the one side, some deny the authority of certain books commonly received, as Canticles and Esther, or Hebrews, James, and Revelation. On the other, some, as the Romanists, affirm the divine authority of certain books known as the Apocrypha, such as Maccabees, Tobit, etc. Here the issue is not as to the nature of inspiration, but as to the claim that particular books have to be counted in the number of the inspired books.

f. *The Rule of Faith*, or the sufficiency of the Scriptures. The rationalists claim that reason is the rule or standard of belief, either alone, or superior to or conjointly with the Bible. Romanists and other traditionalists affirm that the church is inspired as well as the Bible. Its voice is the voice of God. Theoretically, they allege it as only coordinate with the Bible. But practically they establish it as supreme above the Bible. Along with this they make the tacit assumption that they, and those who agree with them, are the church, and they alone. Though admitting an infallible Bible, they put the supposed infallible interpreter in its place. Thus, as so often happens, extremes meet. Rationalism and ecclesiasticism, diverging from the truth, run round the circle till they agree in establishing themselves as the sovereign arbiter—the one class accepting as true in the Bible only what "finds them," that is, suits them. The other makes the church, that is, the hierarchy, that is, themselves and their allies, the vicegerent of the Almighty, the custodian of truth and of salvation.

g. *The Evidences of Christianity*, or the manifold proofs by which the Christian system as a whole is shown to be true and divine.

While all these topics are interwoven naturally with the subject before us, they are distinct from it. It will conduce both to brevity and to fairness and clearness of discussion, to keep them apart, and to confine ourselves now to the topic in hand.

Inspiration Implies Real Supernatural Interposition

For the last hundred years there has been a growing tendency against the admission of anything supernatural. The sophisms of Hume had a wide influence, carrying out some unwarranted inferences from Locke's philosophy, and misusing certain of the metaphysical subtleties of the Scottish school. Afterwards the transcendental philosophy of Germany, the bold pretensions of positivism, and the shadowy theories of pantheism, all tended to furnish avenues of escape, for those who wished them, from the idea of a living, personal, omnipotent God, who interposes freely and effectively in human affairs.

Anti-Supernatural Notions

A more powerful stimulus, however, has been given to the prevalence of these anti-supernatural notions. These have come by the proneness of many students of physical science who apply their favorite methods of investigation to topics outside of their range. They carry the assumptions which seem to be just in dealing with material phenomena into the domain of theology. Because they find, everywhere in the visible universe, law, order, universal principles, they have undertaken to dethrone the Lawgiver, and to exalt on His throne, in His place, law itself. They deny that the Supreme Being can interpose in any way save that which they have ascertained, or are willing to allow, that He has heretofore done. Hence they deny that He can work a miracle.

Some true Christians have yielded to the force of this current, either unreflectingly, or with some vague idea of a compromise, by which they would gain the support of those of science for religion. Without exactly denying miracles, they have set themselves to pare down within credible limits the wonders recorded in the Bible. They will nibble away at the edge of a miracle, chip off a little here and a little there. They seem to imagine that they have removed the difficulty by reducing its size or changing its form.

Let us not be afraid of admitting the idea and the fact of a miracle. The whole system of Christianity is a stupendous series of miracles.

The Existence of Providence of God

With those who deny this we are not now dealing. For them the question is not about inspiration, but about the existence, or else about the providence, of God. This discussion is designed for those who:

- admit that there is a God,

- that He has communicated with men, and

- that the Bible is in some degree or extent His message.

Inspiration May Be Regarded as an Act or Result

It is an influence proceeding from God, and terminating in certain effects. These effects may be affirmed of the men who wrote and spoke, or of the books written. Both may be properly said to be inspired. Originally it was a question as to the men. Practically, for us now, the question is as to the books. Are they a message from God? If so, in what sense, and to what degree?

Limiting the Inspiration

There are some who conceive that the subject is cleared of difficulty by limiting the inspiration to the writings. The men were not inspired, they say, but only their writings; not all they said or wrote, but just these writings. So Paul was not inspired, but the letters to the Ephesians and Romans were. It will be shown hereafter that not all the utterances or writings, not all the opinions or conduct of the sacred writers are divinely sanctioned, but only their official utterances, their teachings and directions. Inspiration was not a personal and inseparable characteristic, attaching to everything they did or thought. It was a divine gift, imparted for a special purpose. There is no proof of its extending beyond the purpose for which it was given, that of making them the accurate and authoritative messengers of God's will and truth to men. Still, in inspiring the record, it pleased God to inspire the men to record or utter it. There is nothing ultimately gained (either to clearness of understanding or facility of proof) by attempting to omit the human link of the chain through which the influence passed. The Scriptures were inspired. The men of God who wrote them were inspired too. They were moved ("borne along") by the Holy Spirit.

Inspiration Implies Both Divine and Human Authorship

The distinction between the divine and the human authorship of the sacred writings is not to be denied in thought, nor ignored in our reasonings. But it is of still greater importance to recognize that both must be distinctly held by the advocates of a true inspiration.

A document or law might be so given from God as altogether to exclude human authorship, or the intervention of any human medium. Then, though divine, it would not be inspired. Such was the Decalogue as originally given. The words were uttered by the divine Voice on Sinai, in the hearing of Moses as well as of the people. He, as well as they, did "exceedingly fear and quake" (See Exod. 20:19–22 and Heb. 12:21.) They were then recorded by the finger of God upon tablets prepared by God. (See Exod. 32:16. Compare with Exod. 34:1, 28.) The subsequent record of them by Moses was inspired.

The Human Element of the Scriptures

The divine origin and authority of the Word is not to be affirmed, so as to exclude or impair the reality of the human authorship, and the peculiarities resulting therefrom. The Bible is God's Word to humankind throughout. Yet, at the same time, it is really and thoroughly man's composition. No attempt should be made (and *we* shall certainly make none) to thrust aside or ignore the "human element" of the Scriptures. They are unmistakably apparent on their very face. No one should wish so to magnify the divine as to crowd this out, or almost out. This is one of the mistakes which good men have committed. Let both be admitted, recognized, accepted, thankfully and rejoicingly. Each contributed to make the Bible more completely adapted to human needs, as the instrument of divine grace and the guide for weak and wandering human souls.

The Word is not *of* man, as to its source; nor depending *on* man, as to its authority. It is *by* and *through* man as its medium. Yet, it is not simply the channel along which it runs, like water through a lifeless pipe. It is *through* and *by man* as the agent voluntarily active and intelligent in its communication. Both sides of the truth are expressed in the scriptural language: "Holy men spake as they were moved ["borne along"] by the Holy Spirit." (See 2 Pet. 1:21.) The men spoke. The impulse and direction were from God.

Theories have been devised, proceeding on various human analogies, and limiting the divine operation to make room for the human, or suspending the human to allow the intervention of the divine. There is a strong temptation to adopt such suggestions. It simplifies the matter so. If the Book were human only, a collection of the thoughts, hopes, desires, guesses at truth, of certain wise men of ancient times, that would be an entirely intelligible supposition. If it were divine only, as the tables of stone, engraved by the finger of God, that would be a perfectly simple proposition. If it were of twofold, independent authorship, part by God and another part by man, the divinity contributing one portion and then retiring, while the human author acts alone, there would be perhaps no objection on the part of modern theorizers to recognize such an intermixture. At any rate, all would be intelligible enough, though there would be serious difficulty in determining which part was from above, and which of the earth, earthy.

The Work of Man

But neither of these suggestions suits the actual phenomena. The Bible will not submit to lie upon this bed of Procrustes, to be crammed and crowded into these molds of human theories. It is all unmistakably the work of man. It is all by singular and accumulated evidences declared to be the Word of God. It was all written by man, all inspired by God. Both points are proved by separate and sufficient evidence. If we undertake to go beyond, and to explain how this was accomplished, we leave what has been made known to us for the barren and uncertain fields of conjecture.

This full recognition of the human authorship of the Scriptures is of prime importance. For much of the force of the argument against a strict doctrine of inspiration consists in proving this human authorship of the sacred writings, which we think is undeniable, and then inferring from that their fallibility.

The Assumption

"Human, therefore fallible," they say. "Fallible, therefore false in some measure."[1] But this favorite line of argument seems to us to be more plausible than powerful. It is a mere *assumption* that their being human forbids their being also divine, that God cannot so inspire and use a human being as to keep His message free from error. That the human origin, under divine control, necessarily involves either falsity or fallibility. This seems to be perfectly plain. Yet this fallacy underlies whole pages of vigorous denunciation and confident appeal.[2]

Double Authorship

Such a double authorship, as we are led by the evidence (hereafter to be submitted) to attribute to the Bible, is a thing utterly unknown in any other book.

A human volume might be the joint composition of two writers:

- one preparing one part, and the other the remainder;
- one suggesting the ideas, and the other clothing them in the language finally adopted;
- one writing originally, the other editing, enlarging, correcting; or
- each doing this revision of the work of the other.

But nothing like either of these is supposed or affirmed as to the divine and the human authorship of the Bible.

If it is objected that we cannot understand how this human and divine authorship was exercised, so that the two elements should be consistent with each other, and that we cannot believe what we cannot understand, we reply:

1. That, if the two things affirmed were plainly incompatible with each other, logical contradictions, so that their union is inconceivable and impossible, the objection would have decisive weight.

2. But suppose that they are of such a nature that, while the combination is, from the nature of the case, not within our experience, and so it is not within our power to comprehend and explain their union, it is not beyond the power of God to effect it. The case then presents a very different aspect, analogous to many others. Where we are compelled to admit the facts, we are utterly unable to explain them. That they are, we know. How they are, we know not. As it has been often and justly said, a man who refuses to believe anything that he does not understand will have a very short creed.

Divine and Human

We recur, then, to the statement that the Bible is throughout divine and human, all inspired by God, all written by man.

This is the current doctrine of Christian people, as set forth substantially by the great body of thoughtful and trusted expounders, of different denominations and of various shades of opinion, with some variations of language indeed, but with great general accord.

Mechanical Inspiration

It is not fair to confound or identify this strict doctrine of inspiration with the so-called "Post-Reformation dogma" of *mechanical* inspiration. This, we think, is not properly inspiration. It is used to sharpen the arguments directed against the current view by invectives at what some are pleased to style the traditional, uncritical, monstrous ideas of the advocates of plenary or verbal inspiration. Some of them have undoubtedly been incautious in statement, or heated in discussion. We need not

attempt their vindication. But that does not impair their substantial agreement in the doctrine as stated here.

A few quotations from some leading authors may suffice on
this point. It is not claimed that all the writers quoted would
accept the views advocated by us in all their minutiae. But, as to
the point now under discussion, their statements are in thorough
accord, and of great weight.

Philip Schaff (Presbyterian). "The New Testament presents in
its way the same union of the divine and human natures as the
person of Christ. . . . The Bible is thoroughly human, though
without error, in contents and form, in the mode of its rise, its
compilation, its preservation and transmission; yet at the same
time, thoroughly divine, both in its thoughts and words, in its
origin, vitality, energy, and effect."[3]

B. K. Peirce (Methodist). "The Bible is not a specimen of the
style of the Holy Spirit as a writer; but the different authors expressed in their own language, and by their own illustrations, the
ideas poured into their minds from on high. . . .The Son of man
was no less a perfect man, hungering, thirsting, sleeping, weep-
ing, because he was the Son of God; and the Bible, with all its
marks of human hands and weakness, is none the less a revelation
of the word and will of God."[4]

B. F. Westcott (Episcopalian). "The human powers of the divine
messenger act according to their natural powers, even when these
laws are supernaturally strengthened. Man is not converted into
a machine, even in the hand of God. . . . The nature of man is not
neutralized by the divine agency, and the truth of God is not impaired, but exactly expressed in one of its several aspects to the individual mind."[5]

Henry Alford (Episcopalian). "The inspiration of the sacred
writers I believe to have consisted in the fullness of the influence
of the Holy Spirit specially raising them to and enabling them
for their work, in a manner which distinguishes them from all
other writers in the world, and their work from all other works.
The men were full of the Holy Ghost: the books are the pouring
out of that fullness through the men, the conservation of the
treasure in earthen vessels. The treasure is ours in all its rich-

ness; but it is ours, as only it can be ours, in the imperfections of human speech, in the limitations of human thought, in the variety incident at first to individual character, and then to manifold transcription and the lapse of ages. The men were inspired. The books are the result of that inspiration."[6]

Edward Garbett (Episcopalian). "If we say that the Bible is the true Word of God, the term 'Word' involves the human element. It denotes at once the fact of a communication, and the channel through which it is made. If we say that the Bible is God's Word, we express it yet more distinctly in the further term 'written.' How is it written but in human words, by human hands, through human materials, and for human readers? To talk of a revelation devoid of a human element is to use words devoid of sense. [After referring to the analogy of the two natures in the personal Word of God, he adds:] If we attempt to confound the divine and human element together, and say that the Scripture is neither human nor divine, but something made up of both, we are corrected by the plain facts of the case; For the distinct human element is palpably there in the language, imagery, and style; and the distinct divine element is also there in the all-pervading unity of design and sublimity of subject. . . . Nor are we any more able to separate the two elements than we are to confound them. For if we say that part of the Scripture is divine and part of it human, we are again contradicted by the facts. In the part we acknowledge to be divine, the human element still survives."[7]

E. P. Humphrey (Presbyterian). "The subject may be opened by pointing out the two elements which coexist in the sacred records, the human and the divine. 'Holy men of old spake,'— there is the human; 'as they were moved by the Holy Ghost,'— there is the divine. Very instructive here is the resemblance between the combination of the divine and human in the person of Christ and in the Scriptures. Both are expressly called by the sacred writers the Word of God: the first is the Word incarnate; the last is the Word written. Again, the manifestation of both proceeded from the Holy Ghost: the first by the way of a miraculous conception; the other by the way of a supernatural inspiration. Next, the Son of God came down from above, and took upon him human nature; even so saving truth was revealed from heaven, and was embodied in human language. Further, in the one person of our Lord, two whole, perfect, and entire natures were inseparably joined together in one person, without conversion, composition, or confusion; in like manner, the Bible is one book, only one, wherein the two elements are inseparably combined in such manner that the divine does not absorb the human, nor does the human adulterate the divine. In Christ the two natures are so related that he is at once the Son of God and the Son of man; in the Scriptures the two elements coexist in such fullness that the whole book is God's word, and the whole is man's word. In neither case are we able to explain the mode of union, but we are not at liberty to solve the problem by rejecting either of its conditions.

We should bear in mind, however, that in Christ the manifestation of the divine is personal, but in the Bible it is verbal. Therefore, we worship the incarnate Word as God over all; we do not worship the written word, but we bow to its authority as the only infallible rule of faith and practice."[8]

J. A. Smith (Baptist). "One of the most beautiful and striking peculiarities of inspired Scripture is the presence there of the various human element, developing itself in all varieties of character and experience, and thus speaking to every reader the vernacular of his own heart and life. It is a different hand, we see, as well as a different theme, when Moses lays down the pen of history, and David takes up the harp of song. When Jeremiah mourns, or Ezekiel thunders from the Sinai of prophecy, it is not as when Isaiah blows glad trumpets. The beloved Apostle is known in the very first words he utters, while no one can mistake the profound and sententious Paul. Each writer is seen in his own proper character and recognized by idiosyncrasies he is known to have possessed. 'But the manifestation of the Spirit is given to every one.' The same divine power pervades all, brings its own gracious design out of each, and gives us in the end a unity as complete as the variety."[9]

Quotations like these might be indefinitely multiplied.

Inspiration Distinguished from Revelation

The supernatural interposition by which the Bible has been given to man implies two things, or consists of two divine operations, which, though usually concurring, are distinguished in their nature:

1. *Revelation*, which is that direct divine influence that imparts truth to the mind.

2. *Inspiration*, which is that divine influence that secures the accurate transference of truth into human language by a speaker or writer, so as to be communicated to other men.[10]

These are not the same, not necessarily united, and ought not to be confounded. They have often been combined in the same person or writing. They must be combined (as we think they are in the Bible) in order to secure the infallible truth and divine authority we claim for it. But it is important to distinctness and accuracy of view to discriminate between them. To illustrate this distinction, we may refer:

a. To those multitudes who heard Christ speak, and thus received a revelation, or to those who listened to the words uttered on Mount Sinai; for truth was presented to them in words by one who was God Himself. But the hearers were not therefore inspired to record or relate these words upon divine authority. Nor were they secured from forgetfulness or error if they attempted to make communications about them. Joseph, the husband of Mary, was warned of God in a dream as to his flight into Egypt and return to Galilee. But we are not informed that he was inspired to record the message.

b. Many inspired men wrote under inspiration things which they knew without revelation. Their record or utterance of these things, however, was divinely controlled. So when Luke records the letter of Claudius Lysias (Acts 23:26–30), he probably transcribes it. When he mentions the decree for the enrollment of the Roman empire for taxation, or when John and Paul record what they themselves said or saw, we have no need to assume revelation as the source of their knowledge.

This distinction may enable us to see more clearly what the precise difference is between the strict and the lax views of inspiration among many who are really evangelical. Both agree that Christianity is true, notwithstanding all objections and difficulties. Both agree that revelation is supernatural, if given at all. And that it has been given, and this notwithstanding their confessed incapacity to understand or explain how it was given. But one class assume, or tend to assume, just at this point, that the writers were left to themselves mainly or altogether in recording what they knew. They allege a divine operation only in imparting to them knowledge on certain subjects. While the other class affirm a divine influence over the writers in their giving forth, as well as in receiving the truth. The former admit revelation freely, but are more or less uncertain or hesitating in affirming inspiration also. The latter affirm God's operation in both.[11]

Inspiration Distinguished from Illumination

It is important also to distinguish both revelation and inspiration from spiritual illumination, such as is common and necessary to all Christians. This last may be defined as that influence of the Holy Spirit under which all the children of God receive, discern, and feed upon the truth communicated to them. This is distinct from revelation and inspiration in several ways:

a. It is promised to all believers, and therefore is what every Christian may expect and pray for.

b. It is dependent on conditions, which may or may not be fulfilled by the individual.

c. It admits of degrees, increasing or diminishing in the same person, and varying greatly as it is actually found in different persons.

d. It is closely connected with personal character.

e. It conduces to and secures salvation.

Neither of these five points is true with respect to revelation or inspiration.

Spiritual illumination is confounded with inspiration by two large and important classes:

1. on the one hand, by the Roman Catholics, and

2. on the other hand, by the rationalists generally.

The former do it for the purpose of maintaining that the church, not only of primitive but of modern times, has an inspiration equal to that which gave the Bible. While theoretically claiming for the Spirit, which is alleged to be residing in the church, equal authority with the Bible, practically they exalt it to a superiority over the Bible. They adroitly add the further unfounded assumption that *they* are this infallible church.

The latter class, claiming more or less to be the devotees of reason, confound this common influence of the Spirit with the extraordinary operations of revelation and inspiration. They do this in such a way as to attribute to the apostles and to the inspired record all the variability, uncertainty, and deficiency which are readily discovered in good men everywhere, acting under the usual leadings of the Holy Spirit in common life.

Inspiration Does Not Necessarily Imply Spiritual Illumination

That inspiration does not necessarily imply spiritual illumination in the sense explained, or insure the possession of saving grace, may be seen in the familiar instances of the prophet Balaam, of King Saul, of the high priest Caiaphas, who all spoke under divine influence, but, so far as we can judge, evidently without renewed hearts.

On the other hand, that spiritual illumination does not imply inspiration is apparent in the consciousness of every truly regenerated person today. It is a transparent fallacy to allege that, because the Spirit that works these two things is the same, therefore the operations are the same. We cannot assume that the Spirit can only act in one way on the children of God in different ages and circumstances. Yet this is what is tacitly assumed, as if unquestionable, by such men as Schleiermacher, Coleridge, Dr. Thomas Arnold, F. D. Maurice, and many others. These are writers of eminent ability and worthy of profound respect. It is a painful duty to differ, but still an imperative duty.

The Distinction

The distinction we have indicated between revelation, inspiration, and spiritual illumination is not only obvious in the nature of the case, and required by the instances given, in which one of these influences is found without the other, but seems also suggested by the express language of the apostle Paul in 1 Corinthians 2:10–14.

- He speaks first (verse 10) of the things naturally unknown which God has *revealed* through the Spirit.

- Secondly, he speaks of the "Spirit which is of God" (verse 12), being received that under its illumination "we might *know* [appreciate or accept] the things that are freely given to us by God," and without which "the natural man *receiveth* not the things of the Spirit of God" (verse 14).

- Thirdly (verse 13), he speaks of the power by which *they uttered* the things that had been revealed to them, "which things also we speak, not in words which man's wisdom teacheth, but which the Spirit teacheth."

Thus, what we have termed revelation, spiritual illumination, and inspiration, are each presented by the apostle in their proper relations and for their appropriate uses.

CHAPTER THREE

Principal Views of Inspiration Now Held

We pass over for the present any minute review of the history and progress of opinion in the past as to inspiration. It could readily be shown how present controversies are but reproductions of the old. The views which have been fairly tried and found wanting might justly be now set aside. It must suffice to state in a summary way the principal views of inspiration prevalent in the present day.

1. Mechanical Inspiration

The first is the theory of mechanical inspiration. It has been termed, the *dictation theory*. This ignores any real human authorship whatever in the Scriptures. Each of the various books, and every part of them, is ascribed to God. In such a sense it leaves no room for human intelligence or activity. The inspired man was as truly and merely a mechanical instrument as the pen with which the writing was done.

This view was vigorously and unmistakably expressed by J. A. Quenstedt. He writes in *Theol. Didactico-Polemica, 4. 2, p. 67*:

> All and each of the things which are contained in the Sacred Scriptures, whether they were naturally entirely unknown to the sacred writers, or indeed naturally knowable yet actually unknown, or finally not only naturally knowable but even actually known, whether from some other source or by experience and the ministry of the senses, were not only committed to letters by divine, infallible assistance and direction, but are to be regarded as received by the special suggestion, inspiration, and dictation of the Holy Spirit. For all things which were to be written were suggested by the Holy Spirit to the sacred writers in the very act of writing, and were dictated to their intellect as if unto a pen *quasi in calamum*, so that they might be written in these and no other circumstances, in this and no other mode or order.

In like manner Carpzovius says, in *Critica Sacra Veteris Testamenti*, Pars 1. p. 43: "He both impelled their will that they might write and he illuminated their mind and filled it by the suggestion of the things and words to be indicated that they might write intelligently. He directed their hand that they might write infallibly, and yet might not contribute anything more to the Scripture than does the pen of the ready writer."

In *Works*, 2. 383, Robert Hooker—the "judicious Hooker"—says: They neither spoke nor wrote any words of their own, but uttered, syllable by syllable, as the Spirit put it into their mouths."

Perhaps Haldane and Carson, among recent writers on the subject, would be regarded as approximating most nearly to this dictation theory. But it is scarcely fair to charge them with holding it. Carson says: "The Bible, as originally given, is divine in every word." But he affirms as clearly as anyone the voluntary and conscious activity of the inspired men.

"The Holy Spirit speaks through man, not as He did through Balaam's ass, or as He might do through a statue, but as a rational instrument. But in all this working of the mind of man, there is nothing that is not truly God's.

"If God has employed them as rational instruments with respect to style, he has likewise employed them as rational instruments with respect to reasonings, thoughts, argument, and words."

He accounts that one would be "frantic to believe that the writers of the Scriptures were unconscious organs." And again he says: "I never met an individual who looked upon the Evangelists as merely mechanical hand-writers. It is universally believed that the inspired writers were rational organs through which the Holy Spirit communicated his mind, though every word written by them in the Scriptures was from God. . . . God can surely speak his words through man in such a way that the words and thoughts shall be the words and thoughts of both."[1]

Ladd's View of Inspiration

Dr. Ladd is certainly the most elaborate, and probably the ablest, of all the recent assailants of the strict doctrine of the inspiration of sacred Scripture. He admits that the view of inspiration which he regards as incorrect because "incompatible with the real authorship of the biblical writers," "has doubtless been, on the whole, most generally prevalent" in the Christian church. "This view of inspiration," he says, "refers the minute peculiarities and variations of the writers, as well as their more important authorial characteristics, to the dictation of the Holy Spirit. This was the prevalent view in the period preceding the Christian era. Not only did the express teachings of Philo and of other authors, make us aware, but also the entire manner of rabbinical interpretation and dialectics from the Hebrew text. We have seen that this was the predominant view among the church fathers.

"In the medieval church (and for a time after the Reformation), this element of the dogma was more loosely held. But it became again an inseparable and vital element of the subsequent Protestant view." He thinks that the discussions which followed have "explicated and exalted the distinctively human elements in all inspired Scripture," and have "proved that the differences in the phenomena cannot in general be referred to the immediate influence of the Holy Spirit."[2]

Without sharing his opinions on that subject, it is safe to say that the convictions of the great body of Christian people in every age have referred the Scriptures as a whole to a divine origin. We do not believe, however, they have intended to deny the real human authorship concurrent with this, however much their language may seem sometimes to look that way.

2. Partial Inspiration

Somewhat as a reaction from extreme statements like those of Quenstedt and others of his time, another class of views arose which may be spoken of together under the title of partial inspiration. This includes all which limit the inspiration to certain parts or sorts of the sacred writings. Under this may be distinguished sundry divisions, as those which ascribe inspiration:

a. *To the doctrinal teachings and precepts*, excluding the narrative and emotional parts; or

b. *To the things naturally unknown* to the writers, and therefore needing to be communicated divinely to them. In all other matters they were left to themselves. They consequently fell into the natural inaccuracies ordinarily incident to all human knowledge and speech, however sincere and honest; or

c. *To the ideas* in their general train, but not to the language used, the illustrations, the quotations and allusions.

Thus it is sometimes said that divine inspiration belongs to the truth conveyed, but not to the framework in which it is set. The kernel is divine, but the shell is human and imperfect.

Among those who would change the statement "The Bible *is* the Word of God," into "The Bible *contains* the Word of God," may be named Le Clerc and Grotius. Their views may be readily traced back to Maimonides, the celebrated Jewish rabbi of the Middle Ages.

Semler says: "It is inconceivable how thoughtful Christians confound the Sacred Scripture of the Jews, and the Word of

God which is here and there contained and enveloped therein."[3] He rejected also whole books as uninspired, such as Chronicles, Ezra, Nehemiah, Esther, Ruth, Canticles, Mark, Philemon, the Apocalypse, as well as numerous narratives of the Old Testament.

The Distinction the Between Bible and the Word of God

Professor George T. Ladd, in his recent learned and able work on the doctrine of sacred Scripture, vehemently maintains the distinction between the Bible and the Word of God. It *"brings* us the Word of God." He thinks it cannot be said to be the Word of God. "The claims and the phenomena of the Bible entitle us to call a *large proportion* of its writings inspired."[4]

"The most obvious and necessary of all the distinctions to be made, as the prerequisite of the dogmatic construction of our idea of Sacred Scripture, is the distinction between the Bible and the Word of God."[5] "Its most untenable extremes" (those of the Post-Reformation dogma) "are all traceable to that fundamental misconception which identifies the Bible and the Word of God."[6]

How then are we to distinguish between the Bible and this "inner Bible"? By the Christian consciousness, is the reply. "It belongs, then, to the Church, in every age, to examine the sacred writings by the light both of tradition and of its own spiritually illumined self-consciousness. By the light of tradition each age discovers what the previous ages have considered to be canonical Scriptures; by the light of its own spiritually illumined consciousness it discerns the Word of God within those Scriptures."[7]

The Word First Preached

Of course, no one doubts that "the Word" was first preached before it was written, and that this phrase is not improperly applied to the general message of the gospel, which message is contained in the Bible.[8]

It is also used in a peculiar sense for the Son of God, the second person in the Trinity, as being the utterance or manifestation of the Father, "the personal principle of divine life and revelation." But neither of these uses need be confounded with the sense in which the Bible (as being the summary of the words of God), is called the Word of God.

Dr. Ladd claims for "the Church" the "right of rejecting from this Word whatever does not satisfy the demands of its ethico-religious consciousness." He perceives that this is liable to the objection that "it attaches to the Word of God a strange and dangerous quality of mutability, and thus places the doctrine and life of the Church in constant jeopardy." He replies, that "a certain mutability necessarily belongs to the precise limits of the Word of God, as scripturally fixed, however we endeavor to determine those limits."

A Question of Canon

But that is a question of Canon, not of the nature of inspiration. If 2 Peter, for instance, be clearly ascertained to not be genuine, not by the apostle Peter, we should not regard it as inspired, or as any part of God's Word. It professes to be from "Simon Peter." If it is not, but from some other author, it bears a falsehood on its face. It is a fraud. There is no room for "pious frauds," or any other sort of fraud, in the Word of God.

How large a part of the Bible this "Christian consciousness" would recognize and admit to be the Word of God is not anywhere clearly defined by Dr. Ladd. "A marked difference must be acknowledged between the Old Testament and the New." The New Testament is "in nearly all its extent the vehicle of the divine Word of salvation." The Old Testament "contains many divine words," nevertheless it "contains also many statements of fact and doctrine which are not thus established, confirmed, and approbated. And in general we must admit that it contains the Word of God only in a preparatory and anticipating way."[9]

3. Different Degrees of Inspiration

Another view is that of different degrees of inspiration. Those who hold this opinion insist that all Scripture was inspired, but not all alike, some parts absolutely and fully, others less completely. And some in such a way as to give considerable room for imperfection and error. Three, four, or five degrees are alleged by different authors. But those usually stated are:

- superintendence,
- elevation,
- direction, and
- suggestion.

The degrees rise respectively in the amount and nature of the divine control supposed to be exercised.

The Mingling of Human and Divine

These authors proceed on the assumption that there is error in the Scripture. This is to be explained consistently with its divine origin by the supposition of a variable mingling of the human and the divine agency in the composition of the Word. So far as the divine element predominated, there was infallible accuracy and authority. But so far as the human element was combined with it there was or might be failure.

Two very different classes of writers, however, have united in the use of this phraseology. There are some who seem eager mainly to exhibit the supposed errors and mistakes of the inspired writers. Others have been evidently actuated by a sincere zeal for the honor of the Word, and the vindication of truth. They have held fast to the integrity and infallibility of the Bible.

Among the eminent writers, generally orthodox, who have been advocates of the theory which lays stress on different degrees of inspiration are:

- Daniel Wilson,
- Philip Doddridge,

- John Dick,
- Leonard Woods, and
- Enoch Henderson.

It is obvious that this theory also may be traced back to the Jewish rabbins, who undertook to explain the division of the Old Testament into the three parts:

- Law,
- Prophets, and
- Hagiographa

by inventing the notion of three degrees of inspiration. These are: (1) the Mosaic, peculiar to him, and highest of all; (2) the Prophetic, by prophets; and (3) the Hagiographa. While the authors of the Hagiographa were not prophets (they had communications chiefly by dreams), they were supposed to know only a part of the truth. This degree they called that of the Holy Spirit. As Havernick truly says: "This asserted diversity of Inspiration appears, even in its definition, to be so vague and inexact that one can hardly form any regular conception of it. Of biblical grounds it is wholly deficient: nay, the New Testament rather decides against it, from the manner in which it speaks of David and Daniel as prophets."[10]

The Number of Degrees

The modern writers who adopt this theory of degrees are not agreed as to the number of the "degrees," nor as to the use they propose to make of the distinction.

Wilson gives *four* degrees:

1. suggestion
2. direction
3. elevation
4. superintendence.

Doddridge omits direction.
Henderson makes *five*:

PRINCIPAL VIEWS OF INSPIRATION NOW HELD

1. a divine excitement
2. invigoration
3. superintendence
4. guidance
5. direct revelation.

J. T. Beck of Basle gives *three* degrees:

1. the *pisteo-dynamical* (Mark, Luke, Acts)
2. the *charismatical*, distributed over the first community of believers, and
3. the *apocalyptic* (the apostles).

Carson objects, with decided force, to this whole theory of degrees. "If this distinction of inspiration be true, the greatest part of the Bible is not the Word of God at all," he writes. "When a pupil writes a theme by the direction of his teacher, with every help usually afforded, and when it is so corrected by the latter that nothing remains but what is proper in his estimation, is it not still the pupil's production? Could it be said to be the composition or the work of the teacher? No more can the Scriptures be called the Word of God according to this mischievous theory. A book might all be true, and good, and important, yet not be the book of God."[11]

4. Natural Inspiration

More recently a view has arisen which may be termed that of natural inspiration. This affirms, in glowing and often complimentary phrases, an inspiration everywhere in the Scriptures, and the same throughout substantially. It is not dictation as the first. Nor is it inspiration in spots, as the second. Nor is it in varying degrees, as the third. But it degrades the whole idea, so as to be little more than a strong excitement or fervor, which all men have in some measure; which many who are not even good men, but simply heroes, poets, or men of genius may share; and which in some vague, poetic sense may be called divine. The inspiration which they allow is such as Milton and Shakespeare, Byron and Shelley possessed, or even Homer, Plato, and

Socrates, in pre-Christian times. It traces all the sacred books of the world to substantially the same origin. It recognizes Christianity as a religion. But simply as *one* of the great religions of the world. It is nothing less, but also nothing more. Such is the view of Kuenen and other rationalist theologians of Holland and Germany, of F. W. Newman in England, and of Theodore Parker in America.

Morell in his *Philosophy of Religion* (pp. 127–79) comes dangerously near to this, if not fully adopting it. "Inspiration," he says, "is only a higher potency of what every man possesses in some degree." Dr. A. H. Strong pertinently replies that "the inspiration of everybody is equivalent to the inspiration of nobody." This view overlooks the fact that man's natural insight into moral truth is vitiated by wrong affections. Unless he is guided from above he is certain to err. It is self-contradictory in admitting inspirations which annihilate each other, the Vedas and the Koran as well as the Bible. It confounds the inward impulse of genius with the impulse from above, man's fancies with God's voice.

Theodore Parker did not deny inspiration to the Scriptures. He did not confine the term to any religious sense. He considered works of intellectual genius also as produced by its influences. Good men of old spake according to the light which was in them.

5. Universal Christian Inspiration

Another view closely allied to this, but still quite distinguishable from it, is universal Christian inspiration. It refers the sacred books, not to the natural suggestions of man, but to the personal influence of the Holy Spirit. But it represents that as the same in kind with the ordinary illumination of every Christian. As the theory last named readily connects itself with Pelagian views of man's nature, so this is not unnaturally associated with those ideas which unduly exalt man's agency, and affirm his cooperation with God in the matter of salvation.

This is substantially the view advanced by Schleiermacher, whose ideas have dominated so largely modern theological thought in Germany. It is held, with some modifications, by Tholuck and Neander. It is also held by Coleridge, Thomas Arnold, F. W. Farrar, Frederick W. Robertson, Martineau in England, and by T. F. Curtis and J. F. Clarke in America.

Something Higher than Human Genius

Schleiermacher regarded inspiration as not infallible, yet as something higher than human genius—"an awakening and excitement of the religious consciousness, different in degree rather than in kind from the pious inspiration or intuitive feelings of holy men."[12]

A Line Drawn Without Authority

Coleridge in his *Confessions of an Inquiring Spirit* contends earnestly that the line of demarcation between the primitive gifts of spiritual inspiration and the inspirations of the Spirit now was a line drawn without authority.

Edward Ivring seems to have received from Coleridge's conversations the start of his fanaticism.[13]

One Department Higher than Another

According to *F. W. Robertson*: "I think it all comes to this; God is the Father of Lights, the King in his beauty, the Lord of love. All our several degrees of knowledge attained in these departments [referring to the Excursion of Anaxagoras, and Newton's revelation of the order of the heavens] are from him. One department is higher than another; in each department the degree of knowledge may vary from a glimmering glimpse to infallibility, so that all is properly inspiration, but immensely differing in value and in degree. If it be replied that this degrades Inspiration, by classing it with things so common, the answer is plain: A sponge and a man are both animals, but the degrees between them are incalculable. I think this view of the matter is important, because in the other way, some twenty or thirty men in the world's history have had special communication, miraculous and from God; in this way, all have it, and by devout and earnest cultivation of the mind and heart may have it illimitably increased."[14]

The Spirit Still Utters God's Oracles

According to F. W. Farrar: "To us, as to the holy men of old, the Spirit still utters the living oracles of God."[15]

Certain Divine Powers

T. F. Curtis divides the views held into three classes:

1. He describes the first as that of absolute infallibility of Scripture in every part, and

2. the second, that which considers "the scientific and historical matter of the Bible as colored by the age and opinions of the writer, and therefore not rendered infallible by inspiration, while yet the *religious* portions are thus absolutely and entirely infallible."

3. He objects to both of these, and classes himself with the third, "who look upon Inspiration as a positive and not a negative divine power; as not destroying but elevating the human element in man [?]; as not conferring a necessary or absolute immunity from all error or infirmity, but as guiding the authors and quickening their writings with a divine life, and clothing them with a divine authority similar precisely to that with which the Apostles themselves were endowed, when commissioned to institute and establish the primitive Church. That is to say, their inspiration gave them certain Divine powers as a whole, leaving their individual and human errors to be eliminated by degrees as necessary for the life of truth."[16]

The church of Christ, he thinks, is an inspired body. "Though the membership of it may be invisible to mortal eyes, it acts with a visible and inspired power and authority upon each age, nation, and community, leading it forward with a heavenly instinct and superior wisdom. There is the home of the Paraclete on earth. Thus all become in measure inspired with the presence of the Saviour, the life of God."[17]

6. Plenary Inspiration

The doctrine which we hold is that commonly styled plenary inspiration or full inspiration. It is that the Bible as a whole is the Word of God, so that in every part of Scripture there is both infallible truth and divine authority.

These two characteristics are distinguishable. Statements might be true, exactly true, yet not conveyed to us on divine authority. The union of absolute truth and divine authority constitutes the claim of the Scripture to our faith and obedience.

This brief statement comprehends the whole of our doctrine on the subject. Nevertheless, in order to promote the clearer understanding of our view, we will present some explanations and distinctions, and to exhibit the doctrine both negatively and positively.

CHAPTER FOUR

Negative Statements of the Doctrine

That our view may be cordially accepted, or even candidly examined, it is important that it should be clearly understood. Hence we beg leave, in further explanation, to submit several negative statements concerning it, to avoid misapprehension.

The Principle of Exclusion

Our business is to get at the facts. This is the true scientific method. We propose to apply the principle of exclusion. In many scientific questions, the beginning of progress is found in ascertaining what a thing is not. Heat, for example, we know is not matter, it is not the same with electricity or light, it is not ponderable, etc. So in other things. Some negative statements may clear the way for future consideration and argument.

Inspiration Is Not to Be Explained as to the Mode of the Divine Influence

It will be perceived that we have given no theory of inspiration, nor attempted to show how it was accomplished. This omission was not from accident or neglect. We expressly avoid and refuse it. The question is one of fact, not of theory. The Scriptures omit to give any theory, any account of the mode of inspiration, any explanation of the phenomenon. They assert it as a fact. They do not tell how it was accomplished. Upon the supposition that it is supernatural, as we have affirmed, it is impossible that there should be any legitimate or adequate theory of it devised by human intellect.

Ill-Judged Attempts

Much of the difficulty supposed to overhang the subject arises from ill-judged attempts at conceiving or describing *how* God inspired men, forgetful of the fact that every supernatural phenomenon is above explanation, and that both revelation and inspiration are so, just as really as the multiplication of the five loaves or the turning of the water into wine.

Revelation

As to *revelation*, we do not know how it was imparted. How would one go about to discover the nature of the divine operation involved? Except the prophet himself, who received the revelation, what man could testify on the subject? There is no possible point of contact by which it can be brought within the sphere of human observation. Even to the prophet was it not still a mystery? Do not all the indications point towards that conclusion? Possibly *he* did not know. Certainly *we* do not know.

Inspiration

So, too, the inspiration is not explicable by us, any more than the condition of the withered hand at the instant it was healed and restored to activity by supernatural power. If the change in the hand or arm was properly supernatural, no explanation as to how it was done can make it more intelligible. No lack of explanation can make it more incredible.

Just so as to the inspiration. We have no reason to suppose that it was understood as to the nature or mode of its operation, even by those who enjoyed it. Much less can it be intelligible to others who never experienced it. Certainly those who had it never undertook to explain its nature for our enlightenment.

Spiritual Illumination

Even spiritual illumination, which seems nearer to us, which has been promised to every age, and which we trust we have individually experienced, is very imperfectly explicable by us. We know the effects. We do not know the way in which the Spirit operates to produce them.

"The wind bloweth where it listeth, and thou hearest the sound thereof, but canst not tell whence it cometh, and whither it goeth. So is every one that is born of the Spirit." If this new birth is inscrutable to us, how can we theorize on the other influences which we have never enjoyed?

Inspiration Is Not Mechanical

A view (that is justly chargeable as mechanical) appears to have been expressed by some of the writers subsequent to the Reformation, such as Quenstedt, heretofore quoted, Calovius, Voetius, and the Formula Consensus Helvetica. They do not leave room for any conscious or voluntary activity of the writers whom the Holy Spirit employed. They regard them as mere machines. They were driven into this extreme, probably, by two causes.

Mere Machines

They were so anxious to claim and defend the divine authorship that they overlooked the human authorship. This is just as, in vindicating the divine sovereignty and efficiency, some Calvinists then and since have overlooked or denied human freedom and responsibility.

Besides, they were in vigorous and deadly conflict with the Papacy. They were in antagonism to the claim of an infallible, inspired church, uttering in every syllable the voice of God. They were eager to set up, in the most uncompromising form, the counter authority of an inspired, infallible Bible—a Bible so purely divine that it excluded all human will or authorship.

It is of this view that Farrar speaks so harshly and in such denunciatory terms.[1] Unfortunately, however, he confounds it with the current or orthodox view, which is not legitimately liable to such charges. He allows himself to say, "From it every mistaken method of interpretation, and many false views of morals and sociology, have derived their disastrous origin. . . . It sprang from heathenism. It leads to infidelity."

In like manner, George T. Ladd, while exercising a marked and admirable courtesy towards all other opponents, never wearies of severe and caustic expressions against the "Post-Reformation Dogma," its "dreadful pressure,"[2] its "monstrous assumptions,"[3] the "stolid predisposition to maintain the Post-Reformation Dogma,"[4] etc.

A Pen in God's Hand

Some of the early Christian writers (commonly called Fathers) used expressions which have been understood to imply that they regarded inspiration as mechanical. But they seem to have used them as illustrations, and in a rhetorical way, rather than as meaning to be strictly interpreted. For example, they spoke sometimes of the inspired man as a pen in the hand of God, or a lyre touched by the musician. Another illustration sometimes used was that of the amanuensis or copyist. But we are not solicitous either to vindicate their soundness or to gain the weight of their great names for our opinions. What does the Word of God teach?

No Scriptural Ground

There is no scriptural ground for either of these figures of speech. The inspired writer is not described either as the pen or the penman. The Bible does not represent verbal dictation to a copyist as the method adopted, either in revelation or inspiration. So far as there is any analogy apparent, the case of dictation to a penman is more like revelation than inspiration. The act of committing to writing that which is dictated differs very much from what we understand to have occurred in writing or speaking what is inspired. The difference is this: that there is, where we dictate, no control over the will of the copyist. Also, there is no aid to his memory, reflection, imagination, or power of expression, on the supposition of his being willing, but unable to give accurately what had been communicated to him. Both the control and the imparted power which we believe to belong to inspiration are lacking.[5]

At Sinai, the people, as well as Moses, heard audible words uttered from the midst of the fire. Though we have no idea how it was done, we unhesitatingly believe this. It is distinctly so recorded.[6]

Direct Divine Utterances

This was dictation, if you please to call it so. But there is no indication that the people were inspired to record what they heard. In like manner, distinct words from heaven were spoken at:

- the baptism of Jesus (Matt. 3:17),

- the Transfiguration (Matt. 17:5),

- Jerusalem during the feast (John 12:28), and

- to Paul near Damascus (Acts 26:14–18).

So much we know as to some direct divine utterances. But we do not believe that this was the method by which the revelations recorded in the Bible were generally given.[7]

Many of the instructions recorded by Moses and the prophets are prefaced by the word: "The Lord spake unto Moses, saying"; or, "The Word of the Lord came to Jeremiah"; or, "Thus saith the Lord to Cyrus." But that there was in these cases any audible voice uttered, I do not see stated or fairly implied.[8]

The Silence of Scripture

The Scriptures observe a guarded silence on this matter. There is generally no hint of the mode of the divine action in imparting, or of the mental activity in receiving and uttering the message. This silence of Scripture is not without significance. It leads to the inference that there is nothing in the communications of human beings with one another that really and fully resembles it. We must stop short then at the boundaries where the Bible descriptions stop. We must not attempt to be wise above what is written.

Inspiration Was Not Destructive of Consciousness, Self-Control, or Individuality

This has often been imputed to the doctrine commonly held, but not justly. There was a heathen idea of that sort as to their oracles. Some of the early heretics, the Montanists especially, fell into similar views. But it has not been at any time the doctrine of the great body of intelligent Christians. It certainly is not the doctrine that we maintain, or that is found in the Bible.

The individuality of the sacred writers, as well as their intelligent, voluntary action, was not superseded by the Spirit's influence. But both these were employed.

The Individuality of Writers; the Spirit's Influence

Every man has a combination of peculiarities which distinguish him from others. That is his individuality. It arises from various sources, from birth, education, environment, one's own will, habit, the grace of God. But from whatever source or sources it originates, it influences his whole being. It molds his thoughts, feelings, expressions. Now this is the material on which we suppose that inspiration acted. As in regeneration, spiritual illumination does not destroy the old faculties and substitute others, but it changes the direction of the currents that flow in the old channels, so in inspiration. If the sacred writers are Hebrew, they speak Hebrew. If Greek, they speak Greek. If Hebrew-Greek, they use Hebrew-Greek. One of them is naturally warm, ardent, impulsive. Another is majestic, deliberate, solemn. One is cultivated. Another is rude. One pours forth a trumpet strain. Another breathes notes soft and enchanting as an Aeolian harp. So of all other peculiarities arising from constitution, habits, age, country, etc. Amos, a gatherer of sycamore fruit; Isaiah, brought up at court; Peter, the Galilean fisherman; Paul, the pupil of Gamaliel; each writes in his own style, under the influence of the same Spirit.

This marked individuality is manifest in every part of the Scriptures. It is the most obvious and primary fact that presents itself to the careful student. We must never lose sight of it.

Inspiration Is Not Merely a Natural Elevation of the Faculties, Analogous to the Stimulus of Passion and Enthusiasm, or to Poetic Genius

Many assert inspiration, meaning by it, however, no more than this. But that is keeping the word, and practically renouncing the doctrine. If the only inspiration which the Bible has is that which is common to all Christians, or even to all men of genius, whether godly or not, or even to all men, as some say, it cannot furnish us with any infallible or authoritative guidance. To make our doctrine clear, and the grounds of it, we must consider at length some distinctions as to that most momentous of theological topics: the influence of the Holy Spirit.

The Influence of the Holy Spirit

There are three spheres or provinces in which the Bible teaches that the Spirit operates:

a. *Nature,* including influences over inanimate things, as where the Spirit of God moved (was brooding) upon the waters (Gen. 1:2); upon animals, in their creation and renewal (Ps. 104:30); and over the human mind and soul. Yet they were falling short of any saving influences. These last are sometimes styled the common operations of the Spirit, because they are shared by believers and unbelievers, by regenerate and unregenerate. Such are the influences which restrain bad men from evil, and urge occasional impulses towards good, even in the worst.

b. *Grace,* where the Spirit operates in originating spiritual life, that is, in regeneration, and in sustaining and elevating it, or in preservation and sanctification. In these, not all men, but all the saved, and they only, share. This influence is needed. It is bestowed to accompany the Word, and make it effective. It is not limited to the natural or moral influence of the truth itself. It is a personal, vital energy, quickening the soul that was dead in trespasses and sins, and illuminating the religious understanding of God's children.

c. *Supernatural,* where the Spirit operates either directly, or by enabling men to perform superhuman wonders. These are of two kinds: wonders of *power,* commonly called signs or miracles, and wonders of *knowledge,* commonly called prophecies, which were usually the effect of revelation and inspiration conjoined.

Often the Spirit united all these forms of the supernatural in one person, as well as the precedent influences of grace. He created and kept the man in being. Then He converted and renewed him, and communicated the truth to him by revelation. He then enabled him to work miracles to attest it. Still further, He gave the supernatural accuracy and authority in recording it which could pertain to none but an inspired man.

But these different influences were not always united. Sometimes they were, but not invariably. Even when occurring together, they can be profitably distinguished and considered separately.

Each of these was distinct both in object and result. On humankind in general, and still more on the lower creatures, the Spirit of God acted and still acts. He acts with no intention to clothe them with authority, or even to make them holy, but to sustain them in being and activity. And as the object in view differs, so the result differs.

- *The realm of nature.* In the first case, in the realm of nature, the result is continued existence, including activity and all that is involved in physical life. The design is no wider or larger than the result.

- *The realm of grace.* In the second case, the realm of grace, the result is salvation. No infallibility is secured to true Christians in general. No absolute exemption from error is promised or is produced. Only God's faithfulness is pledged, and secures that they shall not fall finally or fatally away.

- *The supernatural.* In the third case, that of the supernatural, including both revelation and inspiration, as well as the working of evidential signs, there is a commission to speak and act in the name and by the authority of God.

It would be wrong to say that, in the influences of grace, the men whom God actuates and moves are thereby rendered infallible. That would imply the personal infallibility and absolute sanctity of every truly converted person. It is no less an error to say that, in the supernatural realm, the men whom He actuates and moves are not infallible and authoritative as to the things for which they were commissioned. To secure that was the very object of the influence. The only question of importance is to ascertain when the divine influences belong to the one class, and when to the other. This must be decided by the evidence appropriate to such facts. It cannot be ascertained except by considering the divine promises and the actual results in each case, the claims made, and the sanction or attestation given to the truth of the claims.

Moved by the Spirit

Bezaleel, the architect of the tabernacle, and Samson, the giant champion, were moved by the Spirit. But when we consider the design and the result accomplished, we perceive that He endowed the one with inventive power to devise and execute skillful works in gold and silver for the honor of God in His movable temple. He endowed the other with supernatural strength to fight and destroy the Philistines. But He gave neither of them, so far as we learn, any commission to speak or to write for Him.

By an entirely different sort of influence their respective contemporaries, Moses and Samuel, were moved to speak in God's name. So, even as other holy men of God, they "spake as they were moved by the Holy Ghost."

We freely grant that all good in any person proceeds from the influences of God's Spirit upon him. This, however, does not imply that the influence is the same in all people because the source is the same. Nor does it imply that we must confound all the saving impressions and drawings of the Spirit with the higher influence which produces infallibility in teaching, and confers divine authority in giving commands.

We have dwelt specially, and with some repetition, on these points. It is not uncommon for the opponents of the stricter views of inspiration to err. It is not uncommon for them to lead the unwary into error by confounding these three spheres in which the Spirit operates, and the different influences appropriate to them.

F. D. Maurice, a profound admirer of Coleridge, and prone to recognize the inward light, rather than an objective revelation, as the source of the divine Word and the fountain of all good, virtually denies any *special* supernatural agency in the inspiration of the Bible. He says, for instance, "We must forego the demand we make on the consciences of the young, when we compel them to say that they regard the inspiration of the Bible as generically distinct from that which God bestows on his children in this day."

The English Liturgy very properly says, it is "God's holy inspiration that enables us to think those things that be good." In using the word *inspiration*, not technically, but in that general sense in which it expresses any influence of the Spirit, he asks: "Ought we in our sermons to say, Brethren, we beseech you not to suppose the inspiration of Scripture to at all resemble that for which we have been praying; they are generically and essentially unlike; it is blasphemous to connect them in our minds, and the church is very guilty for having suggested the association."

The Obvious Object of This Appeal

The object of this somewhat extravagant appeal is obvious. It is to lead to the inference that, if Christians *now may* err, so inspired men *may have* done. If the influence from which all good thoughts and all right works do proceed does not, as everybody well knows, secure ordinary Christians from mistake or confer infallibility, he would have us infer, neither does the inspiration which the sacred writers enjoyed.

But it is an utter fallacy to blend all spiritual influences as if they were one, merely because they may be included under a common name. They may be alike, and yet unlike. It may be no blasphemy "to connect them in our minds." Yet it may be perfectly possible and important to *distinguish* them in our minds, to connect or compare them for the express purpose of distinguishing them.

Pantheism

Pantheism (making God and the universe identical) destroys His distinctness from what He created and so ignores His personality. This theory of inspiration, by blending all the voices that proceed from God, raises each to the same pitch and force, preventing us from hearing any. All proper distinction between the Bible and other religious books written by good men is annihilated.

Bibliolatry

A new term of reproach, *bibliolatry*, is invented to stigmatize those that reverence the supreme authority of God's Word. In these strange times into which we have fallen, it is openly affirmed that some of the leading deists are ministers of the Church of England. They are officiating publicly at her altars. However, on the continent, some of the leading opponents of vital Christianity and most energetic assailants of the veracity of the Bible deny that it differs in any essential feature from the Koran or the Zendavesta. These are not only ministers of the established churches. They are also selected and eminent instructors in their theological schools, and trainers of their rising ministry.

The Reverend John Macnaught, a disciple of Maurice, goes indeed further than his leader. He blends in one all the three forms of spiritual influence which we have described. He concludes it to be "the Bible's own teaching on the subject of Inspiration, that everything good in *any* book, person, or thing is inspired; and that the value of any inspired book must be decided by the extent of its inspiration, and the importance of the truths which it well or inspiredly teaches."

Of course, each man is himself the judge of this value. Accordingly, he says that "Milton and Shakespeare and Bacon, and Canticles and the Apocalypse, and the sermon on the mount, and the eighth chapter of Romans are, in our estimation, all inspired; but which of them is the most valuable inspired document, or whether the Bible, as a whole, is not incomparably more precious than any other book—these are questions that must be decided by examining the observable character and tendency of each book, and the beneficial effect that history may show that each has produced."[9]

Hence he has no difficulty in discovering not only books, but inspired books in the running brooks, sermons in stones, and good in everything. There is a true inspiration, he assures us, in the instinct of the owl. Inspiration is heard in the rushing of the wind. It is seen in the springing of a blade of grass. It murmurs in the streams that flow among the hills. The hinds of the field calve by inspiration. And therefore, because there is no evidence of infallibility attaching to these phenomena of nature, Mr. Macnaught argues that there is no such thing as infallibility attaching to the words of writings of God's inspired prophets and evangelists.

Hence a considerable part of his book is occupied, as are many of the commentaries of some German critics, in an elaborate attempt to display the errors of Scripture. He tries to show that to a large extent the Bible, though admitted to be inspired, ought not to be believed! Of what value is such inspiration?[10]

The Inspiration Which the Bible Affirms Does Not Imply that Those who Enjoyed It Had Perfect Knowledge on All Subjects, or on Any Subject. It Affirms Only that They Had Infallibility and Divine Authority in Their Official Utterances

It was limited to the end for which it was given. It was limited by the very nature of the object in view: the communication of divine truth on certain topics by divine authority. It rendered its recipient infallible in nothing else, and authoritative in nothing else. *It did not render him omniscient.*

Overlooking this obvious but important distinction has led to serious mistakes on both sides of this controversy. The opponents of our doctrine of inspiration seem to understand us to maintain that inspired men were personally, absolutely, and universally infallible. They have naturally and forcibly protested against such a view. We agree with them in such a protest.

But not all the advocates of inspiration have clearly perceived the distinction. Some have fallen into embarrassment and into erroneous and inconsistent statements on this point.

Inspiration had nothing to do with Paul's skill or awkwardness as a tent-maker. It did not affect the elegance of his delivery as a speaker, favorably or otherwise. It did not become (as some imagine our doctrine to presuppose) a characteristic in the common affairs of life. It did not preserve its most eminent characters from mistakes in conduct. Nor did it exempt them from sinful feelings at different times, and from the constant need of prayer for forgiveness, and the perpetual, watchful struggle against sin.

Inspiration did not imply the communication to the man of any truth other than that which he was to impart on God's authority to others. It did not imply all truth on all subjects, nor even of all that may be true on any subject. It is not maintained that it secured his infallibility on such subjects, or at such times, as he was not called on to speak with divine authority.

The extent of the inspiration was not necessarily beyond that of the revelation. It might even stop short of it, as when things were made known to Paul which he was not permitted to utter (see 2 Cor. 12:4).

Did They Fully Understand What They Wrote?

Again, inspired men did not know the full meaning of what they themselves taught. We are expressly informed that the prophets "sought and searched diligently" concerning the very salvation which they foretold, "searching what, or what manner of time the Spirit that was in them did point unto." They did not minister to themselves, but to those of later days (see 1 Pet. 1:10–12).

This idea may be illustrated, in some degree, by the case of a telegraph operator, who can accurately transmit messages which he does not understand. His apprehension of its meaning has nothing to do with the exactness of the transcript received at the other end of the wire. Nor has it anything to do with the clear interpretation of the cipher in which it is conveyed.

Accordingly, inspired men, who were the organs of communications concerning the coming glory of Christ and of His kingdom, were still allowed to die without the sight. They also died without fully understanding the things they spoke. But they waited for those things. They delighted in them, longed for them, desired to look into them. They ministered to those of a later dispensation, to whom the key was given by the Saviour's own hand to unlock the dark sayings of their predecessors, so that it could at last be clearly discerned that from beginning to end "the testimony of Jesus is the spirit of prophecy" (Rev. 19:10).

A man might grow in knowledge, though inspired. Peter seems to have done so in regard to the meaning of Joel's prophecy. He had been long familiar with it, but apparently he did not understand it till he received the fullness of the Spirit on the day of Pentecost. Nor did he even then completely apprehend the relation of the Gentiles to the church of Christ. His understanding of that matter was made more full and clear by the communications at Joppa and Caesarea.

Not only might one know more than another, yet not be any more truly inspired, for there are no degrees in infallibility; but the same man at one time would know more than he, himself, knew at an earlier time. Thus, there were all diversities of gifts, but the same Spirit.

Inspiration Did Not Imply Exemption from Error in Conduct, Nor Great Elevation in Spiritual Attainments

This is true also of revelation, as well as of inspiration. Thus, Abimelech, as well as Abraham, received divine communications, that is, had revelations given. Consider: Pharaoh was thus favored, as well as Joseph; Sarah and Hagar, as well as Huldah and Hannah: though the former were not instructed to utter authoritatively, or to record what they received.

So others besides pious men were sometimes, though rarely, authorized to speak for God. They were inspired. Balaam is a striking example of this. He saw the truth, declared the future, yet died an enemy of Israel, fighting and plotting basely against the very triumph he had foretold. So, too, the old prophet in Bethel, and the disobedient prophet that had come out of Judah (see 1 Kings 13), and Caiaphas, who spake "not of himself," (i.e. not from himself, not of his own suggestion), but prophesied as to Christ's dying for the people (see John 11:51).

Though perhaps more eminently pious and zealous than others of the apostles, John and Paul had no higher measure of authority than other inspired men. Excellence of character was not alone a sufficient attestation of divine authority to speak. Nor was imperfection of character a disproof of one's genuine inspiration.

The most eminent and holy of the inspired men were not free from sin. In some cases, they were not free from conspicuous and glaring sin. When we consider the names of Moses, David, and Peter, it is unnecessary to discuss this point further.

Inspiration Is Not Inconsistent with Mistakes in the Subsequent Transcription of the Sacred Writings

The inspiration which we affirm is that of the original text of Scripture. It does not deny that there may have been errors in copying. We have no assurance, nor the slightest reason to suppose, that the supernatural guardianship which insured the correctness of the original record was continued and renewed every time anybody undertook to make a copy of it. The accuracy of our present copies is a separate question, dependent on the ordinary rules of historical evidence. This is examined in the science of text criticism.

Providential Guardianship

There has been a providential guardianship over the Word. It has been preserved remarkably incorrupt, and singularly attested as being substantially the same that proceeded from the original writers. The results of the Herculean labors of modern critics make it evident that, in about a dozen important passages, and in very many unimportant ones, there is reasonable ground for correcting the commonly received text. In a number of others, there is room for discussion as to the true reading. But when all these known errors are correct, and all those doubtful readings are set aside, there is no change in any leading doctrine of fact of the gospel.

The difference is somewhat as if out of a bucket of rain water from the cistern a teaspoonful were taken, and then its place supplied by another teaspoonful of river water. The contents of the bucket would be practically unaltered.

If it be said that these are very trifling and insignificant results to be obtained by all the labors of the eminent text critics who have been toiling for centuries (Bengel, Griesbach, Tischendorf, Tregelles, Westcott, and Hort), we reply that it is no trifle to be assured upon such competent authority, after so painstaking an investigation, that the variations from the originals, or from the manuscript copies nearest to the originals, are so slight. Thus it is that the plain reader may eat his gospel bread in peace, undisturbed by the apprehension that chaff or poison may have been somewhere ground up with the wheat.

It is objected that some adherents of the strict doctrine of inspiration used to affirm the absolute immaculateness of the modern copies of the Scripture, Hebrew points and all. And that they were logically bound to do so. That no other ground is consistent or tenable.

We do not deny that there have been some wild and unfounded assertions on the subject, just as there is even now, with some ignorant persons, an assumption of the infallibility and equality with the original of some particular translation, as the Vulgate, King James's, or Luther's. But we are not responsible for such statements. They are by no means implied in our doctrine. This will be shown when we come to consider this topic in our third part, "Objections to Inspiration."

It is objected, that, if we concede errors in the commonly received text, and the possibility that still other passages are now doubtful and may be found erroneous, this concession weakens greatly the argument for infallible inspiration.

"Why so strenuous for exact inspiration of the words, when you admit there may have been errors of transcription? What do you gain?"

We answer, we gain all the difference there is between an inspired and an uninspired original. We gain all the difference between a document truly divine and authoritative to begin with, though the copies of translations may have in minute particulars varied from it, and a document faulty and unreliable at the outset and never really divine.

Inspiration Does Not Imply the Truth of Opinions or Sayings Stated in Scripture, but Not Sanctioned

There is an obvious distinction between what is recorded and what is taught or enjoined. Errors may be stated only to be condemned and refuted. This position is so nearly self-evident that it is hard to make it plainer than the simple statement. Yet it has been often and strangely overlooked.

The Bible might have presented God as the only speaker—all the words His words, all the acts His acts. On the other hand, it presents a record which introduces men, bad and good, angels, even Satan, speaking and acting according to their own nature. It gives history, dialogue, reasoning, poetry, prayer. It is inspired as a record of these things, but records them as the opinions or sayings of those to whom they are ascribed—not of God, unless it is in some way indicated that they are by authority of God.

- Thus the serpent says, "Ye shall not surely die."
- The fool says in his heart, "There is no God."
- The wicked say, "It is a vain thing to serve God."

The Bible records these as the lies of those who uttered them.

The same thing is true of every history, inspired and uninspired. D'Aubigne's *Reformation* gives the sentiments of papists and of reformers, the cruel and false decisions of the former, as well as the heroic and truthful utterances of the latter. Did any mortal ever doubt which of the two he sanctioned or approved?

The Book of Job contains a protracted discussion between Job and three of his friends, as to the great mysteries of God's providential government. The doctrine and spirit of the three friends, Eliphaz, Bildad, and Zophar, are distinctly stated as their, and not God's, view of the matter. They are clearly and distinctly condemned by the Almighty, Himself, as not right, so that His wrath was kindled against them (Job 42:7). Yet it is from this book that so great a man as Coleridge attempts to draw an argument against the doctrine of inspiration.

"What!" says he;
"Were the hollow truisms,
the unsufficing half-truths,
the false assumptions and
malignant insinuations of the supercilious bigots
who corruptly defended the truth,—
were the impressive facts,
the piercing outcries,
the pathetic appeals,
and the close and powerful reasonings
with which the poor sufferer
(smarting at once from his wounds
and from the oil of vitriol
which the orthodox liars for God were
dropping into them)
impatiently, but nobly and uprightly,
controverted this truth,
while in will and spirit
he clung to it,—
were both dictated
by an infallible intelligence?"

He objects, and justly, against the manner in which both classes of passages are indiscriminately "recited, quoted, appealed to, preached upon, by the *routiniers* of desk and pulpit."

But this heedless misuse and perversion of Scripture must not be set to the account of the doctrine of inspiration. It authorizes no such disregard of plain language and of common sense.

Quotations from Various Sources or Documents

In like manner, we find in Scripture quotations from various sources or documents. For example, in Acts we have a copy of the celebrated letter of Claudius Lysias, and a report of the plausible speech of the orator Tertullus. Both were remarkable for their skill in the art of "putting things," and in their quiet assumption of things that were most probably not so. Does the Bible endorse the truthfulness of what is asserted in these documents? Or does it simply present these as what Lysias wrote and what Tertullus said?[11]

Inspiration Does Not Imply the Propriety of Actions Recorded, but Not Approved

In narrating the actions of men, three or four different courses are adopted in Scripture.

a. Sometimes actions are recorded with express approval. As to them, of course, there is no question now.

b. Sometimes they are recorded, and distinctly condemned. This is usually in the immediate connection, so as to leave no room for mistake or misconception—so David's great sin in the matter of Uriah (2 Sam. 11:2–27), Peter's dissembling at Antioch (Gal. 2:11–14), and his denial of our Lord (Matt. 26:69–75). Sometimes the act is recorded, and the censure is more distinctly given afterwards, as in the case of the sin of Moses and Aaron at Kadesh (see Num. 20:10–12, 24; Deut. 3:26; 32:50–52).

c. The sins both of good men and of bad men are often recorded, without any distinct censure except by the consequences indicated in the history. The greatest crimes and highest virtues are described, often without a word of eulogy or blame, to indicate the emotions of the narrator with respect to them. Yet the judgment of God as to them is indubitable.

Abraham's faith is mentioned, sometimes with and sometimes without special commendation. His lack of faith at other times is recorded. The condemnation, though not distinct or immediately expressed, is sufficiently indicated by the resulting events. A still clearer case of this kind is in the cluster of sins in Isaac's misgoverned and divided family. The evil of each of the parties in the transaction is vividly brought to view in the providential retribution which is subsequently detailed.

d. Sometimes it is left doubtful whether actions so recorded are blamed or approved. Some of the principal instances of this sort will come up for consideration in the reply to objections, in part three. These are cases in which it is difficult to decide whether the actions were not wrong or were not commended, such as

- Jael's slaying Sisera,
- Jephthah's offering his daughter to the Lord,
- Rahab's concealing the spies, etc.

But all that is important for us now to settle is the principle, obvious and undeniable, that the Bible is not accountable for the propriety of actions recorded, but not approved.

CHAPTER FIVE

Positive Statement of the Doctrine of Inspiration

1. The Bible is truly the Word of God, having both infallible truth and divine authority in all that it affirms or enjoins.
2. The Bible is truly the production of men. It is marked by all the evidences of human authorship as clearly and certainly as any other book that was ever written by men.
3. This twofold authorship extends to every part of Scripture, and to the language as well as to the general ideas expressed.

Or it may be summed up in one single statement: The whole Bible is truly God's Word written by men.

PART II

PROOFS OF
INSPIRATION

CHAPTER SIX

Presumptive Argument for Inspiration

In our whole argument revelation will be assumed. It is proved by the general evidences of Christianity, and is admitted by most, if not all, of those with whom we are now discussing. Inspiration, as heretofore distinguished from revelation, is the point to be proved.

It is not incredible, not impossible, but likely, that God, in giving a real revelation to man, would inspire it. That is, He would control, protect from error, and authorize its utterance and its record.

1. This we argue, first, from the nature of God and man, and the relation between them. Suppose that there is a God,

infinitely wise, holy, and good, who loves the rebellious creatures that have strayed into darkness, misery, and sin. Suppose He desires to offer them redemption. It is an object infinitely worthy of such a Being that He should give them clear, accurate, and authoritative information as to truth and duty.

We are not competent to judge of the circumstances and times He might adopt, nor of the form or amount of communications that would be best. But we might certainly expect that they would be *authenticated* as coming from Him, and as *being His message* of love and light. And, while we could not presume to decide in advance what subjects such a revelation should touch, or how fully they should be treated, we would fairly have reason to expect that on whatever subjects it did touch *no error* should be imparted. This much we should naturally expect even of a candid and judicious man, endeavoring to do us good and guide us right.

If the truth was committed, not to merely "earthen vessels," but to vessels of a tainted or poisonous material, so that infusion would corrupt or injure what was placed therein; or if the message was communicated by men who stated simply the result of their own observation, or used the utmost of their native ability, reasoning out as best they could, unaided, what would be useful for man?

In either case, it would hardly comport with what might reasonably be expected. It would not be like God.

2. The force of this argument is increased when we reflect upon the permanence and extent of the object in view. Upon opening the Scriptures, it is evident they were designed, not for one age, but for all the ages, books *of* the times, but *for* all time. While almost, if not quite exclusively, given to one race and nation, they were given for all races of humankind, and all periods. Even those things obviously local and apparently temporary were, as truly as other parts, "written for our admonition, upon whom the ends of the ages are come" (1 Cor. 10:11).

If someone has made some great discovery in science, or has devised some invention which he thinks will be of value to mankind, he is careful to have it accurately described and faithfully preserved. He would not leave its transmission to haphazard, without supervision, to the chances of blunders and misapprehension by those who are to convey the knowledge of it to others. Even if, of necessity, he must use some imperfect instruments or mediums for extending information, he would provide a permanent model or standard of comparison, by which their erroneous or defective statements might always be corrected. Precisely this is what our view supposes to have been done by our heavenly Father.

3. Additional weight is given to this presumptive argument by considering the other supernatural manifestations or acts connected with the giving of the Scriptures. These are recognized by most of those who differ with us as to the doctrine of inspiration.

According to our doctrine, there are three stages of the supernatural in this matter:

a. God communicating to the prophet the truth—revelation.

b. God controlling the record or utterance of this revelation by the prophet—inspiration.

c. God attesting it by divine signs so as to confirm the authority of the prophet as a divine messenger—evidential miracles.

Of these, revelation and evidential miracles are admitted and contended for by our brethren, from whom we differ. They, as much as we, affirm revelation and evidential miracles. Now, if we admit the supernatural at all, in giving man the knowledge of religious truth and duty, it is no more difficult to believe that enough was done to secure completely the result, than to allow that there was a miracle at the beginning of the process, and a miracle at the close, while in the midst, the link of connection was broken by the intervention of uncontrolled human frailty and the liability to mistake.

Supernatural Aid?

If God works a supernatural wonder in giving revelation, and others to authenticate it, then it is not improbable, but likely, that He would exercise such control, and give such supernatural aid as might be necessary to secure the accurate transference of the revelation into human speech, so as to make it just what He meant it should be.

If, on the other hand, revelation had been committed to mere oral tradition, without any writing, it might be seriously corrupted, or might even perish within two generations.

If entrusted to unaided human record, it would have had neither unerring truth nor absolute divine authority at the very first.

If the plan of the Almighty was, by means of one or several persons, to bring all nations into nearness with Himself and acquaintance with His truth, it is reasonable to believe that He would not only superintend the process of their *receiving*, but also that of their *imparting*, the sacred truth. If the divine action ceased with communicating the revelation to them, then *we* have not a revelation at all. We have only a human account of a divine revelation. According to that view, there *was* a revelation, but it perished as such, with the men to whom it was imparted. All that the world has is the fallible impression it made on their minds, or their fallible account of that impression.

The admission of a miraculous revelation not only creates the probability that all further steps would be taken that are necessary to secure the end in view, but also presents a sufficient answer to those who object to inspiration, because it implies the supernatural. A first step of this kind having been actually taken, it is unreasonable to allege that another is impossible or incredible.

4. A further presumptive argument for the inspiration of the Scriptures may be gathered from what we know of the character and circumstances of the writers.

How could these books have been written by such men, in such surroundings, without divine aid? Consider the subjects discussed and the ideas presented. They were hostile not only to their native prejudices, but to the general sentiments then prevalent with the wisest of humankind. The whole system of principles was interwoven everywhere with history and poetry and promise, as well as minute wonders and single excellences of the Word. Our minds are constrained to acknowledge this as God's Book, in a high and peculiar sense.

Creation of Man

If we begin with the Pentateuch, it is evident that its opening pages must be either the floating tradition of human conjectures and guesses at the origin of all things, or else the record of a revelation. The events themselves occurred confessedly before the creation of man. No human testimony was possible, in order to describe what happened before human existence. And the alternative is to regard the account of the creation as a mere human guess, or else as a divine revelation. In the one case, it is of no authority whatever. In the other, it is of complete authority.

Moses' Theology

Whence could Moses have obtained that sublime theology, that condensed summary of ethics, those marvelous precepts? Certainly not from the Egyptian sources, degraded by polytheism and human degeneracy, with which he was familiar by his education. Nor could they have come from the Babylonish traditions, which doubtless may have come down to him through the family of Abraham. A stream can rise no higher than its source. He towers peerless and unapproachable above all the sages and lawgivers of antiquity.

The Psalms

The Psalms are so far above the sacred lyric compositions, not only of any contemporary era, but of all subsequent times. They leave no room for the fancy that these are the foam that crested the waves of Hebrew poetic passion, the utterances of mere national or individual longings, in one of the narrowest and least cultured of the peoples of the ancient world.

Strange that these secluded Hebrews, who scarcely ever passed or looked beyond their own contracted region, unfamiliar with art and unpolished by contact with the literature of other nations, should have given utterance and melody to the deepest feelings of universal human nature!

Strange that the words which linger most tenderly and solemnly on our lips, beside the couches of the dying, or at the graves of our dead, are the words of Moses, the Man of God, or of David, the sweet Psalmist of Israel. These are the words of men who lived thousands of years ago. They belonged to what is often alleged to be the most unsympathetic and isolated of all races! Is there not reason in the claim that the Spirit of the Lord spake by them, and His Word was in their tongue?

The Old Testament Prophets

In the prophets of the Old Testament we find no comparison, but a marked contrast, with the soothsayers and wizards of antiquity, or of today. They were not the paid guardians of pretended oracles, ready for money to issue their ambiguous responses. They were not concealing their unhallowed mysteries in suspicious darkness, and living in luxury on the wages of superstition and vice. Their rewards were more frequently

- contempt,

- derision,

- imprisonment,

- hatred, and

- death.

Their announcements were made in palaces and cities, openly and unshrinkingly, at the gate of the temple, in the high places of the field. They were made without the concealment or caution of conscious imposture, or the studied ambiguity which hides real ignorance under deceptive words. So much might be said, even apart from the foreknowledge of contingent events which is implied in predictive prophecy, and which certainly required divine aid. But if the reality of the numerous minute as well as more extended predictions and fulfillments be conceded, there can be no room for question as to the divine authority and influence under which they spake and wrote. Obviously, what they delivered was not merely for the people of their time. It was to encourage, guide, and sustain those of after days. This could not be available, unless both the precise expressions employed and the record of them were under a divine superintendence and control.

The New Testament

If now we pass to the New Testament, the argument becomes even stronger.[1] We are indeed in the Augustan age of Rome, but in a nook of the empire where the culture of that polished period has scarcely penetrated. We are dealing with writers whose sentences have not been framed on the models of classic Greece or Rome. In the land of darkness, Galilee of the Gentiles, a great light has suddenly arisen. What but inspiration could have lifted these men above their sphere, and given their writings the characteristics by which they have dominated, molded, and quickened the thought of the world, in its most thoughtful and cultured races, from that day to this?

As Dr. E. Henderson well says: "How otherwise can we account for the fact that:
persons of ordinary talent,
untutored in the schools of philosophy,
dull of apprehension,
pusillanimous in spirit,
narrow in their opinions,
secular in their hopes,
and strongly imbued with national prepossessions,
should all at once have displayed
the most extraordinary mental energy,
a superiority to every earthly consideration,
a profound acquaintance with truths
of the most sublime character, and
of the deepest interest to the whole human species,
and an expansion of benevolence which embraced every nation and every human being on the face of the globe?

"To the operation of what causes, within the compass of those principles of action which govern humankind, are we to ascribe the sudden and entire transformation undergone by the plain, illiterate fishermen of Galilee, and the bigoted and zealous disciple of Gamaliel?"[2]

The Four Evangelists

How could these four evangelists, so diverse in their mental peculiarities, have derived the marvelously unique picture which they have presented of the historical Christ, except from its being a reality? No writer of fiction has ever succeeded in so combining the most apparently incompatible characteristics into a harmonious whole.

And how could they, by unaided memory, after fifty or even twenty years, have furnished the incidents and the discourses, some casual and brief, some long and scarcely understood at the time? It is impossible to maintain the absolute historical accuracy of the Gospel historians, without also maintaining their inspiration.[3]

While not unduly pressing these presumptive arguments,[4] it may fairly be claimed that they prepare the way for considering without prejudice the direct proofs of inspiration.

CHAPTER SEVEN

What Direct Evidence of Inspiration Is to Be Expected?

Before proceeding to examine the positive proofs of inspiration, two preliminary questions demand investigation:

1. *From what source* can direct proofs come?

2. *In what form* may they be expected?

I. From what source can direct proofs of inspiration come? We answer: Only from the Bible itself.

The Truthfulness of the Bible

By most writers on the subject, this would be at once admitted as correct. This is involved in the very attempt we are making to ascertain "the Bible doctrine" of inspiration. By others, however, we are met at the very threshold with an objection that is not without plausibility. Yet, when attentively examined, it is entirely destitute of validity. They challenge the admissibility of the witness, the only direct witness that we endeavor to present, or that can be presented. They absolutely rule him out of court. This is bringing the Bible, they say, to prove the Bible, assuming inspiration to prove inspiration, and therefore reasoning in a circle.

Not so. We only assert, in the first instance, and that not without evidence, the truthfulness of the Bible, not its inspiration. Thence we infer that its statements about itself, as well as in regard to other things, are to be believed.

1. We proceed upon data that are admitted. The veracity of the historical record in the Scriptures, the honesty of the writers, the reality of their divine mission, are in general admitted by our opponents. For we are discussing with Christians, not with infidels. Accordingly, we are fairly entitled to argue on these data. If we commenced at the other end, and assumed inspiration to prove credibility, we should be guilty of the fallacy alleged.

But, aside from admissions of many of our opponents, it is evident that this testimony of the Bible as to itself is legitimate; for

2. We are shut up by the nature of the case to such evidence. If there was such a fact as inspiration at all, there could be only two personal witnesses to it: the prophet himself and God. When the Almighty commissioned him to speak His words, there were, in that solitary and awful presence-chamber of Deity, none with the prophet. No testimony on earth except his own, could avail to prove what was done. It is the kind of proof pertinent to the fact, the only kind primarily legitimate, and accessible.

3. The testimony of God is added. We begin in the order of the argument, with the testimony of the man. But we find next the witness of God. This completes the possible personal evidence in the case. (Compare Heb. 2:4, "God *uniting with them* in bearing testimony.") We are standing on the common ground occupied by both parties in this portion of the discussion. There has been a real revelation made to these writers. This is contained in the Bible. The assertions of inspiration made by the

writers as to themselves (or their associates) become authenticated as a fact made known by God. This must be accepted as forming part of the revelation He has given. Their repeated and distinct statements, thus authenticated, cannot be set aside as unintentional and unavoidable error, as part of the "framework," unimportant to the substance of their message. It is fundamental to their message that they *claim to be messengers*. And this claim God, Himself, confirms in manifold ways.

4. To this argument is added, in some cases, the peculiar seal of miracles, which is again the testimony of God in another form. (See Mark 16:20; Heb. 2:4.)

This applies not only to those who personally wrought miraculous signs attesting their words, but to the others also. Even those who wrought no miracle "formed part and parcel of a miraculous system, which cast its halo of light and evidence around the revelation of which their writings were constituents."[1] John the Baptist performed no miracle, but his teachings were amply attested as divine by prophecy going before, and the seal of the Lord Jesus following after. So Luke did no miracle, so far as we know, but his writings seem to have been accepted by apostolic men as of equal authority with their own, before the age of miracles ceased.

5. To this must be added that one inspired writer testifies to another. Thus we have, in still another form, the witness of God, who bestowed the gift upon one, when He confirms and recognizes it through the lips of another. Accordingly, the manifold allusions and references of one part of Scripture to another present the testimony of God in many forms and through manifold channels.

Thus, "across long intervals of time, with many generations lying between, with no personal knowledge of the authors or their qualifications, with no source of information except that which is unseen and from above, one Scripture author may witness to others, and claim to be believed, because speaking by instructions from God. It is thus that a man living in apostolic times, if himself endowed with revelation from heaven, may be a competent witness to the inspiration of records contemporaneous with the judges or the monarchs of the Hebrew people."[2] So the New Testament generally is an effective witness to the inspiration of the Old.

6. This method of argument is only an example of what is both common and legitimate as to other subjects. That is, they build up an argument by successive steps, to advance from a lower point admitted or proved to the higher points really involved in it, or deducible from it.

The successive steps here may be stated as follows:

a. The historical verity of the gospel facts in general.

b. The elevated moral character of the writers.

c. Their freedom from motive to deceive.

d. The impossibility, under the circumstances, of their being deceived.

e. The actuality of the miracles, or supernatural signs.

f. The reality of the revelation, as a whole, that had been so authenticated.

g. The veracity of the statements of the book about Scripture in general, and about special parts of it in particular.

The argument, then, is really cumulative and progressive. It is not like a chain, where the whole depends on each separate link, and consequently the whole is no stronger than the weakest link. But each point proven adds support to all the rest.

7. But if the objection to using the assertions of the Bible as to its own inspiration is evidently groundless, it is equally clear that no fair objection can be made to our drawing arguments from the phenomena of the Scriptures to show their origin and nature. This is the method employed in all physical science, to argue from the facts back to the influences or circumstances under which they were produced. Design is seen in the works of nature. The divinity of the Author of nature is fairly proved by these works. And so the divine authorship of the Scriptures may be seen in its characteristics.

- While the Bible, as a whole, testifies of Christ, Christ testifies to the Bible.

- The apostles testify of Jesus.

- Jesus authorizes and commissions the apostles.

- The church, as a historically established institution, holds the Bible as the Word of truth.

- The Word attests the divine lineage of the church of the Lord Jesus.

Added to all this mutual and interacting strength of testimony, we have the phenomena of Scripture and of early church life confirming each other. Both indicate with the utmost clearness, like the shining sun and fertile earth, that the hand that made them is divine.

II. Another preliminary question relates to *the form* in which this evidence of the Bible concerning its own inspiration is given.

a. The testimony is, sometimes, explicit. We will see some quotations of this kind.

b. It is more generally presented by being implied and assumed all along in what the Scripture says. The tone of authority it uses and the conscious dignity with which it represents the destinies of people for time and eternity are dependent on its acceptance or rejection.

c. The testimony is also found in the phenomena apparent on the very face of the Scriptures. Accordingly, the true doctrine of inspiration is to be gathered by legitimate induction from these, as well as from express assertions.

This is the only truly scientific, as well as the scriptural, method of arriving at the genuine doctrine of inspiration. All the evidence should be admitted. All the classes of phenomena should be examined. We must not only use the inductive method. We must use it legitimately, thoroughly, candidly. Professor Ladd has spoken on this subject with great clearness and force. Yet, as he justly says, "certain postulates must underlie this, as well as every other induction. And whether the induction be genuine and successful, or not, will largely depend upon the character and use of these postulates."[3]

The Bible's Own Claims

The Bible makes on its own behalf high and peculiar claims. This is obvious to even a cursory reader. But the strength of the argument is not in the fact that the assertion of an origin above man is made so expressly or repeatedly. If not directly claimed at all, it would be naturally suggested and fairly inferred.

The student of the Bible feels himself lifted into a region higher than the boundaries of human exploration. It handles the loftiest themes with a quiet simplicity, a regal familiarity which betrays no consciousness of intruding into forbidden mysteries. The assertion of superiority over man is not made in any offensive or supercilious way, but even as Jesus, Himself, who was the pattern of meekness, yet spoke as never man spoke, with authority and not as the scribes.

The Bible does not seem anxious about its own recognition. The divine manifestation in it is much as we find it in creation and providence.

No voice proclaims Him.

No letters of living sunbeam appear on the radiant sky.

No iron pen engraves God's glory in granite rock.

But every harmony of nature is vocal with His praise.

Every mute and motionless rock is inscribed all over with the characters which, if rightly read, reveal the wonder of His power.

The evidences and assertions of its own inspiration in the Bible are usually, then, as they might be expected to be. Not dogmatic formula, not anxious self-indications, but incidental and simple. Such is the general method of doctrinal teaching in Scripture on all subjects.[4]

CHAPTER EIGHT

Direct Proofs of Inspiration

The General Manner of Quoting Scripture in Scripture

This embraces especially the quotations and allusions to the Old Testament in the New. It gives, in a general way, the testimony of our Lord and of the apostles. To bring it out in full would require us to go over the passages in detail. We have a fair sample of the evidence by taking the allusions to the Old Testament in Matthew and Hebrews, and selecting one Gospel and one epistle for comparison.[1] But even this we cannot exhibit at length. We can only present a summary.

As to the Old Testament

When Christ came, there was a body of writings in the hands of the Jews. It was the object of their peculiar reverence and attention. It was recognized not merely as embodying

- the poetry of their antiquity,

- the history of their forefathers, and

- the laws of their nation.

It was above all the Word of God. Not only *their* God, but the God of all the earth, the one only living and true God.

Other ancient writings they had, such as the Apocrypha, were recognized by them all as purely human, yet they were respected and cherished. But these sacred books which make up our Old Testament, though unmistakably human, they regarded as also indisputably divine, and in the strict sense inspired.

Jesus could not be neutral. This universal belief of the Jewish people in these writings could not be overlooked by one who came, like our Saviour, as a teacher, and the Great Teacher, sent from God. It was necessary for Him either to contradict that belief, if not true, or to sanction it, if true.

Upon such a question, He could not be neutral. The gospel, the final embodiment of divine truth, to be presented to the world by Jesus, the only begotten Son of God Himself, could not be planted in the midst of unrebuked error. Least of all could it be built upon error as its basis. And that the New Testament gospel is built upon the Old, and assumes it throughout as its basis, its forerunner, its original and foundation, is unquestioned and unquestionable.

It is a significant and most important fact, therefore, that there is not only no hint anywhere dropped, either by our Lord or by His authorized apostles, that the people have overestimated the authority of the Scriptures of the Old Testament which they had; but there is constantly an appeal to them as an infallible standard in all religious matters. The Great Teacher, the personal Son of God, newly come from the throne of His glory,

- might have at once set aside all previous revelations,

- might have cast them into the shades of insignificance and neglect by His brighter communications,

- might, if He chose, have supplanted, abrogated, consigned them to forgetfulness.

This is precisely what He did not do.[2]

Not only are His discourses significantly full of "echoes from the Old Testament." Not only does He show a constant and affectionate familiarity with its phraseology well worthy of our imitation. Not only does He adopt its language in prayer, comfort Himself thereby in His deep sorrows, and fortify His human nature by it against the assaults of the tempter. Not only does He argue from its minute expressions, and expound its prophecies as having wider applications than the human authors could have had in mind, thereby referring them necessarily to a High Author, who gave them this typical intent. But He takes pains expressly to encourage His disciples to study and reverence the ancient Scriptures as the Word of God.

"Search the Scriptures," He said. Or, if the verb be regarded not as imperative, but indicative, which we prefer, the argument is not at all weakened. He is then commending, instead of commanding, their search.

"Ye search the Scriptures, because ye think that in them ye have eternal life; and these are they which testify of me." (John 5: 39). You sent to John (v. 33); you saw the miracles by which the Father testified (v. 36); you search the Scriptures (v. 39); you set your hope upon Moses (v. 45). But though all these testify of Me, are full of Me, you will not believe. It is right for you to listen to these witnesses, to interrogate them closely, to search them fully, for they are the real methods in which God has spoken. It is your sin and shame that, recognizing them and claiming to heed them, you have not recognized Me by means of them.[3]

The fundamental passage. The fundamental passage, however, in which our Lord expressly sets forth His relation to the law and the prophets of the Old Covenant, is in the Sermon on the

Mount. This is confirmed by the parallel expressions which He subsequently employs, in reference to particular precepts.

In Matthew 5:17–18, Jesus says: "Think not that I came to destroy [unloose, abrogate] the law or the prophets; I came not to destroy, but to fulfill [complete]. For verily I say unto you, Till heaven and earth pass away, one jot or one tittle shall in no wise pass away from the law, till all things be accomplished."

"The law and the prophets" must evidently be regarded, as is generally agreed, to be a summary for the entire Old Testament revelation. He will not abrogate. He will complete them. "To use a figure of speech as old as Theophylact, Christ does not intend to rub out and destroy the sketch in shadow-lines before him, but with true and ideal art will fill it in to the completion of the picture."[4] "The jot and tittle are," as Professor Ladd further and well says, "an inseparable part of an indelible page."

Two things are here distinctly affirmed:

a. the perpetual obligation of the Old Testament, and

b. its imperfection,

so that it needs completion. Dr. Ladd finds, in this primary teaching of Christ, a distinction "between absolute contents of truth and imperfect form, relative to the pedagogic purposes of these content." The truth, he thinks, came from God, while the form is human, fallible, transitory. To us it seems that our Lord makes no such distinction. Both the contents and the form are of divine ordination. The imperfect is not necessarily erroneous. The transitory is not false, or even fallible. All was true and divine so far as it went. For the time for which it was given, it was the best and most appropriate. But the time had come for additions to be made, for germs to be developed, for partial truths to be completed, for the outlines to be filled in, so as to give the more distinct picture. All this might be, without erasing a single line or charging on it a single error.

That this is the correct interpretation of this important and confessedly fundamental passage, is obvious. It is obvious not only from considering its exact expressions, but from the instances of modification of the law, which our Lord goes on to make. *None* of them are *contrary* to it. All *go further in the same direction.*

Killing and adultery. The first two, for instance, as to killing and adultery, are extensions of the Decalogue precept from the outward act to the inward disposition which would prompt it. The next, as to divorce, shows that the original divine law was monogamy. The case of divorce was a temporary concession made under the Mosaic Law to "the hardness of men's hearts." But surely it will not be alleged that in this Moses contradicted the divine will, and acted without sanction from the Almighty. The concession for the time was as truly authorized by God as the original law, and as its subsequent restoration.

The one saying which Jesus condemns is "hate thine enemy." That is *not in the law*, but was one of their traditional additions.

It may be added, that in general the very idea of a progressive, advancing revelation implies a relative imperfection in the earlier parts. This imperfection of incompleteness is perfectly consistent with truth, and with the divine origin of both earlier and later. If otherwise, all progress in divine revelation, which our opponents perceive and affirm as distinctly as we, must be denied.

Our Lord modifies the law. Yes! There are progress and improvement from the Old Testament to the New. Yes! And there are also in the Old Testament itself. Equally also in the New Testament. Even further, can they not be discovered in the personal teachings of our Lord Jesus Himself? There is obvious, deliberate, and intentional advance in His preaching, from that first simple proclamation, which merely repeated the warning and the announcement of the forerunner, "Repent, for the kingdom of heaven is at hand," to the matured and deep instructions of the night of His betrayal. And even those were incomplete. They left "many things" still reserved for the further opportunity of the forty days. They left still others for the communication of the promised Spirit. Imperfect? Partial? Yes, but *not* erroneous!

In the similar expressions found in Matthew 11:13 and Luke 16:16–17, our Saviour reiterates the same teaching. Until John, the law and the prophets had remained the one grand source of divinely authorized information. Now, they are to be, *not* superseded, condemned to failure, but retained and *completed*. Not an item is to be lost, not a jot, not a tittle.

The rich man and Lazarus. Again, our Lord gives a very striking witness to the sufficiency of the Old Testament in the parable of the rich man and Lazarus. Even the resurrection of one from the dead would not convince a man who refuses credence to Moses and the prophets (Luke 16:29–31). The attitude of heart which leads to the rejection of the former appeal will not be changed by even the embodiment of the truth in the resurrection of the Messiah.

The moral purity of Jesus. There is, however, another sense in which Jesus fulfilled the law and the prophets. We do not allude to the fact that He obeyed the precepts with a moral purity and exactness never before found in human beings. Though this was true, it does not seem to be the truth suggested in the Sermon on the Mount. But Jesus completed the law and the prophets, not only by enlarging, elevating, and developing the true meaning really embodied in them, but also by being that to which they pointed, by filling in person the description they had given in word and type.

Age after age, under divine direction, a picture had been growing. The eyes of our first parents, dim with tears as they left the bowers of paradise, had caught and cherished the faint outline of a future deliverer. One stroke after another had been added to the canvas as successive generations passed by. Painter after painter had taken the brush, *obliterating nothing*, but adding here a tint and there a shade, and then died. But the picture lives and grows, century after century, through the long series of revelations; with a marvelous variety, for scores of hands combine to form it; with a yet more marvelous unity, for One controls them all.

And now the picture is finished. But there is not on earth one whom it resembles. There is as yet none even that comprehends it. It is folded away for four hundred years.

In the fullness of time. Then, when the fullness of time is come, strange attention is concentrated on this ancient canvas. The picture is unrolled. It is searched anew by eager, devout, thoughtful eyes. Beside it stands one whom the forerunner recognizes. "See! This is God's Lamb, who takes away the world's sin." There is the old picture! Here is the present reality! All that the law and the prophets promised, He was!

Thus the person and life of Jesus the Messiah, as well as His words and teachings, are seen to rest upon the Old Testament Scriptures. They confirm and verify them in the very fact of appealing to them for testimony.

Did Jesus contradict the law and prophets? It is alleged, however, that our Saviour, while recognizing the law and the prophets, contradicted them in sundry particulars. Let us examine the grounds of this assertion.

In His *teachings as to the Sabbath* (Matt. 12:1–8; Mark 2:23–28; Luke 6:1–5) He does set Himself above the ceremonial law, as a master, not as its servant. But even in doing this He does not subvert it or set it aside. He does not, as Dr. Ladd claims, introduce and apply "a new norm or moral code for the observance of the moral and religious truths contained in the law."[5] He simply gives an *authoritative interpretation* of the law. The act of the disciples, which the Pharisees censured, in rubbing out the ears of wheat, because it was working on the Sabbath, was not a violation of the Mosaic Law. It was in contravention of the rabbinical traditions. Hence, this cannot be pleaded as an instance in which Jesus "must allow to pass from obligation, as a part of that law, many of its special enactments, observances, and established points of view." That the purely ceremonial, typical, and symbolic features of the Jewish ritual ended with Christ, *because fulfilled in Christ*, is agreed. But as to other things, we maintain, the Saviour did not abolish, but rather interpreted, the law.

So here the true meaning of the Sabbatic law is expounded and developed. As Meyer says, it is declared that "*doing well* is the moral norm for the rest and labor of the Sabbath."

In like manner as to the *law of marriage and divorce* (Matt. 19:3–12; Mark 10:2–12), our Lord, it is true, "places his doctrine above that of the schools, and also above the provisions of the Mosaic law itself." But He does so by pointing out that in that law the original and fundamental principle was not only that one man should be joined to one woman, but that they should cleave together, forsaking all others. Prior to the giving of the Mosaic enactments, which were civil as well as moral, great laxity as to the marriage union had sprung up among the people.

Introducing the law among such surroundings, Moses did not *command* divorce, as the Pharisees alleged. He only suffered it, as our Saviour quietly corrects their expression and threw a barrier in the way of the customary unrestrained freedom on the subject. He established a protection to the woman, by commanding that, whenever there was a sending away, there should be a bill of divorcement, a formal, deliberate, legal document. But assuredly we are not to charge this upon Moses as his own act without divine authority. We must not accuse him of "a faultiness of moral judgment." As Dr. Ladd himself says, "The word used by Christ with reference to the act of Moses (suffered), seems rather to place the human law-giver in some sort at that divine point of view from which such concessions are regarded as a necessary part of the divine historic discipline."

On the subject of *ceremonial purifications* and clean and unclean food, it is urged that the Mosaic Law is "at the same time contrasted with the tradition of the elders, and also itself *indirectly accused* of being, in respect to the subject of tradition, on the same unstable ground."[6]

The contrast drawn between the law of Moses and human tradition is certainly plain and important. The indirect accusation we fail to find in anything said by our Lord. He clearly affirms the divine origin of the law. He condemns their unauthorized additions to it. And He develops out of the legal enactments the great principle implied in them. Even as to those ceremonial distinctions between different kinds of food, which were to be done away, they were not in such a sense from Moses as to be in contradiction to God's will. They were *from God*, for the time, as truly as the ethical or any other portions of the law. If our Lord revokes these distinctions, "making all meats clean" (Mark 7:19), this is not because of their human origin. It is because, though divinely given, they had served their end. They must pass away with the dispensation to which they belonged. Because He, as Lord, had and claimed the right to change even the divine law.

Jesus and the ceremonial law of fasting. But Christ, we are told, "seems to take a hostile position toward the ceremonial law of fasting."[7] Not at all toward the *Mosaic* Law of fasting; only to that prescribed by tradition and custom.

It is well known that the Mosaic Law commands only one fast in the year, and that with a ceremonial significance and object, on the great day of Atonement. The Saviour objects earnestly to the multiplied and merely formal observances of this kind which had been added to the "law of Moses."

"A light in darkness." It might be shown abundantly that the apostles, in like manner, only re-echo their Master's reverence for the ancient volume of inspiration. They point the people steadfastly to it, in their preaching and in their letters, as the light to guide them in darkness, as the heaven-descended oracles to lead them back to God.

As to the New Testament.

We proceed to inquire what evidence of this general sort in quotations and allusions may be found as to the New Testament. From the nature of the case, much testimony cannot be expected in one part of the New Testament to other parts of it, as the writings were so nearly contemporary, all within a single generation. But it may be remarked:

1. That such corroborative testimony was scarcely needed. Revelation with inspiration would have impressed the Jew as an unheard of anomaly, in one claiming to be a divine messenger. The communications from on high which were peculiar to the New Dispensation, being recognized as divine on the evidence of miracles, did not require the confirmation of mutual testimony to each other by several witnesses for God. Christ, Himself, had sent them forth, clothed with His authority, to speak in His name.

2. The reappearance of the prophetic order is not only predicted by the Lord Jesus, but distinctly announced by Peter on the day of Pentecost as having actually occurred. This is a peculiar and marked feature of gospel times. For some hundreds of years, confessedly, the nation had been without a prophet. They lamented over the fact. They were disheartened and mortified by the fact. But they still acknowledged it as a fact. There was scarcely anything more startling in the incidents and announcements of the day of Pentecost than the impressive and astounding assurance that the gift of prophecy had been revived. This meant not the mere power of foretelling, but specifically the power of speaking by divine influence and authority.

That this was an extraordinary gift, differing from the gracious blessings which all the devout enjoyed, needed no demonstration to them. That it was temporary, and for special ends and season, requires little proof to us. The equality of the apostles as prophets to those of the Old Dispensation, was thoroughly established, to the satisfaction of all Christians at least. This rendered unnecessary the accumulation of individual attestations from one of them to the other.

3. We may, however, profitably consider the way in which Peter refers to his beloved brother Paul's writings as a part of the Scriptures. (See 2 Pet. 3:16.) This is a remarkable allusion. The familiar expression everywhere else applied to the Old Testament writings is here used as to Paul's epistles, "in which," says Peter, "are some things hard to be understood, which the ignorant and unsteadfast wrest, as they do also the other Scriptures, unto their own destruction."

It has been suggested that this phrase, "the other Scriptures," may include with the Old Testament writings all those portions of the New Testament then in circulation. I do not feel satisfied as to this. But the expression certainly embraces Paul's epistles along with the Hebrew canonical writings, as capable of the same use, and liable to the same perversions and misuse.

4. In 2 Peter 3:2, there is also a clear implication that the commandment of the apostles and that of the holy prophets are equally binding. Writing to the Hebrew Christians, who cer-

tainly believed in the inspiration of the "words which were spoken before by the holy prophets," he conjoins with these, as having similar authority, "the commandment of us, the apostles of our Lord and Saviour."

5. There is another passage (1 Tim. 5:18), in which Paul, referring to provision for the support of the ministry, quotes as Scripture a passage from Deuteronomy 25:4. He apparently quotes another from Matthew 10:10 or Luke 10:7. He writes, "The Scripture saith, Thou shalt not muzzle the ox that treadeth out the corn; and, The laborer is worthy of his hire." The latter quotation is nowhere found in the Old Testament.[8] But our Lord, discussing this same subject, makes this remark on two different occasions, as the evangelists have recorded it. Luke uses the precise language that Paul employs here. If not a quotation strictly, it can only be understood as a proverbial expression used by our Lord, and also used by Paul.

6. No contest, however, is likely to occur on this point, that the inspiration of the New Testament is at least equal to that of the Old. Even without explicit assertions of it, whatever sanctity, whatever divinity, the writings of the Old Covenant may be proved to have, those of the New certainly share in equal degree. In fact, most persons now are disposed to rank the New far above the Old. If, therefore, we succeed in maintaining the true and proper inspiration of the older part of the volume, that of the later will be readily conceded.

Scriptures Which Affirm or Imply the Inspiration of the Scriptures as a Whole

Various titles are used to describe the volume or collection of writings now known as the Old Testament. Under all these titles, its divinity is attested, more or less explicitly.

1. *The Scripture(s)*, as already shown, was in our Saviour's time the well-understood name of a definite body of sacred writings. By this name they are frequently identified with the utterance of God Himself. The phrase, in one or other of its forms, is used about fifty times. It always means the Old Testament alone,

except in the cases already alluded to (2 Pet. 3:2, 16), where Paul's epistles and possibly Luke's Gospel seem to be included with it. Some examples are:

Galatians 3:8: "The Scripture, foreseeing that God would justify the Gentiles by faith, preached the Gospel beforehand unto Abraham, saying, In thee shall all the nations be blessed." Who said those words? God, personally. The manner of the quotation can only be explained on the principle that the Scripture is so identified, in all that it says, with God Himself, that what the Scripture says, God says. A personal utterance of God and a saying of Scripture are simply equivalent.

Romans 9:17: "The Scripture saith to Pharaoh, Even for this same purpose have I raised thee up." But it was God who said it. If this expression, "I have raised thee up," had been represented by the apostle as the saying of Moses himself, it would have sounded strange and startling as identifying Moses and God. But there is no such anomaly in his thus identifying the written Word with God.[9]

In *Hebrews*, it is everywhere assumed that what is said in the Old Testament God said. Constantly the expressions recur, "He saith," "He spake," "He beareth witness," etc.

The living voice of the divine speaker is recognized in the Word. To adopt the language of B. F. Westcott, this usage in Scripture is "as if the author quoting felt in every quotation the actual presence of Him who had inspired it, and spoke through it."[10]

The error of the Sadducees is traced by the Saviour to their not knowing "the Scripture, nor the power of God." (See Matt. 22:29.) If they had properly known and reverenced the one, they would have felt and enjoyed the other.

The minute circumstances, as well as the great burden, of Christ's sufferings, are all represented as necessary in order "that the Scriptures might be fulfilled." (See Mark 14:49; 15:28; John 19:24, 28, 36.) This points clearly to the divine foreknowledge and authority found in those writings.

The expression of our Lord, "the Scripture cannot be broken" (John 10:35), is an impressive instance of argument to the Phari-

sees based on a single word. He says it is in "your law," referring
to a passage in the Psalms (82:6). Thus, He recognizes this as on
a level with that portion of the Scripture to which the Jews gave
the highest honor.

The word "broken" is here the same which we have already
expounded in connection with the Sermon on the Mount. It
means loosed, abrogated. It assures us that "the Scripture, as the
expressed will of the unchangeable God, is itself unchangeable
and indissoluble."[11]

It is furthermore to be noticed that our Lord here argues from
a more profound sense than the ordinary one of the expression
used. He justifies the propriety of such a use of it by the statement, "the Scripture cannot be broken." This means not even a
single word of Scripture can be deprived of its force and meaning.

One of the last acts of Jesus. One of the last acts of our Lord,
before ascending to the skies, was to open the understanding of
the disciples that they might "understand the Scripture." He
says, "thus it is written, and thus it behoved Christ to suffer"
(Luke 24:45–46). These expressions indicate the prophetic character of the ancient Scriptures. It strongly implies their divine
origin and infallible truth.

Second Timothy 3:16: "All Scripture is given by inspiration of
God, and is profitable for teaching, for reproof, for correction,
for instruction which is in righteousness."

The apostle seems to be urging this fact as showing how "the
sacred writings," which Timothy has known "from a babe" are
able to make one wise unto salvation. Perhaps also there is a kind
of undercurrent of allusion, as Chrysostom suggests, to his own
expected decease (2 Tim. 4:6), since he is now "already being
offered," as if to say, "Instead of me you have the divine Scriptures."

Whether the word *theopneustos*, translated "given by inspiration of God," is here to be construed as an epithet belonging to
the subject of the sentence (with the Canterbury revisers), or as a
predicate (with the common version), is not a settled question,
though the weight of recent authority is with the revisers.[12]

But if it is rendered as the revisers prefer, "Every Scripture, inspired of God, is also profitable," etc., the argument remains substantially the same, provided we have due regard to the connection. It implies that *there* is inspired Scripture, and that is the main question. It refers, moreover, unquestionably to *all* "the sacred writings" comprehended under the title Scripture, and with which Timothy is expressly declared to have been familiar from childhood. No distinction is recognized or suggested between Scriptures inspired and Scriptures not inspired, or only imperfectly or partially inspired.

Such a thought is entirely foreign to the context. The passage then stands in its full force, which can scarcely be added to by any comment, and can hardly be taken away by any subtlety or ingenuity of exposition. It may well be pondered.

2. Another expression for the Scriptures in general is *"prophecy,"* or *"the prophets."* By this expression their divine origin is often and distinctly declared. Consider:

- Romans 16:26: "The Scriptures of the prophets, according to the commandment of the everlasting God," and

- 1 Peter 1:10–12: "Of which salvation the prophets have inquired and searched diligently," and "the Spirit of Christ was in them," "to them it was revealed." Furthermore, the same things are "now preached with the Holy Ghost sent down from heaven." Testimony is given here, both to the prophets of the Old Testament, and to the inspired proclaimers of the New, as having the Spirit of Christ in them, and the Holy Ghost sent down from heaven.

What is involved here? This name "prophet" is given from the beginning to those who come as divine representatives, who speak for God, and who do this with supernatural aid, direction, and authority.

Successive stages may be traced in the development of prophecy, but there is no essential change of the nature of the office. Enoch, Noah, Abraham, Melchizedek, each in his own age and own way, stands forth in God's name. But their words for the most part are not recorded. Hence they pass away, as oral utterances naturally do, except as preserved and transmitted by tradition.

The dispensation then changes to a more permanent form. Written prophecy begins with Moses. He stands at the head of this new prophetic line, whose words are to be recorded and preserved for aftertimes.

With Samuel, another stage in advance is reached. A revival of the prophetic order is established. From him a continuous series of prophets is kept up for centuries.

But not until the days of Hosea and Isaiah does it attain its full development. Only then do the prophetic communications generally receive the written and permanent form which enables subsequent ages to profit by them.

At the outset, under Moses, the true nature of the prophetic office is indicated by the analogy of the relation of Aaron to Moses.[13]

A test is given for discriminating the true prophet from the false. Directions are given to punish the pretender with severity. (See Deut. 18:15–22.)

It follows plainly, that what came as an official announcement from an acknowledged prophet was recognized as coming from Jehovah Himself.

Even when no distinct assertion is found, the place of any writing on the prophetic roll established its claim. As Moses, after being once authenticated as a divine messenger, did not need to repeat each time he issued a portion of the divine command, "God ordered me to say this, to write this," so with the prophetic order. When that order was once known and established as a "mouth" for Jehovah, it was sufficient for proving the authority of any word or writing to show that it came officially from the prophets. Such evidence was open to the contemporaries of the Old Testament prophets, to be judged of in each particular case. The reception of the writings by these contemporaries, their being handed down by successive generations, and their recognition and endorsement by our Saviour and the apostles, and the New Testament churches, is the evidence accessible to us.

In Romans 16:26, the apostle gives thanks to God for the mystery (revealed secret) which is now manifested, and "through the prophetic Scriptures, according to the commandment of the eternal God, is made known unto all the nations, unto obedience of faith."

Here the prophetic Scriptures, evidently not meaning some part but the whole, of the older volume of revelation, are set forth as the great source of all Christian knowledge unto all nations. This is by the commandment of the eternal God. They are not superseded or abrogated by Paul's gospel and the preaching of Jesus Christ. They are only confirmed and given a wider extension of influence.

Another passage which seems to express almost in precise terms the doctrine we have been advocating is 2 Peter 1:19–21. "We have the word of prophecy made more sure [confirmed by the gospel evidences], whereunto ye do well that ye take heed, as unto a lamp shining in a dark [squalid or misty] place, until the day dawn, and the day-star arise in your hearts: knowing this first, that no prophecy of Scripture is of private interpretation. For no prophecy ever came [was brought] by the will of man; but men spake from God, being moved by the Holy Spirit."

We may observe here:

1. "The word of prophecy," "prophecy of Scripture," "prophecy," are all expressions to denote the inspired word, the Old Testament, and not merely the predictive portions now commonly called prophecy.

2. This word is confirmed, made more sure, by the subsequent revelations.

3. It is inferior to the gospel light, even as a lamp shining in a dark place is inferior to the sun.

4. Notwithstanding this it is well to take heed to it.

5. It is a principle of first importance that no prophecy is of private interpretation.

6. It is of the very nature of prophecy not to come by human will.

7. But men speak from God, being moved by the Holy Spirit.

Private interpretation. We need only comment on one or two of these points. The expression "of private interpretation" has been variously understood to mean:

a. of separate or detached interpretation;

b. of special interpretation;

c. to be interpreted by the reader himself (as the Romanists expound the passage);

d. to be explained or understood by the prophet himself;

e. of self-solution;

f. the result of private or uninspired disclosure.

The last seems to us the correct view, agreeing best with the force of the words and with the context. The thought is: The prophetic oracles of the Old Testament are worthy of the most profound attention, for they did not originate with man, but with God. The word *idios* (own), translated "private," might be supposed to refer to the prophecy, or the reader, or the prophet. It is the Scripture's own, or the reader's own, or the prophet's own disclosure. The prophecy does not disclose its own meaning. The reader is not to interpret it for himself. The prophet did not disclose it of himself.

This last idea seems to suit the statement of verse 19, for which it gives the ground. We do well to take heed to the word of prophecy, for it did not come from the prophet alone. It is not of his own disclosure. It also agrees with the statement which follows in verse 21, that prophecy came not by the will of man. The use of the verb *ginetai*, and not *esti*, confirms this view. It points to the *origination* rather than the quality of the Scripture. No prophecy has its *genesis*, comes into being, or becomes a prophecy, by one's own disclosure. The word *idios* is used in precisely this sense by Philo. "For a prophet," he says, "advances nothing whatever of his own (*ouden idion*), but is an interpreter, another supplying all the things which he brings forward."[14]

Then, after denying the exclusively human origin of the Word, the apostle describes in singularly appropriate language the combined human and divine authorship which is elsewhere implied. The men spake, the Spirit moved them. They spake, but it was *"from God."* Their own activity, as well as the divine influence that acted on them, is distinctly indicated.[15]

3. Another title applied to the Scriptures of the Old Testament is *the Word of God.*

Our Lord, rebuking the Pharisees for substituting their traditions for God's commandments, and setting aside duty to parents by their rule as to what was *Corban*, or devoted to God, charges them with "making void the Word of God" by their tradition (Matt. 15:8). The commandment of God was what Moses had said: "Honor thy father and thy mother" (Exod. 20:12). And, "He that speaketh evil of father or mother, let him die the death" (Exod. 21:17).

Despising this, or exalting human suggestions or traditions to an equality with it, is rejecting, frustrating, making void the Word of God. Jesus considered that a serious offense.

At the Feast of the Dedication at Jerusalem, when the Jews undertook to stone Him because they said He made Himself God, He said: "Is it not written in your law, I said, Ye are gods? If he called them gods unto whom the Word of God came (and the Scripture cannot be broken) say ye of him whom the Father sanctified and sent into the world, Thou blasphemest, because I said, I am the Son of God?" (John 10:34–36.)

The expression "Word of God" is not here equivalent to the whole of the Scripture. It refers to a portion of it. The passage quoted from the Psalms (82:6) is said to be "written in your law," and this is subsequently called "the scripture." And it is implied that those who had the benefits of this revelation had had the Word of God. God had spoken to them. The judges were called gods as standing, in a judicial relation, in God's stead. (Compare Exod. 21:6, 22:8–9, 28.)

The Word of God. The Word, of course, is primarily oral. But the expression comes naturally to be applied. This is true both in the Old Testament and in the New, to any communication from God, "anything," as Dr. Ladd says, "which God is regarded as procuring or permitting to be said to men."[16]

Any collection of the words of God may be properly styled the Word of God, "because its content is from God, and because God has caused it to be promulgated among men," "because it conveys the truth from God, and seeks the honor of God." Thus the voice of the ancient prophets was the Word of God, which shall stand forever (Isa. 40:8). The preaching of the apostles was the Word of God (Rom. 10:17; 1 Cor. 14:36). It had been sent first to the sons of Israel (Acts 10:36–37). Afterwards it had gone even into Macedonia and Achaia (1 Thess. 2:13). It has a living and abiding energy (1 Pet. 1:23–25).

4. Another term quite similar, and suggesting naturally the same idea, is "*the oracles of God*" (Rom. 3:2), "*living oracles*" (Acts 7:38). The great and overwhelming advantage that the Jews had over the rest of humankind was, that "they were entrusted with the oracles of God." The great sin of the "fathers" was that they would not be obedient unto Moses, "who received living oracles to give unto us." (Compare also Heb. 5:12 and 1 Pet. 4:11.)

These various expressions describe the Hebrew sacred books, some of them recognizing them as a whole, and dealing with them under one designation. All acknowledge their divine origin and authority.

Declarations Which Affirm the Inspiration of Particular Persons or Single Passages of the Word

We can give a few examples of this kind. It is obvious this argument avails mainly to show the nature of the reality of the influence in these instances. By analogy, however, the inference may be reasonably drawn that in other passages or persons a similar influence was exerted. In whatever sense these were inspired, the others were too. For they stand apparently in no respect on a different level from other sacred writings or writers.

A. As to the Old Testament

In Matthew 22:43, Jesus says: "David *in spirit* call[eth] him Lord," referring to Psalm 110:1. This seems to be a distinct assertion that David in that psalm speaks by inspiration, in spirit. Or if the meaning of the language there is doubted by any, because the spirit is not expressly said to be the divine Spirit, the parallel passage in Mark 12:36 makes it unmistakable. It reads "by [literally *in*] the Holy Spirit." (Compare the same Greek phrase in Rev. 1:10; 4:2; and nearly the same in Rom. 9:1 and 1 Cor. 12:3. The same is true of other psalms and of other parts of the Word. There is no peculiarity intimated in this 110th Psalm, distinguishing it as more divine than the others.

"*Lord.*" Further, the argument of our Saviour turns on the precise *word* employed, the word "Lord." It therefore indicates something more than a mere general control of ideas. In fact, we can hardly suppose that David himself, in this and other instances, fully apprehended the meaning of his own words. "It required," says Bannerman, "the foresight of that Omniscient Spirit, through whom our Lord interpreted David's words, to mold them by his inspiration into that form which they actually have, and which, unknown to the prophet, was to afford the materials to build up the proof of the divinity and the incarnation of Him, who was to be both David's Lord and David's Son."[17]

Matthew (in 1:22 and 2:15) represents the ancient predictions he refers to as "spoken *by* the Lord *through* the prophet." This is as precise and accurate a description, according to our view, as could be given of the divine authorship and the human agency involved. "The divine source of the word, its objective verity, and the inspired consciousness of the messenger, are all thus brought before our minds."[18]

In Acts 4:25–26, the apostles and their company (who presently are declared to be all filled with the Holy Spirit), lift up their voice with one accord to God, "who by the Holy Spirit, by the mouth of David thy servant, didst say, Why did the Gentiles rage?" etc., quoting from the second Psalm.

In Hebrews 3:7, a psalm (95:7) is quoted with the introduction. "Even as the Holy Spirit saith." In Hebrews 10:15, "The Holy Spirit beareth witness to us," introduces a passage from Jeremiah 31:33–34.

B. As to New Testament Authors

Acts 4:8: Peter is expressly said to have been "filled with the Holy Ghost" in his address to the rulers.

Acts 10:28: Peter affirms that "God has showed" him the principle on which he is acting as to recognizing the Gentiles, and the truth which he is to declare.

Acts 13:9: Paul is "filled with the Holy Ghost" in his denunciation of Elymas before Sergius Paulus; and his word is instantly confirmed by the miraculous blindness which falls upon the sorcerer.

Further examples might be given, but it is needless to multiply them.

Promises of Inspiration

Promises Given to Old Testament Writers

Among these may be mentioned:

Exodus 4:10–12: "Go, and I will be with thy mouth, and teach thee what thou shalt say." This is the primary promise to Moses. It seems to express in distinct terms all that has been claimed for the divine influence over the inspired man. It is substantially renewed on other occasions.

Deuteronomy 18:18–19: "I will raise them up a Prophet from among their brethren, like unto thee; and will put my words into his mouth; and he shall speak unto them all that I shall command him. And it shall come to pass that whosoever will not hearken unto my words which he shall speak in my name, I will require it of him." The question is whether this refers to the Messiah alone, or to a succession of prophets, or, as is generally believed, to both, to the succession of divinely authorized teachers in the prophetic order first, and to the Messiah ultimately. The contrast with the false prophets in the next verse favors the idea of a plurality of true prophets opposed to them. The singular number, however, is used. But this may naturally be applied, in accordance with a frequent Hebrew idiom, to a collective body or a continuous order. In this view the passage affirms:

1. that the prophetic function is not to cease with Moses, but is to be continued;

2. that the order of prophets will consist of men like Moses, active Hebrews, "of thy brethren";

3. that they are to be raised up from time to time by Jehovah; and

4. that they should have His words put in their mouth, and speak in His name.

Does not this cover the whole ground that we claim? The prophets spoke as God bade them. The Messiah was the summit and climax of the order, the ideal and perfect prophet.

Isaiah 59:21: "My spirit that is upon thee, and my words which I have put in thy mouth." This language describes the nature of the divine influence. The passage proceeds to declare that the teachings thus given shall be permanently preserved in the lips and memories of God's people through all time. [They] "shall not depart out of thy mouth, nor out of the mouth of thy seed, nor out of the mouth of thy seed's seed, saith the LORD, from henceforth and forever."

Jeremiah 1:4–9: "The word of the LORD came to me, saying, . . . I ordained thee a prophet unto the nations. . . .Thou shalt go to all that I shall send thee, and whatsoever I command thee thou shalt speak. . . . Behold I have put my words in thy mouth." Such in general was the idea of the divine prophet among the ancient Jews, a speaker for God, with divine authority, direction, and control.

These quotations may suffice for illustrating the ample and positive manner in which inspiration is promised to the writers of the Old Testament.

It is alleged, however, that the promise of inspiration is made to the "entire faithful people of the covenant," and that "the inspiration of Moses, Isaiah, or Ezekiel is the secondary fact which is dependent upon the primary." The proof given for this is that the Spirit is promised to Israel and to their seed. They are to be a kingdom of priests and a holy nation.

Were all people prophets? Moses *wishes* that *all* the people were prophets. But this last of itself implies that they were not. The other two proofs evidently have nothing to do with *prophetic* inspiration. This idea of the "inspired nation" is scarcely consistent with the conceded fact that every true Hebrew prophet, "by virtue of his office as prophet, *stood between* God and the theocratic people." If all the people were prophets or inspired, how could the prophet stand between them and God? It is also inconsistent with the special divine vocation by which he was to be raised up "from the midst of" the people.

We should remember, however, that other writings besides those which we call "the prophets" were included under that term among the Jews. The historical books seem to have been prepared by those whom the Jews regarded as prophets, from the regular annals of the nation. Hence those books are known in the Hebrew Bible as the former prophets, while our prophetical books are called the later prophets.

Promises of Inspiration to the New Testament Writers

The chain of argument on this important point may be first briefly stated. Then we will turn to the passages themselves.

1. Christ did not plan to carry out His great enterprise on the earth personally. His public ministry lasted only about three years. He committed no word to writing. In this respect He presented a marked contrast to other founders of permanent institutions.

2. He founded an apostolic church, and left it as His representative.

3. He vested in His apostles complete and absolute authority under Himself, as to the administration of this church, and the proclamation of His truth. (See Mark 3:14–15; Matt. 18:18; 28:18; Acts 1:3–9.)

4. To qualify them for this, He gave repeated, special promises of the Holy Spirit.

5. The benefits of these promises were shared with others, who are associated with them and termed prophets.

These promises to the apostles may be conveniently considered in two divisions. The first class were given prior to the last Passover. Though uttered on three different occasions, they are substantially equivalent. They are all recorded in the synoptic Gospels.

- The first is in Matthew 10:14–20, on the occasion of sending forth the twelve, the most appropriate opportunity for describing their authority.

- The second is in Luke 12:11–12, when uttering the discourse to His disciples surrounded by the many thousands that crowded on them.

- The last is recorded in Mark 13:9–11 and Luke 21:14–15, during the crucifixion week.

These promises, thus repeated, may fitly be taken together.

a. A real definite *influence from without* is promised to guide and suggest what they should say. "It is not ye that speak, but the Spirit of your Father that speaketh in you." It was to "be given them" in that hour what they should speak.

b. These promises embrace *all public occasions*, when the apostles must bear testimony of Him, before councils, synagogues, kings. This is not merely for personal defense and rescue, but for a witness to them. This witness is not only to Jews, but it is expressly said to be also to the Gentiles. They are by no means so limited, local, and temporary as has been sometimes alleged.

c. Now take into connection with these the promise of Matthew 18:18, giving them the power of *binding and loosing*, and especially the *commission*, Matthew 28:19–20: "Go, teach [disciple] all nations, baptizing and teaching them all things whatsoever I command you; and lo, I am with you always." In their teaching, then, as well as in their self-defense, He is to be with them. In every exercise of their apostolic office, they are to have His presence, aid, and guidance.

The extension of supernatural guidance. Nor does this extension of the supernatural guidance promised to them seem unreasonable. It is precisely in accordance with the nature of the new phase of their work upon which they are about to enter. If it was important that they should have supernatural guidance in their occasional defense of themselves, in temporary emergencies, before courts, how much more in their permanent instructions to the churches for all time! If "utterance was given" to Paul to make known orally the mystery of the gospel, why might the divine gift not be expected in recording those instructions? What excludes those occasions and exigencies from the promise?

The second class of passages containing the promise of the Spirit may be found in those marvelous chapters (John 14–16) of our Lord's last discourse in the evening before the crucifixion.[19] To bring out their full force, we ought to quote the whole. But since we cannot now do this, let us notice specially the promise of the abiding influence of the Holy Spirit to "bring all things to their remembrance," and to "teach them all things." (See John 14:25–26.) Their testimony as eyewitnesses and companions of the Saviour's earthly life was to be confirmed and supplemented by that of the Holy Spirit given through them. (See John 15:26–27.) Things were to be taught them which they could not yet bear. The Spirit should guide them into "all truth," declare unto them "things to come," take of the things of Christ, and declare unto them. (See John 16:12–15.)

These promises seem to involve both revelation and inspiration, according to the distinction we have drawn between them, and to assure the apostles not only of the divine impartation of truth, which they did not yet know, and could not now bear, but also divine guidance and control in every particular regarding the proclamation of the gospel.

Evidently, however, there is no promise of omniscience, of supernatural information in all human knowledge. And we have no reason to claim or to suppose that this was granted. On this series of promises we have several remarks to submit.

a. The peculiar expression, "the Spirit of Truth," evidently refers to His special office of Revealer and Inspirer. The Spirit's presence might indeed be valuable in other respects. It would give comfort and light. It might confer miraculous powers of various kinds. But this promise seems to point particularly to gifts conferred in His character as the Spirit of Truth, giving them the truth, and enabling them to give it to others.

b. The Spirit was to "bring to remembrance" all that Christ had said. His divine teachings are not trusted to the fallible memory of the men who heard them. These precious deposits are to be insured, repeated, presented afresh, in more condensed form, in more perfect light, in clearer relations to all else that they knew, and especially to the advancing providence and revelations of God. The apostles needed to be enabled to recall and summarize all that the Lord had taught them during His earthly life, and all that He was going to unfold to their opened and enlarged understandings during those wondrous forty days between the Resurrection and the Ascension. This was a period the importance of which must not be estimated by the space given to it in the narrative, but rather by the transforming effects which have been evidently wrought upon the timorous and hesitating disciples of the Passover evening, by the time that we next meet them, on the day of Pentecost.

c. Furthermore, they needed to be qualified to give due proportion and harmony to their preaching. As Lee has expressed it, to "insert in their teaching, without interweaving any heterogeneous element, each particular circumstance as it contributed to the elucidation of the general scheme."[20]

The facts of the gospel history were of course familiar to them. But they needed explanation of the meaning of these facts, as well as the true intent of many of the sayings of our Lord, which they themselves had heard, but which they did not yet fairly or fully appreciate. The relation of these great events to the plan of human redemption, to the divine counsels in the past, and to the progress of the kingdom throughout the ages, was yet to be made known to them. Their own faculties were not to be superseded, however, and disused, but to be used and aided. Their own recollection was to be employed, but guided and reinforced by the Holy Spirit.

d. The Spirit was to "teach them all things," to guide them into "all truth." Our Lord expressly draws the distinction between the things *He* had spoken to them while yet present with them, and the teachings of the Spirit which are to be super-added to them. (See John 14:25–26.) This additional light is not, on the one hand, supernatural information in *every* department of human knowledge, as some have extravagantly interpreted it. Nor is it mere illumination in saving knowledge, such as all converted persons possess, as others unduly limit it. It was not for themselves personally and only, but for them officially, and for the benefit of others. It is expressly connected by our Lord with the intimation that He had many things to say unto them, which *they* were not then able to bear.

A slow and deliberate revelation. Why the revelation of divine truth by God in the Old Testament period should have been so slow and deliberate.

Why, in like manner, it should have been made so gradually by our Lord Himself.

Why it is left incomplete even at this critical moment, when He is leaving the world, and withdrawing from the disciples whom He loved, and the sinner for whom He died, may be an interesting question. But it is certainly a fact. And from considering it, we see the necessity that this added, advancing influence should be given, to finish the unfinished work.

It need scarcely be again remarked here, that incompleteness is not error. The imperfection and inferiority freely acknowledged in the Old Testament as compared with the New, and even in the earlier of the progressive communications of our Lord, or in those of the promised Spirit itself, do not conflict with their being thoroughly divine, and exactly true, as far as they went. That which is imperfect is not necessarily either faulty or false.

e. The Spirit was also promised to "show them things to come," an expression which implies their endowment for predictive as well as declarative prophecy, their ability to describe—what no mere man can know—the future.

f. The earlier promises recorded in the synoptic Gospels are interpreted and confirmed by these later promises. In view of these legacies, both of love and of authority, which our Saviour gives in contemplation of His immediately impending death, it is preposterous to assume that the spiritual aid He had previously promised to them was to be only for their personal defense, and to be confined to the judicial occasions then specially mentioned, as before synagogues and magistrates. The promise is emphasized, renewed, and also enlarged.

It may furthermore be fairly understood, that these additional instructions, given them by the Holy Spirit subsequently to His death, had the same stamp of infallibility as those spoken to them by the lips of the Master Himself.

g. It is only necessary to add that these promises did not extend indefifinitely. Hence the offices both of apostle and prophet came to an end, so far as we can discover, with the apostolic age. There is no proof that either had any successors in office. If like authority is claimed for any others, the claim ought to be supported by adequate, not to say similar and equal, evidence.

The forty days. The meaning of these promises receives further elucidation from the record of the period between the Resurrection and the Ascension. It is evident, as already suggested, that the forty days of our Saviour's mysterious life on earth after the Resurrection were no mere pause in the progress of events. Instead it made a decided advance in the teaching, and in the preparation of the apostles for their great work. Even prior to His death the instructions had become more frequent, more clear, more impressive and precious. They had revolved more about the central doctrines and eternal realities as the Great Teacher approached the appointed death of which He had so tenderly warned them. And now, in this interval, there are plentiful indications that He both opened their understandings, and presented to their opened understandings quickening truths. After their brief course of instruction under this new schooling, the apostles came out widely different men from the vacillating, trembling, earthly-minded fugitives, who, six weeks before, had all forsaken Him and fled. The chiefs of modern rationalism, such as Paulus and Strauss, have not been able to withhold the acknowledgment that this transformation in the character and conduct of the apostles is inexplicable, unless "*something extraordinary* be supposed to have occurred during this interval."

On the very evening which closed that ever memorable first day of the week on which our Lord rose from the dead, He comforted and recommissioned His affrighted disciples. He told them, "Peace be unto you; as the Father hath sent me, even so send I you. And when he had said this, he breathed on them, and saith unto them, Receive ye the Holy Spirit; whose soever sins ye forgive, they are forgiven unto them; whose soever sins ye retain, they are retained" (John 20:21–23). But even this formal imparting of the Holy Spirit is not enough.

It is distinctly recorded that He afterwards not only expounded to them, as He had done before, that all things which are written in the Law of Moses, and in the Prophets, and in the Psalms concerning Him must be fulfilled. But He also "opened their mind, that they might understand the Scriptures" (Luke 24:45). At the same time He renewed the assurance that He would send forth "the promise of the Father" upon them. And He enjoined on them to tarry in the city until they were clothed with power from on high.

The day of Pentecost. In addition to those personal teachings of our risen Saviour, when the day of Pentecost was fully come, the Spirit was given. Too much stress can hardly be laid on this fact. Better even than the presence of Jesus Himself are these promised communications. And they are continued during their ministry, varied and adapted to all the contingencies that arose in their official duties. The apostles, from the notable day, were entirely different men. They were endued anew, and in higher measure than ever before, with power from on high.

Peter at Joppa. An unmistakable example of the influence of the divine Spirit in imparting new truth is the case of Peter at Joppa. He learned by the vision, and by the Spirit's manifestation at Caesarea, the true relation of the Gentiles to the church of Christ. He expressly states that his new position was not something evolved or reasoned out by himself from the truths already known, but revealed to him by God in antagonism to his former prejudices and opinions. God had "showed it" to him (Acts 10:28).

From this whole line of argument, then, it appears that promises of inspiration were distinctly and repeatedly made to writers both of the Old and New Testament. We do not believe that there was any breach of these promises, or that they in any respect failed to be fulfilled.

Assertions of Inspiration by the Sacred Writers

Of course, assertions of this kind by men themselves, unsupported and unattested, would have no weight whatever. Mohammed or Joe Smith could make such assertions.

But the assertions of the sacred writers form an important link in the chain of argument, when taken in connection with the character of the men. This is true when, on the one hand, the divine promises going before are considered, and on the other, the miraculous confirmations accompanying and following, "the Lord working with them and confirming the Word with signs following."

These men are thoroughly authenticated, as in some sense teachers sent from God. That, for Christians, is a settled point. The question now is, what claims, as such, do they make for themselves?

A. In the Old Testament

A few of the passages may be quoted:

Second Samuel 23:2, David says: "The Spirit of the LORD spake by me, and his word was in my tongue."

Isaiah 1:2: "Hear, O heavens, and give ear, O earth; for the LORD hath spoken." (Compare Isaiah 1:20: "The mouth of the LORD hath spoken.")

Jeremiah 1:4–10: "The word of the LORD came unto me, saying," etc. . . . "Then the LORD put forth his hand, and touched my mouth. And the LORD said unto me, Behold, I have put my words in thy mouth."

Jeremiah 15:19: "If thou return, then will I bring thee again, that thou mayest stand before me; and if thou take forth the precious from the vile, thou shalt be as my mouth."

Ezekiel 1:3: "The word of the LORD came expressly to Ezekiel, the priest, . . . and the hand of the LORD was upon him." (Compare 3:4, 10, 11, 17, 27.)

These expressions certainly convey the idea that the prophets claimed to be speaking, not their own words, but those with which they had been entrusted by God.

B. Assertions of Inspiration by the New Testament Writers

It is unquestionable that they do lay claim, in numerous ways and on various occasions, to an authority more than human. No principle can possibly be stated which would limit these claims to those precise occasions, or forbid their extension to other official communications of these same individuals. Their authority rested generally on their well-known character as the accredited representatives of the Almighty, speaking in His name to men. They only repeated or urged anew their claim of divine authority, when it was questioned, or when some special reason required its assertion. Elsewhere it is quietly taken for granted.

While frankly admitting their own fallibility in conduct, and imperfection in grace, and liability to mistake in everything but this for which they are inspired, these writers fearlessly claim to be heard as from God in the proclamation of the gospel, and as to the concerns of the soul. Against any rejection or neglect of that message, they warn men with the utmost energy, and with tearful anxiety and tenderness.

The doctrine which they teach they did not derive from study, did not reason out for themselves. They did not take credit to themselves for acquiring it, or devoting themselves to it. It is all due to the holy impulse and enlightening influence of the Spirit of God.

Their authority they represent as equal to that of the Old Testament prophets. The church is built "upon the foundation of the apostles and prophets" (Eph. 2:20). Now there is no question that the Jews of that time, as well as these Christian teachers, held the inspiration of the Old Testament prophets. If the apostles are found claiming to be regarded as on an equal footing with the prophets, there is no stronger form in which they could assert their own inspiration.

If it is alleged that this guidance and aid were restricted to oral, not written, teachings—

1. We would ask, why? Can any valid reason be assigned?[21]

2. Divine authority is expressly claimed by them for their written word. See 1 Corinthians 14:37: "If any man thinketh himself to be a prophet, or spiritual, let him take knowledge of the things which I *write* unto you, that they are the commandment of the Lord." (Compare John 20:31; 2 Thess. 2:15; and 1 Cor. 2:13.)

Let us now consider some of the passages in which these claims are made by writers of the New Testament.

Acts 15:1–6, 28: The apostles and elders at Jerusalem, in the decision given upon the question from Antioch, say, "It seemed good to the Holy Ghost, and to us."

Romans 16:25–27: The apostle Paul conjoins his own preaching with "the scriptures of the prophets, according to the commandment of the eternal God," as the source of Christian knowledge unto "all the nations."

The case of Paul is somewhat peculiar, and therefore we have in his case special abundance of evidence. He was not one of the original Twelve. His authority, however, is not based simply on the inspiration which men would persuade us belonged to the Christian community as a whole (of which we discover no suitable evidence); nor on that which he might claim as a prophet, which might have been adequate; nor on his adoption into their order, and recognition by the original apostles. It is because of his special call and commission as an apostle by Jesus Christ Himself. He had received the truth not from human sources, even the highest and most direct. He received it from the Lord Jesus personally by an internal disclosure (Gal. 1:11, 16). He has seen the Lord (1 Cor. 15:10; Acts 22:6). He has had abundant evidence subjectively and objectively of his apostleship (Rom. 1:1, 5; 1 Cor. 9:1, 2).

1 Corinthians 2:1–16: In consequence of divisions in the church at Corinth, Paul is led to declare his own apostolic authority. Negatively, he says that his proclamation of the mystery of God was not with excellency of speech or of wisdom. It was not with man's wisdom, not the wisdom of the world. Positively, it was God's wisdom in a mystery, spoken in demonstration of the Spirit, revealed by God through the Spirit. And not only does he thus ascribe to God the communication of the knowledge to him (revelation), but also the words in which it is conveyed by himself to other men (inspiration); "which things also we speak, not in words which man's wisdom teacheth, but which the Spirit teacheth." Here is a clear reference to God, not only of the doctrine taught, but of the form, the words, in which it is taught.

1 Corinthians 14:37: "If any man thinketh himself to be a prophet or spiritual, let him acknowledge the things which I write unto you, that they are the commandment of the Lord." It is a test of discipleship that they acknowledge his regulations in church matters as from the Lord.

2 Corinthians 13:2–3: He claims official control in the church: "I write to them who heretofore have sinned and to all other, that, if I come again, I will not spare: seeing that ye seek a proof of Christ that speaketh in me." And this is not as to some abstract truth which he has declared, but as to the application of the principles of Christian discipline in correcting particular cases of disorder.

Galatians 1:8–12: "But though we, or an angel from heaven, should preach unto you any gospel other than that which we preached unto you, let him be anathema. As we have said before, so say I now again, If any man preacheth unto you any gospel other than that which ye received, let him be anathema. For am I now persuading men, or God? or am I seeking to please men? If

I were still pleasing men, I should not be a servant of Christ. For I make known to you, brethren, as touching the gospel which was preached by me, that it is not after man. For neither did I receive it from man, nor was I taught it, but it came to me through revelation of Jesus Christ."

Nothing but a distinct conviction and assurance from above of his own authority as an inspired man could warrant the claims Paul here puts forth. He had not received his doctrine from men, not even from the other apostles. And if any proclaim a different gospel—even if he himself should, or if an angel from heaven should do it—he denounces with the utmost severity such a departure from the gospel which he had proclaimed.

Ephesians 2:20: In this Scripture, the apostles and prophets are classed together, and are represented as the foundation on which Christians are built, Jesus Christ Himself being the chief corner stone. It is immaterial here whether the prophets be understood to be those of the Old Testament or of New Testament times. The authority which Paul attributes to "the prophets" is well understood. He ranks the apostles with them, and places both in fundamental connection with Jesus Christ Himself. This teaching of the apostles and prophets, then, is a sure foundation, infallibly true and certain.

Ephesians 3:1–7: Paul claims that God by revelation made known to him the mystery "which in other ages was not made known unto the sons of men, as it is now revealed unto his holy apostles and prophets by the Spirit;" and that of this gospel he was "made a minister, according to the gift of the grace of God, given unto [him] by the effectual working of his power." It is by the agency of the Spirit, by the effectual working of divine power, that this knowledge has been communicated to him, and to the other apostles and prophets.

1 Thessalonians 2:13: He thanks God that "when ye received the word of God which ye heard of us, ye received it not as the word of men, but as it is in truth, the word of God." It was divine teaching, though received by them from human lips. It is matter of continual rejoicing that they received it as such. Here is a sharp contrast between simply human instruction—persuasion,

argument, the word of men—and divine instruction, authoritative assertion, the Word of God. The apostolic teaching is expressly said to be of the latter kind.

1 Thessalonians 4:2, 8, 15: "Ye know what commandments we gave you by the Lord Jesus." "He therefore that despiseth, despiseth not man, but God, who hath also given us his holy Spirit." "This we say unto you by the word of the Lord," giving a statement as to the wondrous future events at the resurrection day.

2 Thessalonians 2:13–15: He points to the two-fold influence exerted in their salvation by "sanctification of the Spirit and belief of the truth." To this they had been called by "our gospel," and accordingly they are to "stand fast, and hold the traditions which ye have been taught, whether by word, or by our epistle."

The power of the Spirit and that of the truth are here intimately associated. That truth they had learned through the preaching of the apostle. If they are to stand fast in the salvation they have received, it is to be by faithful adherence to the teachings they had obtained from Paul. Moreover, it makes no difference whether these teachings were oral or written. They were equally binding, equally authoritative, equally connected with salvation.

1 Peter 1:10–12: The inspiration of the Old Testament writers is here shown to be no mere modification or exaltation of their own unaided faculties, but the impartation of capacity and authority, by "the Spirit of Christ which was in them," to speak on subjects which they did not otherwise understand, and to record things the meaning of which they were still left to search and inquire diligently into. Furthermore, the proclamation of the gospel in New Testament times was "by the Holy Spirit sent forth from heaven."

2 Peter 3:1–2: An equal place is claimed in the attention and confidence of the people for "the words that were spoken before by the holy prophets," and "the commandment of us the Apostles of the Lord and Saviour." The Canterbury Revision adopts a different reading, and translates the last clause "the commandment of the Lord and Saviour through your Apostles." This

would not vary materially the evidence, but presents our doctrine in rather more distinct terms.

Revelation 1:1–3, 10–11, 19: Revelation opens with a vision of God, and a command to John, (such as had been formerly given to Moses), to write in a book what he sees. The assurance is afterwards given that this communication is from the same Almighty One, "the Lord God of the holy prophets."

Revelation 22:6–7, 18–19: The angel says, "These words are faithful and true; and the Lord, the God of the spirits of the prophets, sent his angel to show unto his servants the things that must shortly come to pass." There is added a most solemn warning against adding to, or taking away from, the words of the book of this prophecy, on peril of incurring all the plagues, and forfeiting all the blessings of the eternal world.

Considering this whole series of claims put forth by the apostles and their associates, it is impossible to overlook:

- *the formal and public position* assumed by the apostles as the introducers, under the authority of Jesus Christ, of the new revelation;

- nor the *distinct connection* of this with the old revelation, their reverence for which is well known and universally acknowledged;

- nor the *tone of authority and command* which men, who were not ambitious but humble, not self-seekers and worldly, but self-sacrificing and spiritual, assume in addressing their fellow men as to the concerns of their souls.

Passages in Which the Union of the Human and Divine Authorship of Portions of Scripture Is Expressly Recognized

The special feature of our doctrine of inspiration, (which may probably excite question among those unfamiliar with the subject), is the thorough-going ascription of a divine character to those parts of the Bible which are most obviously and unmistakably human.

According to our view, indeed, there is no part of the Bible which does not show clearly the marks of human origin. This is the first and most obvious of the "phenomena" and also of the "claims" of Scripture—that it is written by Moses, David, Isaiah, Paul, and other men; and this is equally true of those portions the human authors of which are unnamed and unknown. But we have endeavored to show that this is not inconsistent with the real divine authorship.

The Divine Origin, the Human Agency

The divine origin is as strongly and as distinctly affirmed as if there had been no human instrumentality involved. The human agency is also as clearly and unmistakably presented as if there had been no divine interposition in the case. We believe that much of the error and difficulty that have arisen in the minds of devout and earnest inquirers are due to looking exclusively at one or the other of these classes of facts. It may be useful to present some passages of Scripture where the union of the human and the divine element in the same utterance is distinctly stated or recognized. Here the same words are quoted and ascribed indifferently and equally to God and to man as their author.

Consider:

- The commandment, "Honor thy father and thy mother" (Exod. 20:12), is quoted (Matt. 15:4) under the expression, "God said"; and again (Mark 7:10) the Saviour is represented as saying, "Moses said."

- The language of the Psalm (110:1), "The Lord said unto my Lord," etc., is quoted (Mark 12:36) with the expression "David . . . said by the Holy Spirit," which really presents both sides of the truth in the single statement. In the succeeding verse (Mark 12:37) the same evangelist informs us that our Saviour adds, "David . . . himself calleth him Lord." Compare Matthew 22:43, "How then doth David in the spirit call him Lord?" It is difficult to see in what more explicit language both the authorship by David and the inspiration by the Spirit could be affirmed. Or what higher testimony could be adduced than that of Him who was at once both God and man.

- The argument of our Lord from the expressions in which Jehovah is called "the God of Abraham, the God of Isaac, and the God of Jacob" (Exod. 3:6, 15), is worthy of special attention. He gives it (Matt. 22:31) as that which was "spoken unto you by God"; again (Luke 20:37), as what "Moses shewed at the bush," etc.; while Mark (12:26), who is noted for giving minute details and precise circumstances, combines both ideas, and presents the language, "Have ye not read in the book of Moses, how in [the place concerning] the bush, God spake unto him, saying, I am the God of Abraham?" etc.

It is not necessary to our purpose here to vindicate our Lord from the charge of using "rabbinical dialectic" and illogical argumentation. God had spoken thus to Moses (Exod. 3:6), and bade him speak the same things to the people (Exod. 3:15). Luke shows that our Lord emphasized the fact of its coming through Moses—"Even Moses showed." Our Lord authoritatively expounds the passage in a deeper sense than the obvious one, and shows that "the Eternal would not make and avow such a covenant, save with those whose existence is permanent."[22]

- That frequently quoted passage (Isa. 6:10), in reference to the fat heart, and heavy ears, and closed eyes of the people, is referred to by Paul (Acts 28:25): "Well spake the Holy Spirit by Isaiah the prophet unto your fathers," etc.; while John (12:39–41) declares, "Isaiah said again," and, "These things said Isaiah, because he saw his glory."

- Peter, in like manner, says, "It was needful that the Scripture should be fulfilled, which the Holy Spirit spake before by the mouth of David concerning Judas" (Acts 1:16); thus combining both ideas in the one phrase. (See Acts 4:25.)

- So too Matthew (1:22; 2:15) employs, in quoting, the expression "spoken by the Lord, through the prophet"; not "of the Lord by the prophet." It was unquestionably intended to convey precisely what we understand it to mean, namely, that the speaking was primarily and fundamentally the Lord's, and that the utterance of this divine message was through the prophet speaking for him. No line of discrimination is to be drawn between the human and the divine portions of Scripture.

- In Hebrews, not only portions from the express words of Jehovah as recorded in the Old Testament are quoted with the expressions, "God saith," "the Holy Spirit saith," "the Holy Spirit also is a witness to us," but even the words of Jeremiah and David. Each of the three great divisions of the Scriptures (the Law, Prophets, and Psalms) is thus referred to.[23]

- Turning to the New Testament apostles and prophets, in their inspired testimony, it is apparent that their human characteristics and circumstances are intended to be employed as natural means of enforcing their witness and giving it the utmost credibility. The fact of their being personal eyewitnesses is again and again insisted on. Yet this human personality of theirs is not in the slightest degree incompatible with their utterance being at the same time the message of God. And the combination of the two testimonies is expressly brought to view in such passages as John 15:26–27, "When the Comforter is come ... he shall bear witness of me; and ye also bear witness, because ye have been with me from the beginning." Luke 24:48–49, "Ye are witnesses of these things. And behold I send forth the promise of my Father [the Spirit] upon you: but tarry ye in the city, until ye be clothed with power from on high." And among the very last words spoken to them by our Lord on Olivet, just before He ascended, He said, "Ye shall receive power, when the Holy Spirit is come upon you; and ye shall be my witnesses . . . unto the uttermost parts of the earth" (Acts 1:8).

Accordingly, the apostles, in the presence of the council, declare: "And we are witnesses of these things; and so is the Holy Spirit, whom God hath given to them that obey him (Acts 5:32)." And, when assembled for consultation at Jerusalem, on the subject of circumcision, they give their decisions under the form, "It seemed good to the Holy Spirit and to us" (Acts 15:28); which style, observes the judicious Hooker, "they did not use as matching themselves in power with the Holy Ghost, but as testifying the Holy Ghost to be the Author, and themselves but only utterers of that decree."[24]

The doctrine indicated in these passages is precisely what we have been endeavoring to advocate, and to show to be the Scriptural doctrine of inspiration. If we have succeeded in proving this, our end has been attained. Those for whose special benefit this discussion has been designed will readily admit that whatever representation the Scriptures make on the subject is the true one.

In conclusion, we have to observe that the force and effect of the various arguments exhibited are not to be obtained by considering each apart, but by taking the whole result. Each one does not bear alone the whole weight of the conclusion. As Bishop Butler has well said of the evidence for Christianity, so the evidence of inspiration combines many things "of great variety and compass, . . . making up, all of them together, one argument; the conviction arising from which kind of proof may be compared to what they call *the effect* in architecture or other works of art, a result from a great number of things so and so disposed, and taken into one view."[25]

It has been shown that there is a reasonable presumption that God in giving a revelation, as it is agreed He has done, would inspire it; that the proper source and kind of evidence to prove that He has actually inspired the Bible is in its own statements and phenomena; that this conclusion is established:

1. by the general manner of quoting Scripture in Scripture;

2. by passages which affirm or imply the inspiration of the Scriptures as a whole;

3. by declarations affirming the inspiration of particular persons or passages;

4. by promises of inspiration to the sacred writers;

5. by assertions of inspiration by the sacred writers;

6. by passages in which that union of the human and the divine authorship which we have seen to be implied, is expressly recognized.

Thus the Bible statements on the subject have been considered, in general and in detail, as classified and part by part. It remains only to submit our minds frankly and lovingly to the combined influence of *all God's words about His Word*, and to join with peaceful confidence in the prayer and the assurance of our Lord Jesus—"Sanctify them in the truth: Thy Word is truth."

PART III

Objections
To Inspiration

It remains only that we give a brief, but full and frank consideration of the principal objections that have been urged against the doctrine of plenary inspiration, which we have endeavored to expound and establish.

CHAPTER NINE

Objections from Scripture

Certain passages of Scripture are urged, in which it is alleged that some of the sacred writers disclaim inspiration, at least in the cases mentioned. From this it is attempted to infer, somewhat illogically, that the disclaimer applies equally to all that is contained in the Bible, even if written by entirely different men. Let us candidly examine these passages, and see what they imply.

Supernatural Assistance

Luke 1:3: It seemed good to me also, having traced the course of all things accurately from the first, to write unto thee in order. . . ."

To some, this claim of careful and accurate inquiry seems to conflict with the idea of assistance or direction from a supernatural source. They assume apparently that there could be no inspiration except as to the record of such things as were derived exclusively from revelation. But this is an unwarranted assumption. And certainly that is not the view of inspiration for which we contend.

If Luke had denied that there was any other source of information than these inquiries of his, or that he had any aid from above in the arrangement of the materials, however gathered, this objection might have some validity as against the revelation or inspiration of the two historical books of his composition. Though even then it would be necessary to show that this denial affected the other books of the Bible.

But there is no positive disclaimer of that sort, nor even any implied denial here. While asserting this diligent search and comparison of information, he nowhere distinguishes between the authority of the things so derived, and the facts concerning which he makes no reference to such sources.

The case might be illustrated by supposing that Peter, while claiming to have been an eyewitness of the Redeemer's transfigured majesty, and therefore worthy to be believed in reference to that event on the ground of his personal testimony, had denied, instead of affirming, that on other subjects he "preached the Gospel with the Holy Ghost sent down from heaven." If he had denied it, there would have been evidence of the absence of divine agency or authority. But as he makes no such distinction between the different parts of his teaching, and no disclaimer of inspiration as to any part, this reference to his personal observation and experience on a particular point does not invalidate his general authority.

Neither does Luke's allusion to his diligent investigations invalidate his authority. He was as really controlled in the record of what he knew naturally by personal observation, and of what he learned by inquiry and diligent research, as in the communication of what he received by direct revelation. And this control is what we mean by inspiration.

The question is a different one, when it is asked on what ground Luke's writings are accepted as inspired, when he was not an apostle. That question belongs to the subject of the Canon, and does not properly come up here. But it may be remarked that the general recognition of his Gospel and of the Acts by the churches during the lifetime of the apostles, and his intimate association with Paul, lead to the inference that he was to be classed among the prophets or apostolic men to whom inspiration was granted. The same thing substantially may be said in regard to the Gospel according to Mark, who was similarly associated with Peter.

1 Corinthians 7:6–25: In this passage the apostle gives directions concerning sundry practical questions of difficulty, as to marriage, separation of married people, etc., about which the Corinthians had written to him.

In reference to the propriety of marriage in general for most people, he says, verse 6: "I speak this by permission, [or by way of permission] and not of commandment," i.e. in the way of an indulgence or allowance to you, not as a commandment which I enjoin. There is no reference, as some have imagined, to the difference in the authority by which he speaks in the different cases, as if the origin or nature of that authority were in question.

Even if the meaning were, that in this case he was only permitted, not commanded, by the Spirit to utter what he did, the objection would have no weight against the doctrine of inspiration. Because, if this teaching was permitted by the Spirit, it could not be opposed to the truth and to the will of God as expressed in his other teachings. But both the language itself, when properly translated so as to be free from ambiguity, and the connection of the argument, make it clear that the contrast intended is not between things which Paul is permitted and other things which he is commanded to speak. It is between things which Paul in his apostolic character permits or allows, but does not command, and other things which he commands. To marry is not wrong, nor to abstain from marriage. "Marry, if you think best; I speak this by way of permission, not as a commandment."

We may compare with this a corresponding expression in 2 Corinthians 8:8, 10. Addressing the Corinthians, and commending to their imitation the great liberality of the churches of Macedonia, he says, "I speak not by commandment, but. . . . I give my advice: for this is expedient for you."

So far the matter is really quite plain. All respectable commentators agree as to the meaning. The real difficulty, or the point on which the objection is based, begins in the tenth verse of the passage in 1 Corinthians 7:10–25.

In verse 10, the apostle says, "I command, yet not I, but the Lord": in verse 25, "concerning virgins I have no commandment of the Lord: yet I give my judgement."

God's Commandment, Men's Suggestion?

It is alleged that this is a contrast between different portions of what he speaks, as being part of them of divine origin and authority, and part his own opinion, human, fallible, and therefore uncertain. Part God's commandment, and part men's own suggestion merely.

This is evidently not the contrast intended. It is not a distinction between what is authoritative and what is not so. It is between that which he speaks simply reiterating the express words of *the Lord Jesus*, personally uttered, and that which he speaks by inspiration, not having any words of Jesus to quote. Both are authoritative, both divine. But the first comes from Christ primarily. The other comes in the first instance to Paul himself, and through him to the Corinthian church.[1]

It need scarcely be remarked that "the Lord," in Acts and the Epistles, is the standing and habitual designation for the Lord Jesus personally. This is well understood and admitted by all careful students of the New Testament.

There are three questions here as to the law of marriage. These arose in the early Christian churches, in their hand-to-hand conflict with heathenism. These questions pertained:

1. to the married in general (v. 10);

2. to the special cases of mixed marriages, where one party was a believer and the other not (v. 12); and

3. to the unmarried (v. 25).

The Married

As to the first, the Lord Jesus had personally laid down the law. (See Mark 10:2–12.) From that there was no appeal, and to that nothing could be added.[2] To those already married, Paul says, "I command, yet not I, but the Lord." He simply repeats and enjoins what Jesus the Lord had commanded with His own lips.

Mixed Marriages

As to the other two cases, Christ had given no specific commandment. These questions had scarcely arisen during his brief personal ministry. So the apostle proceeds to give his own decision as to mixed marriages. This he clearly means to be authoritative. He adds: "So ordain I in all churches" (1 Cor. 7:17). It is not a mere individual opinion, thrown out casually, uncertain, local and temporary in its application. In the Old Testament dispensation a somewhat different law had prevailed as to mixed marriages. According to the Mosaic Law, such a union was not to be formed at all between Israelites and Gentiles, between Jehovah's worshipers and idolaters. When formed, under the peculiar circumstances prevailing, for example, after the exile, such heathen or foreign wives were to be resolutely and invariably put away. This was done even in cases which seemed to involved great severity and distress. (See Ezra 10:2–19; Neh. 13:23–27.) But Paul enjoins that now the believing or Christian party shall *not* abandon the other, a rule which needed direct, original, divine authority to establish and enforce it, as he does "in all churches."

To the Unmarried

As to virgins, the unmarried, he has no commandment of the Lord. That is, no express word of Jesus to quote. But he proceeds to give advice suited to the peculiar circumstances. He gives suggestions but lays down no universal rule. He closes this discussion (1 Cor. 7:40) by saying, "I think also that I have the Spirit of God."

There are some who regard this passage as expressing Paul's doubt of his own inspiration. Because Paul says he thought he had the Spirit of God, they are quite sure that he had not. They represent it as implying uncertainty in his own mind as to his divine authorization, or as to his possessing the Spirit. This is certainly not its meaning.

So far from that, in this same epistle, having referred to the existence of miraculous gifts in the church, one of which was the discerning of spirits, he says, "If any man think himself to be a prophet, or spiritual, let him acknowledge that the things *that I write unto you* are the commandments of the Lord" (1 Corinthians 14:37).

Romans 6:18–19: "I speak after the manner of men." What does the apostle mean by this? He had just spoken of the believer as the *slave* of righteousness. He adds that this is but a human illustration, drawn from human affairs, and must not be misapplied.

The expression "slave" must not be strained to imply severity, compulsion, reluctance, injustice. It only conveys the idea of the relation of entire ownership and consecration, in which the Christian delights to stand towards holiness and God. "I have used an illustration," he would say, "drawn from human relations, on account of the intellectual infirmity of your flesh. You need such figures to set the truth vividly before you." Thus he is speaking after the manner of men, but with no renunciation of the divine authority with which he speaks.

2 Corinthians 11:17: "That which I speak, I speak not after the Lord, but as in foolishness." Does he mean that he is speaking nonsense? Is he deliberately and purposely making himself a fool? Certainly not. Just before he had said, "I say again, Let no man think me foolish; but if ye do, yet as foolish receive me, that I also may glory a little."

It is the outgushing of his ardent, affectionate heart, grieved that he should be misjudged and mistreated by those for whom he had toiled so devotedly. Yet he only poured forth more freely out of that pierced and wounded heart the zealous desires he had ever felt for their welfare.

"Grant that I am a fool. Put me in the position of a fool, if you will. It has been for your sake that I have acted thus. And even if counted by you as foolish, I deserve *your* sympathy and consideration."

The language is plainly ironical, assuming, for the sake of argument, that what some of them are charging him with is correct, and showing that even on that ground he could boast, if so inclined, of more abundant labors and sacrifices for them and for the gospel. But it is said, he alleges that he speaks not only "as in foolishness," but "not after the Lord"; and that this must mean that he is at least then not under the influence of inspiration. If this interpretation be correct, and if he here disclaims it in regard to this apparent self-boasting to which he is compelled by the unworthy and ungrateful depreciation of his labors among the Corinthians, would not the express exception in this case only confirm more incontestable the general claim that elsewhere he is speaking the mind of the Lord?

But it is admitted, even by those (as Meyer and Alford) who regard Paul as in this passage denying "the theopneustic character of the utterance in the stricter sense," that this is done "without his laying aside the consciousness of the Spirit's guidance, under which he, for his purpose, allows the human emotion temporarily to speak."

Meyer adds that "Bengel aptly says: But even this passage, and the exception peculiar to this passage, he so wrote according to a *rule of divine propriety*, being instructed by the Lord."

Paul's Self-Praise

On the other hand however, Hodge thinks as we do that, even in this very passage,

Such an utterance is not inconsistent with the Apostle's claim to inspiration. For the simple end of inspiration is to secure infallibility in the communication of truth. It does not sanctify, nor does it preclude the natural play of the intellect or of the feelings. Even if therefore this conduct of Paul was due to human weakness, that would not prove that he was not under the inspiration of God. But such an assumption is needless. There was nothing wrong in his self-laudation. He never appears more truly humble than when these references to his labors and sufferings were wrung from him, filling him with a feeling of self-contempt. All that the expression implies is, that self-praise, in itself considered, is not the work of a Christian; it is not the work to which the Spirit of Christ impels a believer. But when it is necessary to the vindication of truth or the honor of religion, it becomes a duty.[3]

Must we not accept the testimony of the apostle, that even in this glorying "the truth of Christ is in [him]" (2 Cor. 11:10), and that his object in what exposes him to misconstruction is a pure and noble one, so that he can appeal confidently to the divine judgment in the matter—"God knoweth" (v. 11)?

2 Corinthians 12:2–3: "Whether in the body, I cannot tell; or whether out of the body, I cannot tell: God knoweth"; literally "whether in the body, I know not; or whether out of the body, I know not; God knoweth."

Those Things Paul Did Not Know

This passage is adduced to show that there were some things which Paul admits he did not know. From this confessed limitation of his knowledge, it is inferred that he cannot have been inspired.

But this inference would only be just on the ground that inspiration implied omniscience, which no one attempts to claim. That there were some things which God knew, and which Paul did not, does not invalidate his real inspiration.

Does it?

If it did, would any real inspiration be possible or conceivable in any man? Is it not obvious that the objection is grounded on such a notion of inspiration as is utterly impracticable, and such as no intelligent advocate of inspiration holds?

Paul's Faulty Memory

1 Corinthians 1:16: "I know not whether I baptized any other." A somewhat similar argument is based on this passage as upon the one last mentioned. It is said: Here is a matter on which Paul's mind is in doubt as to a matter of fact. He remembers distinctly that he baptized Crispus and Gaius, and the household of Stephanas, in whose providential and helpful presence he is rejoicing. He does not remember whether he baptized any other.

His memory is at fault.

Hence, says Alford, "the last clause is important as against those who maintain the *absolute omniscience* of the inspired writers *on every topic which they handle.*"

But we do not allege their omniscience on every subject, or even on any subject. Only that all that they say is accurate, and is uttered under divine direction and authority. As Hodge says, "We learn that inspiration was an influence which rendered its recipients infallible, but it did not render them omniscient. They were preserved from asserting error, but they were not enabled either to know or to remember all things."

CHAPTER TEN

Objection from the Existence of Difficulties

The general fact of the existence of difficulties and obscurities in the Bible is urged as a proof that it cannot be inspired. It is assumed by some that, if it were inspired, there would be none; that everything coming from God must necessarily be perfect, in the sense of being free from all deficiency, and therefore from all obscurity as well as liability to error.

We answer, that this is an unwarranted assumption. On the contrary, it might be expected that there would be difficulties in the Bible, notwithstanding it is inspired; and this is reasonably inferrible—

a. From the nature of *human language*, which is an incomplete medium for the expression of thought, ambiguous often, changeable in the lapse of time, and always liable to be misinterpreted.

b. From the nature of the *mind*, which is limited in its capacities, defective in the power of steady attention, frequently partial and one-sided in its investigations even when thoroughly sincere, and often prejudiced unconsciously. Some obscurities arise from the eye that sees, rather than from the nature of the object seen. Better eyesight would lay many a ghost, and clearer minds would remove many difficulties.

c. From the nature of *the truths revealed*. "A Bible without difficulties would be a firmament without stars." Such a one would have to omit many subjects on which the Bible instructs and cheers man, and could not touch some of the sublimest truths that the Bible actually presents. Some of these things are abstruse and elevated, some apparently conflict, but having their connections and harmonious relations established, where they meet up yonder in a sphere higher than human observation can now reach.

d. From the nature of *God Himself,* who from His infinity cannot be thoroughly comprehended by any finite intelligence. All that we are competent to understand of Him is just what He has revealed—part of His ways. The man who thinks he absolutely comprehends anything infinite only shows the shallowness of his comprehension.

e. From the *analogy of all God's communications* to man in nature. The obscurities in His Word and those in His works correspond. The same characteristics are found in both revelations—in the Bible and in the universe. The grand work of Bishop Butler, his *Analogy of Natural and Revealed Religion,* is chiefly devoted to exhibiting this fact, and specially shows that like obscurities are to be expected, and are found in each. That book has been before the world of thinkers for several generations. It has not been answered or set aside, and it is safe to say it never will be.

f. From the *corruption of mankind*, by which the understanding has been darkened, and rendered averse to truths that would be amply clear and satisfactory to a pure soul.

CHAPTER ELEVEN

Objections from Alleged Discrepancies or Mistakes

The subject is a very large one. A full discussion of it would take one over almost every part of the Bible. It would be inconsistent with the limits of a volume like this.

1. Some general suggestions in regard to these alleged mistakes, as a mass, may be profitably made. For example:

a. Many of these are founded on misinterpretation of Scripture. It is said that the New Testament writers misunderstood and misapplied the Old Testament. They were controlled by the false prejudices of their age. They were guilty of illogical argument. But these allegations cannot be sustained by fair exegesis. Particular expressions have been interpreted so as to imply some scientific or historic error. Thus the word *firmament* in Genesis has been supposed to convey the idea common in ancient physical science, that the starry universe was fixed in a firm, spherical covering revolving round the earth. That idea is naturally suggested by the Latin *firmamentum*, and by the Greek *stereoma*, of which it was a translation. But it is entirely absent from the original Hebrew word *raqia*, which means simply something spread out or expanded, an *expanse*. So the expressions as to the sun's rising (literally *breaking forth*) and setting (*going in*) are no difficulty to the candid reader. It is interpreted phenomenally, just as are similar phrases in use everyday among ourselves.

b. Many objections rest on misapprehension of the facts of history. Many of these have been already satisfactorily cleared up. We are thus led to expect the solution of any that remain obscure. Research has shown, in numerous instances, that it was the objectors who were mistaken and not the sacred writers. It used to be alleged, for example, that Daniel was certainly in error in representing Belshazzar as ruler in Babylon, and slain when it was taken. Whereas profane historians give the name of Nabonidus as the last king, and affirm that he was not in Babylon, but at Borsippa, where he surrendered to Byrus, and was continued in authority as a subordinate ruler. The difficult seemed formidable, until recent discoveries revealed the name Bil-shar-uzur on a brick of the period. It indicated that he was the son of the reigning monarch. He may then be fairly supposed to have been joined with him in dominion, and left in charge of the city of Babylon.

This explains what had formerly been another puzzle. In promising to exalt Daniel to the highest dignity, he proposed to make him *third* ruler in the kingdom. He himself was only the second ruler.

In like manner, Luke was long charged with error as to Cyrenius being governor of Syria at the time of the enrollment for taxation. Cyrenius was known to have been governor ten years later. It now appears from the researches of Zumpt that he was twice governor of Syria. It seems reasonable to suppose that that earlier period was the one referred to by Luke.

c. Many of the objections are based manifestly and confessedly upon our ignorance. The sacred writer states a portion of the facts. Another writer, sacred or profane, presents another portion. The intervening or connecting links are not given by either. They have to be conjectured or left unsupplied. If we knew more, the difficulty would be diminished, or might disappear altogether. This is obviously the case in all historical accounts. It is always unsafe and unfair to say that a thing *cannot* be, merely because we do not understand *how* it was. Every juggler's exhibition affords numerous instances of apparent incompatibles, where it only needs the knowledge of some slight unobserved circumstance to explain the mystery.

Balaam

The two accounts of Balaam (Num. 22–24, and 31:8–16) are different, but not incompatible. They present the same man in different periods of his history, under different circumstances. At first he was a backslider in heart, but still clinging with one hand to God. All the while, he grasped with the other hand after the rewards of his unhallowed greed and ambition. Afterwards having thrown off all restraints, he did evil with both hands earnestly. Why must this be rejected, on purely internal grounds, as not "a trustworthy history of facts"? The intervening fact, fairly supposable, if not inferrible from the narrative, is that God deserted the prophet who, though he spoke the truth, loved a lie. He left him to his miserable and corrupt self.

Contradictions

It is painfully common to find some commentators making out of every difference of view or statement a contradiction, when nothing of the sort is fairly implied.

- Mark and Luke give the details as to the paralytic let down before Christ through the roof. Matthew simply describes his being brought. Therefore even Weiss represents that he conflicts with Mark.

- Matthew mentions two demoniacs. Mark mentions only the more prominent and remarkable one. If there were two, there was one. Where is the contradiction?

- Matthew and Mark name Thaddeus as one of the Twelve. Luke calls him Judas. He says he is the brother of James, to distinguish him from Judas Iscariot. Is this any discrepancy? He had two names, as was so common in those days. He was Judas Thaddeus, Judas the beloved. And Lebbeus, which some manuscripts read, is probably only another endearing epithet, which Jerome says meant *corculum*, or darling. A hundred instances of this sort might be given.

d. Some alleged discrepancies arise from the different objects had in view by the different narrators, or from the different circle of readers or hearers addressed. The four Gospels are not only thus a four-sided view of our Lord's history from as many different directions, but are adapted to as many different classes, as may be seen in all recent comparative studies of the evangelists. This is obvious not only in the selection of the incidents narrated, and in the special details given, but in the arrangement of the materials. It is evident that Matthew, for instance, is guided, not by a chronological, but by a topical principle in the order he adopts. He groups together things of similar nature, or incidents that naturally suggested each other.

"That the Evangelist's mind should thus have worked according to the natural laws of suggestion, is altogether compatible with the inspiration of his narrative; for every part of the Bible bears the impress of human thinking, only preserved by the Spirit from error and guided into all truth, so that the inspired writer says precisely what God would have him say."[1]

Differences in Narrative

An interesting example of the natural and legitimate difference in the narrative, produced by different circumstances and audiences, may be found in the three accounts of the conversion of Paul, as given by Luke, in the course of his history (Acts 9:1–18), by Paul himself to the Jews at Jerusalem (Acts 22:1–21), and again by Paul to Festus and Agrippa (Acts 26:9–23). The variations cannot be urged as discrepancies that mark error or falsehood. They all occur in the same brief book. He would have been a heedless and unskillful falsifier indeed who, in forging a story would have failed to avoid, or smooth away and remove, such obvious grounds of objection. But when the three accounts are carefully compared, when the points omitted at this time and inserted at the other are considered, the verisimilitude of the whole is decidedly confirmed. Compare any of the recent commentaries on Acts. And on this general subject, see Westcott's *Introduction to the Study of the Gospel*, Da Costa's *Four Witnesses*, and Gregory's *Why Four Gospels?*

e. Some apparent discrepancies arise from counting years from different eras or starting points; from the use of round numbers or approximate numbers; from the counting of parts of years or days as years or days, etc. Such methods of computation are in accordance with recognized custom in all speech, are common, legitimate, necessary. The laborious arithmetical criticism of Bishop Colenso on the Pentateuch, though expanded over seven volumes to manufacture and magnify the mistakes of Moses, derives its plausibility mainly from ignoring these obvious principles.

f. Some disagreements and difficulties arise apparently from errors in the transcription of our present copies, notwithstanding all the care that has been taken, and the general accuracy with which the sacred books have been preserved. This is probably the explanation of such cases as the fifty thousand and seventy men dying at the small village of Bethshemesh (1 Sam. 6:9), where the fifty thousand are omitted by Josephus, and by Thenius, Reinke, Wellhausen, and Keil; and the statements of Stephen as to the places of burial of the patriarchs (Acts 7:16). So with many of the discrepancies between Kings and Chronicles as to the years of the kings of Judah and Israel, and similar matters.

2. The most satisfactory and useful method of answering this class of objections, if we had time to go into detail, would be to take up the particular cases of alleged discrepancy; or, if not all, at least those among them that seem strongest or most important.

Thus we might subject the matter to a practical test. If we examine, for instance, the different accounts as to the genealogy of our Lord, the inscription on the cross, or the words spoken at the baptism of Jesus, it is readily seen that these present no insuperable obstacle to our accepting the plain testimony of the Scripture as to the authority of the inspired writers. Yet they certainly should be allowed, as part of the phenomena of Scripture, to aid in shaping our doctrine as to the nature of the record thus inspired, and to lead us to recognize it as thoroughly human and individual, at the same time that it is sent forth with divine authority. It is believed that the failure to do this by some advocates of inspiration, in their arguments and statements, is what has led many devout and earnest students to array themselves against the commonly received, but sometimes unfortunately presented, doctrine of inspiration.

It is evident that the testimony of the evangelists, for instance, should be compared and put together on the same legal principles as the testimony of the several witnesses before a court of justice, each stating the facts from his point of view, each modifying, enlarging, or supplementing the impression derived from the account of the other, so that the result of the whole testimony is presented. Thus the celebrated jurist, Judge Greenleaf, has reviewed on legal grounds the witness of the four evangelists in his well-known work.

Professor George P. Fisher, in his *Beginnings of Christianity* (pp. 406–12), has selected and briefly discussed five out of the whole mass of alleged contradictions in the Gospels, as those most apparently insuperable on the ordinarily received view. These are:

- the Sermon on the Mount, as given in Matthew and Luke;

- the healing of the centurion's servant;

- Peter's denials;

- the healing of the blind man at Jericho;

- and the time of the Last Supper, in John and the Synoptics.

These particular cases have been ably discussed by President Bartlett in the *Princeton Review* for January, 1880. An elaborate and valuable work by Reverend J. W. Haley, on *The Alleged Discrepancies of the Bible*, has been published by Draper of Andover. It gives, in the first part, an excellent and instructive chapter on the origin of the discrepancies. It then treats of their design and results.

In the second part, he discusses them in detail, as doctrinal, ethical, and historical discrepancies. While in the numerous and varied cases mentioned we may not always prefer the explanation to which he seems inclined (and there is great room for difference of opinion in such matters), the work deserves earnest commendation and study for its laborious research, its condensation of results, its candor and courtesy, as well as its decided ability.

We cannot now go into the details. They are discussed, not only in the works mentioned, but in any good commentary. It is sufficient here to say that there is no case that does not seem to us to admit of a reasonable explanation, consistent with true inspiration.

3. After one has considered and explained the particular discrepancies alleged as most forcible or troublesome, we are sometimes met by an inquiry like this: "I grant that this and that case admits of a fair, or at least a probable explanation. That would not be sufficient to hinder me from believing in the inspiration of the Scripture. But suppose we should find a case of insuperable discrepancy, or discover by some Assyrian or Egyptian monument a clear historical error in the Bible? What would become of your doctrine of inspiration?" Our answer is, we propose to wait till such a case arises before we shape our doctrine, not from the facts and teachings of God's Word, but to meet an imaginary contingency which may never arise.

And the fact that such discrepancies and errors have been so often and so confidently alleged, and one after another have been found to admit of a reasonable explanation, is a ground of confidence that in the future it will be as in the past.

CHAPTER TWELVE

Objections on Moral Grounds

Actions deemed censurable, or laws and principles of actions regarded as immoral, are found in Scripture. Therefore it is argued that it cannot be inspired. Most of these points of objection are really urged, as by Tom Paine and Ingersoll, against accepting the Scripture as from God in any sense at all. It is thought, by some defenders of the Bible, that the defense is made easier and more impregnable by adopting a view of inspiration which gives up these to the assaults of the enemy, as only belonging to the human element, for which the divine is not responsible. These things are thrown overboard, as tubs to the whale, while the ship, lightened of them, pursues its course unimpeded. A wiser course, it seems to us, is to meet the difficulties squarely.

1. The objections on moral grounds to the actions narrated may be classified under four different heads. It may be doubtful, sometimes, to which class a particular transaction should be referred. But the general propriety of the distinction proposed is clear.

a. Many acts are recorded without specific censure that are certainly not approved. Their occurrence in the narrative gives no moral sanction to them, either expressed or implied. Everyone concedes that in most cases this is so. It is claimed, however, that in certain objectionable acts, such a sanction is implied, as in the cases of Jephthah's daughter, the killing of Sisera, and Rahab's falsehood. We think that in these there is no divine sanction of the conduct referred to. Others prefer to admit the commendation, and to justify the actions. Opinions may differ, as to that. Practically, however, the difficulty remains substantially the same, whatever view of inspiration we adopt.

b. Some of the actions objected to are not really censurable, when properly examined.

- The slaying of Agag, the Amalekite king, by Samuel (1 Sam. 15:33),

- the "spoiling" of the Egyptians by the Israelites on their departure (Exod. 12:35–36),

- the alleged falsehood of Elisha to the Syrian army that came to take him (2 Kings 6:19).

Agag deserved death for his manifold slaughters and rapines, and had been divinely condemned. Samuel was but the executioner of a penalty sanctioned at once by human and by divine law in such a case.

As to the "spoiling of the Egyptians," there is no countenance in the original to the idea of borrowing and lending unfortunately and erroneously suggested by our common translation. The Israelites *asked*, and the Egyptians gladly gave, to get rid of these terrible people, whatever they asked. There is no implication of any promise or obligation to return the things given, no fraud or deceit in the case. Elisha's conduct might be regarded as among the stratagems allowable in war. But aside from that, he did lead them to the man whom they sought, as he said he would. And he dismissed them without harm.

c. Some actions, which would now and ordinarily be wrong, were right under the peculiar circumstances of the case. Or they were made right by specific divine authority, modifying the general law. Instances of this kind may be found

- in the marriage of brothers and sisters in the beginning of the race,

- the extermination of the Canaanites under Joshua,

- the imprecations in the Psalms and Prophets by inspired men, where God's retributive interposition is denounced or implored against foul and persecuting cruelty.

d. There are numerous cases where, though the general character or conduct of persons is approved, no sanction is given to the various errors or the crimes into which they fell. It is sufficient to mention, without further comment, the cases of Noah, Abraham, Jacob, David, Peter. They were good men, but, as all others on earth, imperfect good men.

2. Besides specific actions like these, in regard to which the principles of explanation are clear, whatever differences of opinion may exist as to the particular view to be taken in each case,

- there are more general moral objections on the ground that morally faulty conceptions, enactments, or institutions are inwrought into the Scripture;

- that, in certain of the writings (those of Solomon especially) a low moral tone prevails, not religious but purely selfish, prudential, and worldly;

- and that in others such fierce, bloody, and cruel ideas are sanctioned, or positively inculcated, as are inconsistent with divine authorship.

Special objection is made to the Old Testament teachings with reference to polygamy, divorce, war, and slavery, and to such laws as that of strict retaliation upon a malicious false swearer, death for the idolater or seducer to idolatry, etc.

As to the law of retaliation, like for like, it is sufficient to say that it is difficult to see how a fairer retribution could be assigned, or one more likely to deter from such a crime, than that a malicious perjurer, who expected by his false swearing to injure another, should have exactly that same suffering inflicted upon him that he thought to bring on the other. A rigid law strictly enforced is mercy to the innocent, however hard upon the guilty. It is far more beneficial to those who might otherwise have been criminals, by deterring them from crime, than impunity in wrongdoing would be.

Idolatry

In reference to the punishment for idolatry, it is to be remembered that the Jewish state was a theocracy. In a government where God was the King, promoting idolatry was high treason and fitly to be punished by the highest penalty known to the law.

Polygamy, Etc.

As to polygamy, easy divorce, slavery, and war, they all existed in the state of society into which the earliest revelations came. They were modified, controlled, and have been greatly ameliorated by the progressive influence of the Mosaic and the Christian systems. They have not yet been entirely abolished.

The complaint against the Bible is, that it did not instantaneously and at the outset annihilate evils, already entrenched in such strongholds of human passion and interest and habit as even the boasted nineteenth century cannot utterly demolish. If it be said that any partial correction of evil is compromise and connivance—that everything proceeding from God must be absolutely perfect, and that everything temporary, transitional, preparatory, must be ascribed to the fallible human instruments, and not to the divine Designer who used them—we reply that we do not concede these points. God does make millions of incomplete, imperfect things, of all shades and degrees approximating perfection. He does correct evils progressively and gradually. It is *His* wisdom, and not the folly or mistake of the instrument employed, which secures the adaptation of the successive phases and stages of revelation to the needs of humankind. The skill of an architect may be expended as well upon the temporary scaffolding as the permanent structure, and may be seen as truly in the rough foundation as in the polished column or carved ornaments.

The relative imperfection of parts of a progressive system may be an element of that real perfection which consists in its adaptation as a whole to the people and the circumstances for which it was designed, and to the object which it was to accomplish. Taking men as they were, sunk and degraded in ignorance and vice, it was necessary for their deliverance that God should stoop to their need. That He should construct a ladder, the lowest rounds of which should not be too far above the "Slough of Despond" in which they were sinking. That He should send down a law that would reach them, and lift them up, *where they were*. Would it have been more divine had it stopped short of them, in order that it might conform to some abstract conception which we may imagine of perfection? Certainly not. The success of the divine moral government as a unity, and yet a progressive unity, was dependent on such a use of gradual steps and processes. As Dr. Ladd has well said:

> Imperfect human ways of thinking and speaking, and ethically low and imperfect customs, institutions and laws may be taken up into, and more or less changed and assimilated by, the forces of revelation and inspiration. Such must the historical process, indeed, be, if God is to get his moral and religious ideas realized in human life. . . . It resembles all the methods of the divine government, to take man in hand for legal discipline in the condition in which he is found, and to deal with him by starting from this condition [1]

But if we thus recognize "these concrete divine words and definite commands as the forms into which the divine ideas cause the crude material to crystallize";

if the fact "that the ideas take these forms is, indeed," as Dr. Ladd says, "a proof of their divine origin and nature";

if in this adaptedness to man's case consists their perfection for their purpose, and

if this relative imperfection was really necessary to its end, and wisely, mercifully, lovingly, adapted to that end,

why must we ascribe that peculiarity to the fallible man rather than to the all-wise God? Why attribute this exact suitableness in the instrument for its end to the instrument itself, and account it a token of fallibility, rather than to Him who both made and chose and used the instrument, and shows His wisdom thereby?

We admit the imperfection in these laws and institutions. The immorality, however, we deny. If the Mosaic law not only recognizes its own preparatory and partial and incomplete nature, but points to and provides for its own completion in the subsequent stages of revelation, this seems to us far from indicating an origin inferior to the mind of Him who saw the end from the beginning, and had it in view in the very first steps of His divine self-revealing.

Progressive Revelation

We may be permitted to quote and adopt the forcible words of Reverend Dr. Frederic Gardiner:

Revelation was progressive, because only in that way was it possible that man could receive it. Nowhere is it possible for him to attain, or even to comprehend, perfect truth at a bound. He is obliged to gain first one elementary fact or principle, and then by means of this to advance to another, which must often seriously modify his conception of the first.

In the study of language, he must master the rule before he can learn the exception. The Ptolemaic system in astronomy was the necessary means of systematizing observations until they should lead to the Copernican; the Copernican must begin by the assumption of circular orbits and uniform motions of the planets, until these could lead to the discovery of elliptical orbits and the doctrine of the radius vector.

Still our present knowledge is imperfect. The law of gravity and the observed facts of astronomy are not in perfect accord. Each new discovery, as of the asteroids and of Neptune, brings about a closer harmony; but we cannot expect to see in nature a perfect realization of the law until we can look out upon its completeness from the footstool of the throne of the Omniscient.

The same thing is true of chemistry and of all other natural sciences, and indeed of all human knowledge. As already said, the elements, the most essential points, must be thoroughly fixed in the mind before it can receive their modifications. Were the process reversed, and the fuller truth set at once before the untrained thought, the result could only be disastrous, and positive misconceptions take the place of simple imperfect apprehension. The child now, as well as the race in its childhood, must learn the unity of God, before it can be profitably, or even safely, taught the doctrine of the Trinity. Any other course will be sure to lead to the error of Tritheism.[2]

Substantially the ideas suggested above apply to the other allegations against the morality of the Bible. We must be allowed, however, before passing from the subject, to protest against the charge that certain of the proverbs "show so much of shrewdness as scarcely to escape the charge of being immoral, when considered from the Christian point of view (see Prov. 17:8, 18:16, and 21:14)."

These are simply statements of what is a fact of common observation and experience, that gifts are both used effectively and abused. They do not give any commendation or advice of bribery. Also we fail to discover any "asceticism" in Paul's judicious suggestions to the Corinthians (1 Cor. 7). They seem to us quite suitable, as he said, "by reason of the present distress." They are not at all out of harmony with the cheerful views of God and man, of human life and enjoyment, in his discourse at Lystra (Acts 14:17), or his charge to the rich (1 Tim. 6:17).

"Moral Feebleness?" "Cowardice?"

That the record of religious experiences, of the conflicts of minds grappling with the great problems of life and thought, is not unfit for a revelation designed for the instruction of those who are called to similar experiences and conflicts, is apparent enough. There is no more effective way of teaching the ignorant, guiding the perplexed, and comforting the despondent or tempted, than by such examples. Yet the use of this very method in psalms like the sixth has been regarded as an exhibition of "moral feebleness amounting almost to cowardice," and in the seventy-third as a "complaint against the divine dealing," regardless of the triumphant issue of these conflicts of soul indicated in Psalms 6:9 and 73:17–26.

Dr. Ladd, though censuring these passages, says very forcibly and justly in another place:

> In these cases [of religious experiences] we surely can find no fault either with the contents of the writing, or with the moral consciousness of the author, for furnishing to us an accurate and sympathetic picture of facts. Even the saints, both of ancient and of modern times, do often doubt the word of the Lord, waver in their judgment of his justice and mercy, and wander in the dark places of rebellion and despair. The story and the picture of these experiences may well form a part of the ethico-religious contents of Sacred Scripture; for the use of the story and the picture have, in all subsequent times, been both ethically and religiously purifying. And when the narrator of the experience, or the painter of the picture, comes at last into the confidence of trust and into clearness of moral vision, we may well believe that the Spirit of all truth and light has been with him all the way. We may well assign the record of such moral and religious experiences to a notable position among the revealed ethico-religious truths of the Bible. Such remarks as the foregoing are more or less applicable to the books of Job and Ecclesiastes, to many of the Psalms, to numerous portions of the prophetic and historical writings, and to certain passages of the New Testament.[3]

We need scarcely add anything to these truthful and appropriate suggestions.

Our reply so far has been limited to discussing, first, the particular actions complained of as immoral, and, secondly, the general objections to the ethical teachings of the Bible. It is time that we turn to a large view, and contemplate those teachings, not in fragments or scraps, but as a whole.

3. The moral grandeur of the ethics of the Bible, whether taken singly as a system, or compared with any other system that has ever been presented to man, bespeaks its divine origin. In the

search for flaws on the beautiful vase, men may fail to observe its matchless symmetry, its richly variegated hues, and the skillful blending of tints. In looking for spots in the sun, one may be blind to the magnificence of that glorious orb itself. And thus we may be so absorbed in finding, or even in refuting, paltry objections against the ethics of the Bible, as to fail to take those impressive and affecting views that we should of its sublime moral teachings.

It remains a fact, that after all the highest exertions of the human mind on moral questions, and all the wildest vagaries of invention and combination, no moral teaching has ever been devised which has

- so ennobled man,

- so purified life,

- so liberated captives and overthrown tyranny,

- so lifted up the degraded and invigorated the weak, and

- so comforted the bereaved and animated the despairing.

During an age when comparatively enlightened and cultivated nations were still groping in darkness on moral questions, the Hebrews received, and have transmitted to all succeeding ages, a code of ethics that still furnishes the foundation for all ethical teaching for humankind. There is such simplicity, such grandeur, such regal breadth of control, and divine adaptation to the human heart, (in the Decalogue and the subsequent precepts based upon it), as to cast utterly into the shade all the injunctions and advices that have come from heathen sources, and make them seem entirely empty. Every renewal or acceleration of moral life in the world, every quickening of worn-out nationalities, or amelioration of savage tribes, may be traced directly to the influence of the Bible. The decadence which has occurred, in numerous distressing cases, in Christendom itself, is no less distinctly connected

- with the neglect of the Word,
- with departure from its plain precepts, and
- with holding it back systematically from the people.

By their fruits ye shall know them. "The infallible test of all religious teaching," says L. Abbott, "is its practical result in the lives of those that receive it. The answer to modern eulogists of Buddhism and Confucianism is India and China." The most terrible and overwhelming refutation of atheism is France in the Revolution. The most invincible argument against the substitution of the Church of Rome for the authority of God's Word is sullen, stagnant, sinking Spain. And the effect of even the partial introduction of the Scriptures is to be seen in the awakening of Italy, and the dawn of a brighter day for that priest-ridden land.

CHAPTER THIRTEEN

Objections on Critical Grounds

Under this head are classed sundry objections arising out of the alleged discoveries and conclusion of modern criticism as to the origin and authorship of certain books of the Bible, and as to their transmission to the present time.

What Does Criticism Mean?

The word "criticism" has received several different significations. Primarily a critic means a judge, from *krino*; and one who examined anything carefully, so as to judge of its character or its meaning, was called a critic. So criticism was used in a very wide sense, including interpretation or exposition.

At present, in reference to the Bible, criticism is commonly limited to various subsidiary topics which precede and prepare for interpretation. In this sense it is customary to distinguish between text criticism and higher criticism. The former signifies the discussion as to the agreement of the present form of the sacred text with the originals as they proceeded from their respective authors.

The latter embraces all inquiries, especially internal evidence, as to the authorship of the writings, their age, circumstances of composition, object, etc., thus covering a considerable part of the subject of investigation usually considered in what is termed "special introduction."

Of course it is beyond our scope here to take up all the objections that might arise in connection with criticism in its widest application. We shall endeavor to discuss briefly those which are based on text criticism and higher criticism.

Text Criticism

1. It is objected, that, with all the researches of text criticism, it is not possible in all cases to be certain what was the original text. Hence it is allege:

- that, even if the original was infallible, our present text is not;

- that plenary inspiration, were it granted, would be useless and unmeaning, if the writings were not preserved miraculously and absolutely (as they evidently have not been) from the accidents of time and of careless copying; and

- that it is not probable that God would supernaturally confer complete accuracy and authority, if the documents were then to be left to the usual possibilities of error in transmission to future ages.

To these objections we reply:

a. The facts present a valid argument against the unfounded claim that was once made, that every letter, syllable, and even every vowel-point and accent of our present received copies of the Bible must be regarded as inspired. But they do not affect our doctrine, for we make no such claim. The inspiration of the original Scriptures is what we affirm. This is an entirely different question from the accuracy with which copies of them have been preserved. It is now well known that the Hebrew vowel-points are of later origin than the Christian era (probably about the fifth or sixth century). They can only be regarded as representing the carefully preserved, but not authoritative, tradition as to the pronunciation. The consonants alone form the ancient text.[1]

Also it is thoroughly understood that the manuscripts both of the Old and New Testament have been subject to the defects necessarily incident to the most careful copying. What we affirm is, that the sacred Scriptures, as they came from the respective authors, had the characteristics of accuracy and authority, as messages from God.

b. The Scriptures, though subject to the necessary perils of transcription, were specially protected, not only by a general providential guardianship, which it is fair to assume and which history confirms, but by several favoring circumstances of no small importance.

Among these are:

- the reverence with which from the beginning they were regarded, occasioning more frequent copying than in the case of any other book in the world, and more careful and affectionate effort to be accurate;

- the number of manuscripts, which naturally increases the number of various readings to be noted, but also greatly increases the opportunity of detecting errors, and arriving with much confidence at the original text;

- the publicity of these documents by their being read repeatedly and reverently in worship, which also tended to insure the discovery and correction of errors;

- the numerous translations, early and late, which called attention to the minutiae of their language and expression;

- the habit of delivering discourses based on them, and of making extensive quotations from them, in speaking and writing;

- the elaborate expositions and commentaries, the harmonies and comparisons of parallel passages, and even the searches, friendly or hostile, after discrepancies and difficulties, beginning at an early period, and kept up with unwearied perseverance and microscopic minuteness;

- the wide diffusion of copies in different lands, and often in the hostile custody of warring sects, prompt to detect and eager to expose any falsification or corruption.

All these circumstances have tended to secure in a very high degree substantial accuracy and purity in the transmission of copies of the sacred writings.

c. The limits of error, within which we are practically sure of our ground, may be very confidently fixed. They leave little opportunity of mistake as to the teaching of Scripture in regard to any fact or doctrine or precept. This is especially true of those parts of the Bible on which faith and duty chiefly rest. If there are "textual uncertainties," as we frankly admit, there are also textual certainties. These are ample enough for guidance through the snares of earth and to the glories of heaven.[2]

On this subject the emphatic testimony of Westcott and Hort, the most recent, and certainly among the most competent of text critics, is adequate, without further discussion. They say:

> With regard to the great bulk of the words of the New Testament, as of most other ancient writings, there is no variation or other ground of doubt, and therefore no room for textual criticism; and here, therefore an editor is merely a transcriber. The same may be said with substantial truth respecting those various readings which have never been received, and in all probability never will be received, into any printed text. The proportion of words virtually accepted on all hands as raised above doubt is very great, not less, on a rough computation, than seven eighths of the whole. The remaining eighth, therefore, formed in great part by changes of order and other comparative trivialities, constitutes the whole area of criticism. If the principles followed in the present edition are sound, this area may be very greatly reduced. Recognizing to the full the duty of abstinence from preemptory decision in cases where the evidence leaves the judgment in suspense between two or more readings, we find that, setting aside differences of orthography, the words in our opinion

still subject to doubt only make up about one sixtieth of the whole New Testament. In this second estimate the proportion of comparatively trivial variations is beyond measure larger than in the former; so that the amount of what can in *any sense be called substantial variation* is but a small fraction of the whole residuary variation, and can hardly form more than a *thousandth part* of the entire text. [3]

With this weighty testimony agree the well-chosen words of Dr. Philip Schaff, the chairman of the American Committee of the Revisers.

> This multitude of various readings of the Greek text need not puzzle or alarm any Christian. It is the natural result of the great wealth of our documentary resources; it is a testimony to the immense importance of the New Testament; it does not affect, but it rather insures, the integrity of the text; and it is a useful stimulus to study.

> Only about 400 of the 100,000 or 150,000 variations materially affect the sense. Of these, again, not more than about fifty are really important for some reason or other; and even of these fifty not one affects an article of faith or a precept of duty which is not abundantly sustained by other and undoubted passages, or by the whole tenor of Scripture teaching. The *Textus Receptus* of Stephens, Beza, and Elzevir, and of our English Version, teach precisely the same Christianity as the uncial text of the Sinaitic and Vatican manuscripts, the oldest versions, and the Anglo-American Revision. [4]

Richard Bentley, the ablest and boldest of the earlier classical critics of England, affirmed that even the worst of manuscripts does not pervert or set aside "one article of faith or moral precept."

Dr. Ezra Abbot, of Harvard, who ranked among the first textual critics, and was not hampered by orthodox bias (being a Unitarian), asserted that "no Christian doctrine or duty rests on those portions of the text which are affected by differences in the manuscripts, still less is anything *essential* in Christianity touched by the various readings. They do, to be sure, affect the bearing of a few passages on the doctrine of the Trinity; but the truth or falsity of the doctrine by no means depends upon the reading of those passages."

The same scholar spoke on the subject more fully, with special reference to the English Revision:

This host of various readings may startle one who is not acquainted with the subject, and he may imagine that the whole text of the New Testament is thus rendered uncertain. But a careful analysis will show that nineteen twentieths of these are of no more consequence than the palpable errata in the first proof of a modern printer; they have so little authority, or are so manifestly false, that they may be at once dismissed from consideration. Of those which remain, probably nine tenths are of no importance as regards the sense; the differences either cannot be represented in a translation, or affect the form of expression merely, not the essential meaning of the sentence. Though the corrections made by the revisers in the Greek text of the New Testament followed by our translators probably exceed two thousand, hardly one tenth of them, perhaps not one twentieth, will be noticed by the ordinary reader. Of the small residue, many are indeed of sufficient interest and importance to constitute one of the strongest reasons for making a new revision, which should no longer suffer the known errors of copyists to take the place of the words of the evangelists and apostles.

But the chief value of the work accomplished by the self-denying scholars who have spent so much time and labor in the search for manuscripts, and in their collation or publication, does not consist, after all, in the corrections of the text which have resulted from the researches. These corrections may affect a few of the passages which have been relied on for the support of certain doctrines, but not to such an extent as essentially to alter the state of the argument. Still less is any question of Christian duty touched by the multitude of various readings. The greatest service which the scholars who have devoted themselves to critical studies and the collection of critical materials have rendered has been the establishment of the fact that, on the whole, the New Testament writings have come down to us in a text remarkably free from important corruptions, even in the late and inferior manuscripts on which the so-called "received text" was founded. While the helps which we now possess for restoring it to its primitive purity far exceed those which we enjoy in the case of any eminent classical author whose works have come down to us. The multitude of "various readings," which to the thoughtless or ignorant seem so alarming, is simply the result of the extraordinary richness and variety of our critical resources.[5]

d. It is not true that plenary inspiration of the original would be useless, unless the copies were secured by a perpetual miracle against the effects of time and of careless and corrupt transmission. A truly divine original, even if copied with no more than ordinary human care and fidelity, is vastly superior to an original, however accurately preserved, that never had divine authority. And obviously the fact that it was recognized and accepted as from God would serve greatly to insure its being preserved with more than ordinary care.

e. Neither can it be justly said that there is no probability that God would supernaturally inspire the writings, unless He also miraculously preserved them from erroneous transcription. He might do the one, which He alone could do, and leave the other, as in so many other matters, to the faithfulness of His servants entrusted with that responsibility. We know that the oral teaching of our Lord Jesus not reported by our evangelists was directly and thoroughly the voice of God. We believe that the oral and unrecorded instructions of the apostles in their official work were inspired. Yet there is no reason to affirm any miracle of preservation for either. The voice of God in these forms was limited, except indirectly, to the audience or the generation that heard it. The accidents and corruptions of oral transmission did not render either impossible, or improbable, or unmeaning, or useless, the divine authority with which they spoke. Why should the similar but smaller periods of written transmission render it incredible that God should inspire, in the fullest sense, the records of His grace?

2. The objections on critical grounds that are most urgently and confidently pressed against the doctrine of inspiration are those arising from what is called the "higher criticism."

This is a region of thought and inquiry almost entirely modern, in which much is still vague, and dependent largely on subjective impressions and presuppositions, rather than ascertained facts, but where positive assertion is often furnished with surprising liberality in the absence of definite information. The remark of Professor Ladd on this subject is eminently just, as pointing out the weaknesses of both the older and the newer criticism.

> That the former dogmatic manner of regarding these critical questions, while it claimed to weigh carefully the purely external and historical sources for its affirmations, was in reality largely subjective in the worst sense of the word, there can be no dispute. But there ought to be just as little dispute, that much of the more modern criticism, whether it please to call itself external or internal, or neither, is just as largely subjective, in quite as bad a sense of the word. The difference between the older so-called critics and many of the more modern ones consists largely in this: the former had a childish trust in untrustworthy traditions, while the latter have a conceited confidence in the vagaries of their own minds.[6]

We have no need nor disposition to undervalue either the legitimate method or the fairly established results of modern critical research. Much may be learned, much has been learned, by the patient, elaborate comparisons on which it proceeds. A true "higher criticism" may be just as valuable as a false or misguided attempt at it may be dangerous and delusive.

It is impossible, of course, to give here a *full* discussion of many, or in fact of any, of the questions arising on this topic. Our aim is only to present such general considerations as may show how far those questions apply to our present subject.

a. It is highly important to distinguish between criticism and the critics. We are often assured vehemently that "the verdict of criticism" is thus and so. Even when perhaps it is only the sentiment of a few critics, possibly, when sifted, of a single man of eminence, re-echoed and repeated by several other persons. Doctors disagree, and so do critics.

b. Some critical theories of large extent and pretension are based on cool assumptions of what is utterly devoid of proof. For instance, the views of Graf and Kuenen are avowedly based on the denial of anything really supernatural, the ignoring of any actual miracle or prophecy. Whatever appears to be such must be either ingeniously explained away, or set aside contemptuously as *unhistorical*, the polite modern term for false. The Leyden school of theologians have attempted to do for the Old

Testament what the Tubingen school with equal confidence proposed to do for the New, that is, to revise the history of divine manifestation with the divine omitted, like the play of *Hamlet* with Hamlet left out. In our judgment both have failed. Their verdict is that of certain critics, but not at all that of criticism. The presuppositions on which they are based are emphatically denied.

c. A large part of the questions discussed by the higher criticism, whichever way they may be decided, have nothing to do with the doctrine of inspiration, or with the acceptance of the books concerned as a part of the sacred Word. There are a number of the biblical books, such as Kings and Chronicles, concerning the authorship and period of which the Bible itself gives no distinct indication. Whether they are concluded to be by one author or by several, whether earlier or later, can have no decisive bearing on our investigations.

d. As to some of the critical questions most discussed, it is apparent that they bear rather on the Canon of Scripture than on the inspiration of Scripture. It is fair to say that, if the results of careful inquiry should make it necessary to reject or surrender certain books as not a genuine part of the Word of God, it would only deprive us of those books themselves, not cast any doubt or obscurity over the value and authority of the remainder. Thus, if, as the result of candid investigation, 2 Peter or Jude must be given up, if Esther or Canticles (Song of Solomon) cannot be vindicated as entitled to a place in the sacred volume, the evidence for the inspiration of the other books, and their utility for every Christian, would not be thereby in the least weakened. And the question of the extent of the Canon must always be carefully distinguished from the other question, which is the one immediately under consideration, viz. what authority belongs to the books that are recognized as inspired or canonical.

e. There are books in regard to which serious doubts are urged as to authorship, but no consequences materially affecting their inspiration would follow, if the decision should be adverse to the common opinion. Thus, if Ecclesiastes be by some later author personating Solomon, or the second part of Isaiah (chaps.

40 to 66) be by a later Isaiah than the well-known prophet of Hezekiah's day; or, if the Letter to the Hebrews should be judged not to be by Paul, it would not be necessary to relinquish the inspiration or the canonical authority of these writings. We do not accept the alleged proof against the genuineness of either of these writings according to the received view of their authorship. But if we did, it would not destroy their value or their divinity for us.

f. There are other books, however, on which an adverse decision as to authorship would have a wider range, and consequences more disastrous upon the whole system of revealed truth, as commonly understood and received. Professor Ladd does not hesitate to say, that "we should regard the Pentateuch differently, if we could consider it as coming in its present form from the speech or pen of the great inspired lawgiver, Moses;"[7] and "there can be no doubt, that, in the narrow and more technical sense of the word, we should pronounce the Pentateuch 'inspired,' as we cannot now, if we could show that it was written by Moses."[8] On the other hand, he declares that "complete critical proof of the spuriousness of the Fourth Gospel would profoundly change our conception of Sacred Scripture, and would not leave untouched our conception of Christianity itself."[9] He as earnestly denies that Moses wrote the Pentateuch, as he affirms that John wrote the Gospel. He frankly recognizes the logical consequences of the decision in both cases.

The Mosaic authorship of the body of the Pentateuch (aside from the addition to Deuteronomy which records his death, and possibly a few brief notes, geographical or historical, which may have been inserted by some later hand), seems to us of profound importance. It is so thoroughly assumed and recognized elsewhere in Scripture, that to deny it leads naturally, we think, to a denial of the reality of Old Testament history, and to a subversal of the whole scheme and system of divine revelation. If the Pentateuch, as we are told by some, is "not a work, but a growth," of exceedingly composite authorship and mainly post-exilian origin; if it is a compound of Babylonish legends and pious frauds, whether gotten up for selfish interest, or class aggrandizement, or with broader and more patriotic purpose; if it not only gives indications, as we think it does, of diverse sources traditional or documentary, employed under divine direction by Moses himself, but also contains, as we think it does not, contradictions and marks of falsehood; if Moses himself is, as some contend, a mythical personage, and the Exodus never actually occurred as described—we can scarcely vindicate the verity of the subsequent history, or the allusions of Jesus and the apostles to these writings.

So, if the genuineness of Daniel is successfully assailed, and it must be dragged down from the position of a true history and prophecy to be a legend of the era of the Maccabees, a *vaticinium post eventum* a fiction designed to inspire the patriotic ardor of the Jewish rebels against Antiochus Epiphanes, we cannot, it seems to us, logically stop short with that. We must either exscind it from the Canon, in spite of its recognition by Jews and Christians and by our Lord Himself, or else maintain such moral enormities as an honest lie, a fraud of divine origin.

In like manner, the authorship of the Fourth Gospel by John seems to us not only to have been triumphantly vindicated from the ingenious and vehement assaults it has encountered, but to be vital to the system of Christianity, as a divinely inspired whole. This Gospel is, as Dr. E. H. Sears has well styled it, "the Heart of Jesus Christ."[10]

CHAPTER FOURTEEN

Objections on Scientific Grounds

The progress of the physical sciences in late years, and especially in the present century, has been indeed marvelous. It has opened up new avenues for industry and new fields for thought. If the "oppositions of science falsely so called" (1 Tim. 6:20) were a dangerous snare to young preachers of the early church, the peril of them has not passed away. It is renewed and increased with all the wider research, the rapid advance of discovery, and the daring freedom of investigation characteristic of these later generations. The Christian soldier of today needs to acquaint himself with all the lines of assault adopted by the enemy, and to arm himself at all points. Especially should he familiarize himself earnestly with those methods of attack which seem most in accordance with the spirit of the age, which are most fortified by appeals to the modes of argument and inquiry that have yielded such admirable results, and that claim to be associated with the advance of truth and light and free investigation. These are noble words, *Truth* and *Light* and *Freedom:* they are watchwords of progress. And the ideas they represent are justly dear to the hearts of all, and not less dear to us, as lovers of the Bible, which has so greatly promoted that advance.

The Bible and Physical Science

It is not our purpose to consider in detail the various points of alleged discrepancy between the Bible and modern physical science. This is the business of elaborate treatises on science and the Bible. All that is practicable for us here is to state some general principles as to the relation between God's two revelations, in His works and in His Word.

All Truth Is Consistent with All Other Truth

The human mind is so constituted as to desire to perceive this consistency, in order to produce and maintain conviction. No system of belief can command intelligent confidence, unless we have the conviction that it is in harmony with whatever else we know. We do not affirm that we will always be able to *see* the points of contact between truths, each of which is satisfactorily proved by its own independent line of argument. The meeting place of the two may be out beyond the sphere of our vision. But all truth, rightly understood, is harmonious.

There are truths, the full connection of which with each other, or with other truth that we know, may not be clearly seen, yet concerning which we do not doubt. Such are the existence of evil compared with the divine attributes of goodness and omnipotence; the divine efficiency considered in connection with human freedom and responsibility; the Trinity, three persons in one God, and similar doctrines. But these do not at all invalidate the general principle that all truth is consistent with all other truth. A thing cannot be true in theology and false in fact, or reliable in science but wrong in practice, any more than it can be both true and false at the same time, or than black can be white.

The Bible Does Not Profess to Teach Physical Science

That does not come within the scope and object of Scripture. Its grand design was the manifestation of God in His revelation to man. In revealing this it touches, at numerous points, human history and affairs. All that can be expected of the Bible is, that, when it makes allusions to matters outside of its special topic, the statements shall be correct so far as they go. Omissions of things historical or scientific, however important and interesting these things might be to the general scholar, may naturally be expected. They are unavoidable, in accordance with the plan on which the Scripture was given. So far from being fairly objectionable, they form a part of the fitness of the Bible to its end, as could readily be shown.

It was never objected to Euclid's work on mathematics, that it did not contain an account of the dramatic performances of that age. Or that it was defective because it gave no sketch of physics or metaphysics, as expounded by Aristotle. It would be equally futile to object to the Scriptures that they fail to give an account of the science of that day, whether correct or incorrect. They do not profess to teach that thing. They were not intended to do it. There was no need that they should, in carrying out their grand and spiritual design. It would have been a palpable turning aside from the great theme of revelation, and unsuited to the end in view; i.e. to meet the moral necessities of man, and restore him from the ruins of the fall.

Our Interpretations of Scripture Are Not Scripture

Though they may seem to us quite obvious, though they may be hallowed by long traditional belief, or sanctioned by the judgment of many of the good and great, our interpretations of Scripture may be erroneous. We may have mistaken its meaning.

If apparent discrepancy arises, either with other Scripture or with facts otherwise made known, let us re-examine, and see what the passages really mean. Let us compare Scripture with Scripture, and find out the total aggregate result of such comparison. One text is often limited or interpreted by another. This passage, if considered alone, might seem to assert a particular idea. But, by comparing it with others, it is seen that that would be a misinterpretation. Another passage may have been erroneously translated, and the apparent inference will be at once set aside on considering the real meaning of the original. Or facts of nature or of secular history may have come to light, which help to fill up the deficiencies of our apprehension, which point to new and better interpretations of misunderstood or obscure texts. The true biblical scholar will welcome light from whatever source, old or new, hostile or friendly. His reverence for God and for His truth will bind him, instead of repelling, to accept whatever is fairly proved. Only let us be sure that it is proved, and not merely asserted.

In Like Manner, Scientific Conclusions and Opinions Are Not Always Correct

We must wait for science to have reached a settled conclusion before any legitimate argument, or any well-grounded objection to the Bible, can be fairly deduced from it. How opposite to this, and how inconsistent with candor and common sense the course usually pursued by opponents of revelation, we need scarcely pause to describe. As soon as any idea has been started by some scientific man which seems to conflict with the received views of Christians, an idea thrown out, perhaps, as a mere conjecture, or a theory, novel, peculiar to himself, and as yet untested, some are ready to exclaim, and to trumpet it in all the newspapers, "Ah, Moses was mistaken! The Bible is in error. The learned Professor So-and-so has just discovered it. There can be no mistake about it *this* time. Science never lies."

Science Never Lies

True: science never lies. And so, figures never lie; but they often deceive, they are often misinterpreted and misapplied. They tell no untrue story, but we take from them an untrue meaning. Our inference, our understanding, our observation of the facts, or our induction from the facts, may have been fallacious.

In this, as in other topics, we must draw the distinction between science and scientists, as we have to draw it between theology and theologians. Certain critics say so and so; therefore that is the verdict, we are told, of criticism, of *modern criticism*, of advanced criticism! Therefore, it is unquestionable. Some geologist, or biologist, says thus; therefore geology or biology testifies to that conclusion. Perhaps not!

The Conflict of Science with Science

Much of what has been called the conflict of science with religion was really the conflict of science with science, the overthrow of one false opinion after another, which Bible readers as well as others of their day had adopted, not from the Bible, but from their predecessors or contemporaries.

As long as human knowledge continues to be progressive, such experiences may be repeatedly expected.

The Language of Scripture in Describing Physical Facts Is the Language of Common Life, the Language of Appearances

The Bible describes phenomena, not the essence or abstract nature of things. We cannot see how it could well do otherwise. If it used any other language than that of common life, it would be misunderstood, or not be understood at all, by plain people. It would fail to accomplish the purpose for which it was given. And as we do not look for what is called scientific precision in the colloquial use of everyday terms, so we need not be surprised to find the same sort of terms used in the Bible. No one counts you an ignoramus, or charges you with a blunder, because you speak of the sun's "rising and setting," as if that necessarily implied your belief that the sun is high, i.e. more remote from the center of the earth, at one time of day than at another, or as if it indicated your ignorance of the revolution of the earth on its axis. You are using, as every sensible man does on such subjects, whether philosopher or not, phenomenal expressions.

The Language of Appearances

The language of science itself is also, for the most part, the language of appearances. Very often also it contains etymologically some implication, which originally represented a crude, temporary, erroneous phase of scientific opinion. What are oxygen and hydrogen, electricity, magnetism, galvanism, rays, reflection, refraction, focus, and the like, in fact, almost all the familiar terms of science, but words that wrap up in them allusions to ancient theories, some of them exploded, or references to men and ideas of a past age?

May I not speak of rays of light, without being chargeable with ignorance that the undulatory theory of light is now generally preferred to the corpuscular? Must I necessarily be understood to allude to amber whenever I use the term electricity, because the word *elektron* means amber?

Had the Scriptures used the language of modern science, itself subject to perpetual modifications and even revolutionary transitions, with reference to the common physical phenomena incidentally mentioned, they would have been unintelligible to those to whom they were at first given, and no more instructive to us of modern times. There was no alternative, then. It would have been necessary, if that idea was carried out, to occupy the pages of revelation with merely scientific statements and explanations of physical facts, and so to make it a book of scientific rather than religious teaching; in which case it would either have been so brief and fragmentary as to be utterly unsatisfactory, incomplete, and obscure, or else so huge a volume as to be practically inaccessible. Even then it would have been obscure, because the world was not prepared for it.

The Only Reasonable Plan

The plan adopted was the obvious, the practical, the only reasonable plan. It was to use the language of the appearances of things and of common life—not as endorsing any errors which may be supposed to be involved in the etymology of the words, but simply to become intelligible. In speaking to humans, the terms they used and understood at the time must be employed.

Had the other course been adopted, it is easy to see, not only that the book must have been extremely burdensome in bulk, but that its communications would have been as sure to meet with opposition at one period from being ahead of the age, unintelligible and preposterous to their minds, as at another from being behind the age.

Its scientific communications, if it undertook to teach science, must have been complete, anticipating even those brilliant and now unimagined discoveries which await the zeal of future explorers of the twentieth, or perhaps the thirtieth century, when the science and the scientific phrase of today may be as much the jest and scorn of the learned world as medieval ideas on such subjects are now. The student who graduated from college even forty years ago would find himself today bewildered and utterly at a loss, in reading the text books or attempting to use the apparatus of instruction in chemistry, if he had not diligently kept up with the progress of research and the changes of technical nomenclature.

God does not reveal either scientific or moral truth in the way that the objectors demand; not all at one time, and especially not all the first time. He gives scope and need for the exercise of our own powers of research. He gives us faculties, and expects that we shall use them.

There was sound philosophy in the answer of the little five year-old girl, when someone teased her about curling her hair, instead of leaving it to her Maker. She replied, "When I was little, He curled it for me. But now He thinks I am old enough to curl it myself." God leaves us something to do, in searching into His works and His Word.

Bearing these ideas in mind, it will not be difficult to apply fair principles in interpretation to both records, that of science and that of revelation. Both volumes were written by Almighty direction. The latter was recorded and unfolded by degrees, during centuries of human progress, but now lies before us complete and full. The other began to be recorded far earlier, but is even as yet only partially unfolded and read by us. God permits human hands to open and reveal it to our view, under the guidance of His providence. Some of the pages have been turned, and earnest minds are at work deciphering their meaning. More remain to be brought to light, and read in the progress of science. How many, we cannot tell, and what is in them we cannot imagine.

As we advance in the process of investigating and comparing the teachings of these two records, these two divine volumes, God's Word and God's works, it may well be that seeming contradictions will arise. But as leaf after leaf is turned and offered to our perusal, as fact after fact falls into place in the great system of inductive truth, we find fresh instruction arising. We may be sure that ultimately, when both are correctly understood, the two records will thoroughly agree.

This has been actually the experience of devout and patient students of both records, in age after age. There has been no period, perhaps, in which some apparent contrarieties have not been either discovered or imagined. But each generation has seen some difficulties solved, and new ones arising, to be soon relieved by further investigation.

The Number of Remarkable Agreements Between Science and Scripture Is Very Great

It is far more difficult for these unexpected coincidences to be explained, on the principles of the unbeliever, than for any of the apparent contradictions to be cleared up, which are so boastfully alleged. It would be easy to point out a number of these in detail, and to show how science, in each of her departments, is casting light on revelation. At present it may suffice to give a single example taken from an able article by Dr. McCosh, president of Princeton College.

> The correspondence between Genesis and Geology as to the order of creation has been expounded scientifically by the three men on this continent most competent to speak on the subject: viz. Professor Dana of Yale, Dr. Dawson of McGill University, Montreal, and Dr. Guyot of Princeton. . . . I doubt much whether any geologist in the present day could, in so brief a compass, give as accurate a compendium of the changes which our earth has undergone as is in these thirty-one verses in the opening of our Bible. Except on the supposition that the Scriptural statement is inspired, it is impossible to account for its being written and published three thousand years before science made its discoveries.[1]

The same point is presented by the Hon. William E. Gladstone, in his memorable discussion with Mr. Huxley in the *Nineteenth Century*, in 1886. We quote simply a few sentences:

> I do not suppose it would be feasible, even for Professor Huxley, taking the nebular hypothesis and geological discovery for his guides, to give, in the compass of the first twenty-seven verses of Genesis, an account of the cosmogony, and of the succession of life in the stratification of the earth, which would combine scientific precision of statement with the majesty, the simplicity, the intelligibility, and the impressiveness of the record before us. Let me modestly call it, for argument's sake, an approximation to the present presumptions and conclusions of science. Let me assume that the statement in the text as to plants, and the statement of verses 24 and 25, as to reptiles, cannot in all points be sustained; and yet still there remain great, unshaken facts to be weighed.

> First, the fact that such a record should have been made at all.

> Secondly, the fact that, instead of dwelling in generalities, it has placed itself under the severe conditions of a chronological order, reaching from the first *nisus* of chaotic matter to a consummated production of a fair and goodly, a furnished and a peopled world.

> Thirdly, the fact that its cosmogony seems, in the light of the nineteenth century, to draw more and more of countenance from the best natural philosophy; and,

Fourthly, that it has described the successive origins of the five great categories of present life with which human experience was and is conversant in that order which geological authority confirms.

How came these things to be? How came they to be, not among Accadians, or Assyrians, or Egyptians, who monopolized the stores of human knowledge when this wonderful tradition was born; but among the obscure records of a people who, dwelling in Palestine for twelve hundred years from their sojourn in the valley of the Nile, hardly had force to stamp even so much as their name upon the history of the world at large, and only then began to be admitted to the general communion of humankind when their Scriptures assumed the dress which a Gentile tongue was needed to supply?

It is more rational, I contend, to say that these astonishing anticipations were a God-given supply, than to suppose that a race, who fell uniformly and entirely short of the great intellectual development of antiquity, should here not only have equaled and outstripped it, but have entirely transcended, in kind even more than in degree, all known exercises of human faculties.[2]

The Absence of Definitely Established Contradictions So Far Is a Remarkable Phenomenon

Many have been alleged, and some insisted on with great zeal and positiveness. *All* the dogmatism and boldness of assertion has certainly not been confined to the theologians. But, when closely considered, many of the contradictions claimed have disappeared under the re-examinations of a wiser exegesis of Scripture. Many have been removed by the advancing discoveries in science or history, showing that it was not the Bible that was mistaken, but its assailants. All have admitted some fair and reasonable explanation.

This may encourage us, when new difficulties are alleged, to wait candidly, patiently, and hopefully for further light.

The Bible: More than Human Wisdom

But furthermore, this fact is itself a tribute of no small importance to the accuracy of the Bible, and a proof that more than human wisdom has presided over the composition of its pages. Here is a volume made up of sixty-six different books, written in separate sections, by scores of different persons, during a period of fifteen hundred years. It is a volume antedating in its earlier records all other books in the world, touching human life and knowledge at hundreds of different points. Yet it avoids any absolute, assignable error in dealing with these innumerable themes. Of what other ancient book can this be said? Of what book even one hundred years old can this be said?

The sacred books of India, of Zoroaster, of Mohammedanism, reveal their human origin by the obvious human errors they distinctly affirm, by the misconceptions and falsehoods which are wrapped up inextricably in their theological systems.

In like manner, the works on systematic theology so late as the Reformation period, and equally with them the philosophical and scientific writings of the same era, or even of four or five generations ago, are marked by blunders of fact, or errors of theory, which can be exposed by the schoolboy of today.

These books are comparatively little read now. Their mistakes are unknown to the masses of even well-informed men. They are only noticed by scholars who know how to account for them, and to appreciate the value of the works, notwithstanding these deficiencies.

Not so with the Bible. Every line in it has been subjected to a minute, jealous, microscopic scrutiny, by friend and by foe, such as no other writing has ever experienced. The fires of criticism have kindled all around it and over it, hot enough to detect and to burn out the dross, if there was any. It stands today the book in all the world most loved, most hated, most studied, most misused; the book upon which the converging light is cast from every source, from every science and from every age of human research, and to which the concentrated attention of the most vigorous minds of the race has been directed for centuries. It is only simple justice to say, that it stands a monument of marvelous accuracy.

Men of Science of the
Highest Rank Sustain the Bible

Finally, let it never be forgotten that, if there be scientific men who assail the Bible, there are others, equally eminent or more so, who defend it; men not less honest in their love for truth, not less zealous and candid in their search for it, and not less bold and frank in declaring it when found. If there have been a Voltaire and a Diderot to assail it, there have been on its side a Newton and a Davy, a Hugh Miller, an Agassiz, a Maury, and a Guyot. If there was a Huxley and an Ingersoll to attack, there are a Hitchcock, a Silliman, a Dana, a Gray, and a Dawson to defend and honor it, men in whom devotion has not blinded the eye of science, nor learning palsied the heart of piety. Even among the votaries of pure science, who have no professed acquaintance with theology, or who take no distinct religious position, they that are with us as to the divine origin of the Bible are more and mightier than those that are against us.

CHAPTER FIFTEEN

Objections from Insignificant Details

Did the Holy Spirit dictate such details, it is asked, as the minute instructions for the tabernacle and the temple, the genealogies of private families and petty tribes, in the Old Testament; or such as the salutations to friends at the close of several epistles, Paul's medical counsel to Timothy as to taking remedies for his stomach and infirmities, or the communications with which he charges him as to his parchments and the cloak he had left at Troas?

1. This objection, it appears to us, wholly misconceives the doctrine which we advocate, ignoring the fact that we affirm and vindicate the thoroughly human quality of the books. This feature we claim for them as earnestly as their divine authority. The objection might be of force against a mechanical theory of

inspiration, which admits no real human authorship, but it has no validity against our doctrine.

2. The objection also ignores the obviously beneficial and valuable design of some of these alleged "insignificant details" e.g., the typical object of the Mosaic ritual, and of the temple services, and the indispensable importance of the genealogies as evidence in tracing the descent of the Messiah.

3. Further, the objection fails to do justice to those historical passages which it charges with insignificance. It fails to appreciate those details which it calls trivial. It is just in these slight circumstances of the history that character speaks out, oftentimes, in the most affecting and instructive way. But for these affectionate greetings to beloved friends, we should have lacked evidence of the genuine tenderness of the apostle's soul, and we might have been told that Christianity left no room for the virtue of friendship. The practical common-sense advice to Timothy is no encouragement to intemperance, but, on the other hand, a strong evidence that Timothy was abstemious in principle and practice, since it needed apostolic suggestion and urgency to induce him to use even "a little wine," and that when it was medicinally necessary.

The Character and Personality of Paul

Again, Paul's concern about his parchments and other books, and his cloak, is to our minds as interesting a circumstance as that other petty but instructive incident of the little old man, practical, helpful, considerate for others, after the shipwreck on the island of Malta, bustling around to gather up fragments of sticks to make a fire for the chilled and dripping company that had been rescued from the waves. We would not be willing to spare or lose either, on any consideration. They reveal to us the man, Paul. They bring us nearer to him in actual, real life.

Consider the case about this much-complained-of cloak. Here is a man who, some thirty years ago, renounced ease, fortune, popularity, brilliant prospects, all for Christ, in order to do good to the souls of men. He has had his reward all along, from the world and from his nation, in stripes, in rod beatings, in stonings, in imprisonments, in treachery and deadly conspiracy, in unblushing falsehoods, in unassuaged malice. And now his end is near. He is advanced in years, in his last prison, his usefulness accomplished, his course finished. He is just awaiting the sentence of death. Bravely, cheerfully, triumphantly, he writes his last letter to his dearest friend, his son in the gospel. Not a note quivers, not a word hints of gloom or regret.

But he is shivering with cold. Winter is commencing. He is in want of clothes. And in that prison he is lonely. He cannot solace himself by talking, as of old, to the guard to whom he was chained; nor can he, as formerly, have interviews with the hostile Jews, and strive to convert them, or with the loving Christians, and endeavor to comfort them. He is shut off from such intercourse. Some of the Christians themselves are afraid or ashamed now to stand with him. Others are debarred from doing what they would for him. Only Luke is with him, sharing apparently his imprisonment for the sake of alleviating his sufferings— Luke, who had been with him in his imprisonment at Caesarea, and again in his first imprisonment at Rome. *He is used to it*: he has come to stand by him to the last. But the good man wants his books, especially certain beloved precious parchments. They would cheer his lonely hours. He needs his cloak, he wants his manuscripts. Is there nothing touching, nothing affecting in this?

We read with emotion about Jerome of Prague, "shut up for three hundred and forty days in the prisons of Constance, in the bottom of a dark and fetid tower, and never allowed to leave it except to appear before his murderers"; and our hearts go out in sympathy with the martyr. We read of the venerable Bishop Hooper in old England, "dragged from his disgusting cellar, covered with wretched clothes and a borrowed cloak, tottering on his staff, and bent double with rheumatism on his way to the stake," for the testimony of Jesus; and our hearts kindle anew with admiration and devotion. We read of Judson at Oung-pen-la, in extremest peril and destitution, ministered to by that godly wife, his life only saved at the risk of her own; and we feel afresh the impulse to rise to similar heroism. And shall not these venerable martyrs, these noble missionaries, remind us also of our brother Paul, shut up in prison, suffering from loneliness and from cold, and asking for his cloak? And shall his example fail to stir our hearts, or excite our sympathy?

"We behold him," says Haldane, "standing upon the confines of the two worlds—in this world about to be beheaded as guilty, by the emperor of Rome, in the other world to be crowned as righteous, by the King of Kings; here deserted by men, there to be welcomed by angels; here in want of a cloak to cover him, there to be clothed upon with his house from heaven."

We put a high value upon that cloak, and the little passage that alludes to it.

In like manner we might take up, as Gaussen has done very instructively,[1] the greetings at the close of the epistle to the Romans, and show the manifold and precious instructions which come to us from them. Mere lists of names, we are told; personal reminiscences of his friendships; dry nomenclature of eighteen people, all in oblivion otherwise. To give these needed no inspiration.

On the contrary, we are specially thankful for these very sixteen verses, giving us a living picture of a primitive church, and casting a flood of light on the reorganization of heathen society under the influence of Christianity. And we do not see why inspiration might not suggest, as well as affection prompt, these kindly fraternal allusions.

But we almost shrink from pursuing this line of argument, for it seems as if, in such defenses of what is contained in the Word of God, we are in danger of exalting ourselves to the position of judges of what should and what should not be contained in a revelation from God. A man who is fully competent for such judgment is competent to make a revelation.

As Gaussen has said, "It strikes us that there is no arrogance to be compared with that of a man who, owning the Bible to be from God, then makes bold to sift with his hand the pure in it from what is impure, the inspired from what is uninspired, God from man. This is to overturn all the foundation of the faith; it amounts to placing it no more in believing God, but in believing ourselves."[2]

> There are those today [says Mr. McConaughy] who know just what God ought to do, and their judgment, rather than what he pleases, is their criterion. They measure their God with a yardstick. They sound him with a plumb-line. They calculate him by mathematics. They bring him to the test of science. They regulate him according to right reason—that is, their own. They prescribe the exact limits within which he may work; and then, having made him altogether such a one as themselves, having robbed him of his Godhead, they fall down and worship the God of their own hands.[3]

Conclusion

We have now completed the plan we proposed. We have attempted to set forth, *first*, the doctrine of inspiration, with such distinctions and explanations as seemed proper to make it clear; *second*, the proofs, indirect and direct, by which we believe it is sustained; and *third*, the objections most commonly urged, with such replies as appeared suitable and practicable within our brief space.

The result of the whole investigation has been, we trust, adapted to remove difficulties which have been in the way of many thoughtful and earnest students, who had a general conviction of the divine authority of the Scriptures, but did not see how this was to be reconciled with some of the conclusions of modern scholarship. Our labor was commenced with a distinct belief that thorough and candid inquiry would subserve the interests of the cause of Christ; that truth has nothing to lose, but everything to gain, from fair investigation; and that to one who earnestly and prayerfully seeks, God will give guidance and satisfaction.

Having found the subject cleared up to our own mind by these studies, we have ventured to submit them to the inspection of friends, and now of the general public, in the humble hope that they may convince opponents, and reclaim the doubting to a real and rejoicing faith in the Bible as God's Word to man.

Questions for Group Discussion and Personal Reflection

Chapter 1

1. Manly writes: "Christianity is the religion of the Book. It is not an external organization, nor a system of ceremonies, nor a philosophy . . . . nor a vague inquiry and aspiration, nor a human invention for man's own convenience or advantage."

   What does Dr. Manly mean by this statement? Do you agree or disagree? Why?

2. Discuss the possible meanings of Manly's *facts*, *doctrines*, *commands*, and *promises*.

3. Manly asks the question: Is the Bible the Word of God? Why is this question of the highest importance to Christians? Why does the answer affect our life and work and all that we do?

4. "The Bible, the Bible only, the religion of Protestants." Why does Manly refer to this "watchword of victory" as the "battle-cry of freedom from ecclesiastical domination"?

5. Discuss Manly's statement: "We must go for guidance, not to the Fathers, but to those who were earlier and greater than the Fathers . . . . to the apostles, and above all to the Lord Jesus Christ Himself."

   Ponder and discuss the meaning of this statement.

6. "The difference between an inspired and uninspired Bible is . . . . closely connected with the question whether we are following God or men; whether our religion is of divine or of human origin." What did Manly mean by this statement?

7. Discuss the three serious defects of an uninspired Bible.

8. Why would an uninspired Bible "furnish no infallible standard of truth"?

9. Why would an uninspired Bible "present no authoritative rule for obedience, and no ground for confident and everlasting hope . . . . and give no firm ground on which to base our convictions, to build our hopes, or to order our life"?

10. Why would an uninspired Bible "minister to the pride of reason, instead of to the culture of faith . . . generate perplexity instead of repose, conflict instead of submission, and resistance instead of reverence"?

11. Why is inspiration not "essential . . . to the historical credibility of Scripture"?

12. Manly holds that doubts regarding the inspiration of Scripture originate in three sources. In your own words, what are those sources? Do you agree or disagree? Discuss.

13. Describe in your own words Manly's description of the "unwary advocate" and the "kind-hearted, liberal man," and the results of each.

Chapter 2

1. Why is an attempt sometimes made "to embrace at one view . . . all the manifold questions which arise in the study of the Canon, of text criticism, higher criticism, hermeneutics, biblical history, and its connection with secular history"?

2. Discuss Manly's "genuineness of the Scriptures" . . . the question of authorship.

3. What does Manly mean by "text criticism, or integrity of the Scriptures"?

4. What is "higher criticism"?

5. When Manly discusses the "authenticity of the Scriptures," what does he mean?

6. What does Manly mean when he refers to the "Canon of Scripture"?

7. Discuss Manly's "Rule of Faith." What does he mean by the term "sufficiency of the Scriptures"?

8. What does Manly mean by "the evidences of Christianity"?

9. Concerning the supernatural, Manly describes the following as a "more powerful stimulus." "A more powerful stimulus, however, has been given to the prevalence of these anti-supernatural notions. These have come by the proneness of many students of physical science who apply their favorite methods of investigation to topics outside of their range. They carry the assumptions which seem to be just in dealing with material phenomena into the domain of theology. Because they find, everywhere in the visible universe, law, order, universal principles, they have undertaken to dethrone the Lawgiver, and to exalt on His throne, in His place, law itself."

What does Manly mean by this statement?

10. In light of the Toy Controversy (see Introduction), discuss what Manly, no doubt, means by this statement: "Some true Christians have yielded to the force of this current [anti-supernatural notions], either unreflectingly, or with some vague idea of a compromise, by which they would gain the support of those of science for religion. Without exactly denying miracles, they have set themselves to pare down within credible limits the wonders recorded in the Bible."

11. Manly writes concerning miracles: "Let us not be afraid of admitting the idea and the fact of a miracle. The whole system of Christianity is a stupendous series of miracles."

    Do you agree? Discuss.

12. Why does Manly believe that inspiration is really about the existence and providence of God?

13. Explain Manly's meaning of this statement: "There are some who conceive that the subject [inspiration of Scripture] is cleared of difficulty by limiting the inspiration to the writings."

14. Ponder and discuss the following: "There is nothing ultimately gained . . . by attempting to omit the human link of the chain through which the influence passed. The Scriptures were inspired. The men of God who wrote them were inspired too. They were moved ('borne along') by the Holy Spirit."

15. "Inspiration implies both divine and human authorship." Do you agree? Discuss the significance of this statement.

16. "The distinction between the divine and the human authorship of the sacred writings is not to be denied in thought, nor ignored in our reasonings."

    Why or why not?

17. If time permits, explain and discuss what happened in Exodus 20:19–22 and Hebrews 12:21.

18. "The Bible is God's Word to humankind throughout. Yet, at the same time, it is really and thoroughly man's composition."

    What are the implications of this statement? Discuss.

19. "The Word is not *of* man, as to its source; nor depending *on* man, as to its authority."

    Do you agree with this statement? Discuss.

20. "If the Book were human only, a collection of the thoughts, hopes, desires, guesses at truth, of certain wise men of ancient times, that would be an entirely intelligible supposition." Why would that be "an entirely intelligible supposition"?

21. "If [the Bible] were divine only, as the tables of stone, engraved by the finger of God, that would be a perfectly simple proposition."

    Why would that be a "perfectly simple proposition"?

22. Considering the time in which Manly wrote, ponder and discuss the following statement.

    "If [the Bible] were of twofold, independent authorship, part by God and another part by man, the divinity contributing one portion and then retiring, while the human author acts alone, there would be perhaps no objection on the part of modern theorizers to recognize such an intermixture."

    Why would the "modern theorizers" of Manly's time voice no objection here?

23. "[The Bible] is all unmistakably the work of man. It is all by singular and accumulated evidences declared to be the Word of God . . . . all written by man, all inspired by God."

    Why, according to Manly, is this statement of utter significance?

24. Referring to biblical inspiration, Manly writes concerning the reasoning of his day: "Human, therefore fallible," they say. "Fallible, therefore false in some measure."

    Why does Manly say "It is a mere *assumption* that their being human forbids their being also divine"?

25. Discuss Manly's argument that leads up to his conclusion: "We recur, then, to the statement that the Bible is throughout divine and human, all inspired by God, all written by man."

26. What is meant by the "so-called 'Post-Reformation dogma' of *mechanical* inspiration"?

27. In one sentence, try to summarize the opinions of the following men:

a. Philip Schaff: _____

_____

b. B. K. Peirce: _____

_____

c. B. F. Westcott: _____

_____

d. Henry Alford: _____

_____

e. Edward Garbett: _____

_____

f. E. P. Humphrey: _____

_____

g. J. A. Smith: _____

_____

_____

28. Discuss Manly's definitions of "revelation" and "inspiration."

29. Why is it "important to distinctness and accuracy of view to discriminate between [revelation and inspiration]"?

30. How does Manly distinguish "inspiration" from "illumination"?

31. "Spiritual illumination is confounded with inspiration by two large and important classes: . . . the Roman Catholics and . . . the rationalists."

What are Manly's arguments about these two classes? Do you agree?

32. If deeper study is desired, study the writings of Schleiermacher, Samuel Taylor Coleridge, Dr. Thomas Arnold, and F. D. Maurice. What did they believe about the way the Spirit can act on the children of God? Why does Manly single out primarily these particular "writers of eminent ability"?

Chapter 3

1. Discuss the principal views of inspiration held by J. A. Quenstedt, Carpzovius, and Robert Hooker as Manly addresses them.

2. What does Manly say about Haldane and Carson regarding the dictation theory?

3. What was the doctrine of sacred Scripture according to Dr. Ladd?

4. "It is sometimes said that divine inspiration belongs to the truth conveyed, but not to the framework in which it is set. The kernel is divine, but the shell is human and imperfect."

   What does Manly mean with this statement regarding partial inspiration?

5. Discuss what is meant by these statements: "The Bible *is* the Word of God," and "The Bible *contains* the Word of God."

6. Explain Professor George T. Ladd's distinction between the Bible and the Word of God, when he writes: It "*brings* us the Word of God. . . .The claims and the phenomena of the Bible entitle us to call a *large proportion* of its writings inspired."

7. How does Manly say we are to "distinguish between the Bible and this 'inner Bible'"?

8. According to Dr. Ladd, what "places the doctrine and life of the Church in constant jeopardy"?

9. Explain what Dr. Manly means by his term "pious frauds."

10. Discuss the following statements written by Carson. What is the argument he tries to make here?

"When a pupil writes a theme by the direction of his teacher, with every help usually afforded, and when it is so corrected by the latter that nothing remains but what is proper in his estimation, is it not still the pupil's production? Could it be said to be the composition or the work of the teacher? No more can the Scriptures be called the Word of God according to this mischievous theory. A book might all be true, and good, and important, yet not be the book of God."

11. What is meant by the following:

a. mechanical inspiration
b. partial inspiration
c. different degrees of inspiration
d. natural inspiration
e. universal Christian inspiration
f. plenary inspiration or full inspiration?

Explain each and discuss its significance and meaning.

12. Discuss Morell's definition of inspiration.

13. Ponder the meaning of the following:

"Schleiermacher regarded inspiration as not infallible, yet as something higher than human genius—'an awakening and excitement of the religious consciousness, different in degree rather than in kind from the pious inspiration or intuitive feelings of holy men.'"

14. "Coleridge in his *Confessions of an Inquiring Spirit* contends earnestly that the line of demarcation between the primitive gifts of spiritual inspiration and the inspirations of the Spirit now was a line drawn without authority."

What does Coleridge mean by this statement?

15. Discuss the following: "The doctrine which we hold is that commonly styled plenary inspiration or full inspiration. It is that the Bible as a whole is the Word of God, so that in every

part of Scripture there is both infallible truth and divine authority."

Chapter 4

1. Discuss the argument Manly is making with this lengthy statement: "As to *revelation*, we do not know how it was imparted. How would one go about to discover the nature of the divine operation involved? Except the prophet himself, who received the revelation, what man could testify on the subject? There is no possible point of contact by which it can be brought within the sphere of human observation. Even to the prophet was it not still a mystery? Do not all the indications point towards that conclusion? Possibly *he* did not know. Certainly *we* do not know."

2. Ponder the following: "Even spiritual illumination, which seems nearer to us, which has been promised to every age, and which we trust we have individually experienced, is very imperfectly explicable by us. We know the effects. We do not know the way in which the Spirit operates to produce them."

   Do you agree or disagree? Discuss.

3. Read the following statement: "Some of the early Christian writers (commonly called Fathers) used expressions which have been understood to imply that they regarded inspiration as mechanical. But they seem to have used them as illustrations, and in a rhetorical way, rather than as meaning to be strictly interpreted. For example, they spoke sometimes of the inspired man as a pen in the hand of God, or a lyre touched by the musician. Another illustration sometimes used was that of the amanuensis or copyist."

   Ponder the implications of the Fathers' statements. Can you think of other illustrations the Fathers used that might possibly speak of mechanical inspiration?

4. Manly ascertains: "The inspired writer is not described either as the pen or the penman. The Bible does not represent verbal dictation to a copyist as the method adopted, either in revelation or inspiration."

Do you agree? What does Manly mean here?

5. Do you see this statement as a logical argument? "There is, where we dictate, no control over the will of the copyist. Also, there is no aid to his memory, reflection, imagination, or power of expression, on the supposition of his being willing, but unable to give accurately what had been communicated to him. Both the control and the imparted power which we believe to belong to inspiration are lacking."

In your own words, what does it mean?

6. Read the following Scriptures and then Manly's statement. Read Exodus 19:19; 20:1, 19, 22; Deuteronomy 4:33, 36; 5:4, 22. "At Sinai, the people, as well as Moses, heard audible words uttered from the midst of the fire. Though we have no idea how it was done, we unhesitatingly believe this. It is distinctly so recorded."

What is your opinion? Why do we "unhesitatingly" believe this? Do you consider it "dictation"?

7. "There is generally no hint of the mode of the divine action in imparting, or of the mental activity in receiving and uttering the message."

What is the significance of this "silence of Scripture"? Do you agree with Manly that "it leads to the inference that there is nothing in the communications of human beings with one another that really and fully resembles it"?

8. Explain the meaning of Manly's statement: "The individuality of the sacred writers, as well as their intelligent, voluntary action, was not superseded by the Spirit's influence. But both these were employed."

9. What is Manly's definition of "individuality"?

10. "Inspiration is not merely a natural elevation of the faculties, analogous to the stimulus of passion and enthusiasm, or to poetic genius."

What does Manly mean by this statement? Discuss. Do you agree?

11. According to Manly, what are the "three spheres or provinces in which the Bible teaches that the Spirit operates"?

12. What are the two kinds of supernatural wonders, and what were they the effects of?

13. Ponder the following: "On humankind in general, and still more on the lower creatures, the Spirit of God acted and still acts. He acts with no intention to clothe them with authority, or even to make them holy, but to sustain them in being and activity. And as the object in view differs, so the result differs."

    In your own words, what does this statement mean? Do you agree?

14. Why would it "be wrong to say that, in the influences of grace, the men whom God actuates and moves are thereby rendered infallible"? What would that imply?

15. Read, ponder, and discuss the relevance of this statement:

    "Bezaleel, the architect of the tabernacle, and Samson, the giant champion, were moved by the Spirit. But when we consider the design and the result accomplished, we perceive that He endowed the one with inventive power to devise and execute skillful works in gold and silver for the honor of God in His movable temple. He endowed the other with supernatural strength to fight and destroy the Philistines. But He gave neither of them, so far as we learn, any commission to speak or to write for Him. By an entirely different sort of influence their respective contemporaries, Moses and Samuel, were moved to speak in God's name. So, even as other holy men of God, they 'spake as they were moved by the Holy Ghost.'"

16. Discuss pantheism and its implications, according to Manly.

17. Discuss Manly's "new term of reproach, bibliolatry." What does it mean, according to Manly?

18. Recall the year 1888, when Manly wrote these words. What was happening in that era that would bring Manly to make the following statement? Who do you think are some of the "ministers" he is referring to and why?

"In these strange times into which we have fallen, it is openly affirmed that some of the leading deists are ministers of the Church of England. They are officiating publicly at her altars. However, on the continent, some of the leading opponents of vital Christianity and most energetic assailants of the veracity of the Bible deny that it differs in any essential feature from the Koran or the Zendavesta. These are not only ministers of the established churches. They are also selected and eminent instructors in their theological schools, and trainers of their rising ministry."

19. Why does Macnaught argue that there is no such thing as infallibility regarding the words/writings of God's inspired prophets and evangelists?

20. Discuss Manly's following thesis: "The inspiration which the Bible affirms does not imply that those who enjoyed it had perfect knowledge on all subjects, or on any subject. It affirms only that they had infallibility and divine authority in their official utterances."

21. What is the major point Manly makes in the following statement?:

"Inspiration had nothing to do with Paul's skill or awkwardness as a tent-maker. It did not affect the elegance of his delivery as a speaker, favorably or otherwise. It did not become (as some imagine our doctrine to presuppose) a characteristic in the common affairs of life. It did not preserve its most eminent characters from mistakes in conduct. Nor did it exempt them from sinful feelings at different times, and from the constant need of prayer for forgiveness, and the perpetual, watchful struggle against sin."

22. Ponder the following statement: "Inspired men did not know the full meaning of what they themselves taught."

Do you agree?

23. How were Peter's understandings of the Gentiles to the church of Christ made more full and clear by the communications at Joppa and Caesarea? Discuss.

24. Consider what Manly means when he writes: "There are no degrees in infallibility."

25. "Inspiration did not imply exemption from error in conduct, nor great elevation in spiritual attainments," Manly writes.

    Why is this true of revelation as well as of inspiration?

26. Discuss the implications of the following: "We have no assurance, nor the slightest reason to suppose, that the supernatural guardianship which insured the correctness of the original record was continued and renewed every time anybody undertook to make a copy of it."

    Why does Manly say the accuracy of our present copies is a separate question?

27. What does Manly mean with his "rain water" and "river water" illustration? Do you consider it an appropriate illustration to the point he is making? Why or why not?

28. Consider and discuss: "Inspiration does not imply the truth of opinions or sayings stated in Scripture, but not sanctioned."

29. Why, according to Manly, is there an obvious distinction between what is recorded and what is taught or enjoined?

30. "The Bible is not accountable for the propriety of actions recorded, but not approved."

    What does Manly mean by this statement?

Chapter 5

1. Discuss Manly's three points for the positive statement of the doctrine of inspiration:

   a. The Bible is truly the Word of God, having both infallible truth and divine authority in all that it affirms or enjoins.

   b. The Bible is truly the production of men. It is marked by all the evidences of human authorship as clearly and certainly as any other book that was ever written by men.

    c. This twofold authorship extends to every part of Scripture, and to the language as well as to the general ideas expressed.

2. How does Manly sum up biblical inspiration in one sentence? Would you agree with him?

Chapter 6

1. Discuss the following statement by Manly: "Suppose that there is a God, infinitely wise, holy, and good, who loves the rebellious creatures that have strayed into darkness, misery, and sin. Suppose He desires to offer them redemption. It is an object infinitely worthy of such a Being that He should give them clear, accurate, and authoritative information as to truth and duty."

2. What is the powerful impact of Manly's thesis here: "If the truth was committed, not to merely 'earthen vessels,' but to vessels of a tainted or poisonous material, so that infusion would corrupt or injure what was placed therein; or if the message was communicated by men who stated simply the result of their own observation, or used the utmost of their native ability, reasoning out as best they could, unaided, what would be useful for man? In either case, it would hardly comport with what might reasonably be expected. It would not be like God."?

3. What are the "three stages of the supernatural" regarding "the other supernatural. . . acts connected with the giving of the Scriptures"? Why are they essential?

4. "If God works a supernatural wonder in giving revelation, and others to authenticate it, then it is not improbable, but likely, that He would exercise such control, and give such supernatural aid as might be necessary to secure the accurate transference of the revelation into human speech, so as to make it just what He meant it should be."

Do you agree? Discuss.

5. Why does the "admission of a miraculous revelation not only [create] the probability that all further steps would be taken that are necessary to secure the end in view, but it also presents a sufficient answer to those who object to inspiration, because it implies the supernatural"?

6. Discuss the point Manly makes in using the example of the Psalms in his presumptive argument for inspiration. He writes:

"The Psalms are so far above the sacred lyric compositions, not only of any contemporary era, but of all subsequent times. They leave no room for the fancy that these are the foam that crested the waves of Hebrew poetic passion, the utterances of mere national or individual longings, in one of the narrowest and least cultured of the peoples of the ancient world. Strange that these secluded Hebrews, who scarcely ever passed or looked beyond their own contracted region, unfamiliar with art and unpolished by contact with the literature of other nations, should have given utterance and melody to the deepest feelings of universal human nature!"

7. Why does the argument for inspiration become even stronger in the New Testament?

8. Discuss the beauty of Dr. E. Henderson's thought and words when he writes:

"How otherwise can we account for the fact
that persons of ordinary talent,
untutored in the schools of philosophy,
dull of apprehension,
pusillanimous in spirit,
narrow in their opinions,
secular in their hopes,
and strongly imbued with national prepossessions,
should all at once have displayed
the most extraordinary mental energy,
a superiority to every earthly consideration,
a profound acquaintance with truths
of the most sublime character, and
of the deepest interest to the whole human species,

and an expansion of benevolence which embraced every nation and every human being on the face of the globe?

"To the operation of what causes, within the compass of those principles of action which govern humankind, are we to ascribe the sudden and entire transformation undergone by the plain, illiterate fishermen of Galilee, and the bigoted and zealous disciple of Gamaliel?"

9. Why is it "impossible to maintain the absolute historical accuracy of the Gospel historians, without also maintaining their inspiration"? Discuss.

Chapter 7

1. Why must these two preliminary questions be examined:

   a. *From what source* can direct proofs come?
   b. *In what form* may they be expected?

2. "The veracity of the historical record in the Scriptures, the honesty of the writers, the reality of their divine mission, are in general admitted by our opponents."

   Why is this data "admitted"?

3. "John the Baptist performed no miracle, but his teachings were amply attested as divine by prophecy going before, and the seal of the Lord Jesus following after. So Luke did no miracle, so far as we know."

   Why were the writings and teachings of these men accepted by apostolic men as of equal authority with their own?

4. Ponder the following statement and discuss:

   "One inspired writer testifies to another. Thus we have, in still another form, the witness of God, who bestowed the gift upon one, when He confirms and recognizes it through the lips of another."

5. Manly asserts that an argument be built up by successive steps. In other words, one should advance from a lower point admit-

ted to the higher points really involved in it. Discuss the successive steps one by one that he lists.

6. Manly writes that "the argument, then is really cumulative and progressive. It is not like a chain, where the whole depends on each separate link, and consequently the whole is no stronger than the weakest link. But each point proven adds support to all the rest."

   Discuss the chain image Manly uses to prove his point.

7. "While the Bible, as a whole, testifies of Christ, Christ testifies to the Bible."

   Do you agree with this statement? Why?

8. What does Manly mean by the terms "legitimate induction" and "express assertions"?

9. How does Manly form this conclusion? Do you agree?

   "The Bible does not seem anxious about its own recognition. The divine manifestation in it is much as we find it in creation and providence."

Chapter 8

1. The general manner of quoting Scripture in Scripture "embraces especially the quotations and allusions to the Old Testament in the New. It gives, in a general way, the testimony of our Lord and of the apostles."

   Why is this statement true? On what does Manly base this statement?

2. Discuss the major significance of this statement:

   "This universal belief of the Jewish people in these writings could not be overlooked by one who came, like our Saviour, as a teacher, and the Great Teacher, sent from God. It was necessary for Him either to contradict that belief, if not true, or to sanction it, if true. Upon such a question, He could not be neutral. The gospel, the final embodiment of divine truth, to be presented to the world by Jesus, the only begotten Son of

God Himself, could not be planted in the midst of unrebuked error. Least of all could it be built upon error as its basis. And that the New Testament gospel is built upon the Old, and assumes it throughout as its basis, its forerunner, its original and foundation, is unquestioned and unquestionable."

3. Describe what Jesus means here when He discusses the Scriptures: "It is right for you to listen to these witnesses, to interrogate them closely, to search them fully, for they are the real methods in which God has spoken. It is your sin and shame that, recognizing them and claiming to heed them, you have not recognized Me by means of them."

4. Reread Jesus' Sermon on the Mount and then discuss the meaning of this statement: "The fundamental passage, however, in which our Lord expressly sets forth His relation to the law and the prophets of the Old Covenant, is in the Sermon on the Mount." Do you agree? Why or why not?

5. Discuss this statement and explain what Professor Ladd means: "To use a figure of speech as old as Theophylact, Christ does not intend to rub out and destroy the sketch in shadow-lines before him, but with true and ideal art will fill it in to the completion of the picture."

6. Explain the following: "Our Lord modifies the law. Yes! There are progress and improvement from the Old Testament to the New."

7. Explain the importance of the following statement by Manly: "Until John, the law and the prophets had remained the one grand source of divinely authorized information. Now, they are to be, *not* superseded, condemned to failure, but retained and *completed*. Not an item is to be lost, not a jot, not a tittle."

8. What questions would you personally ask of this statement: "Our Lord gives a very striking witness to the sufficiency of the Old Testament in the parable of the rich man and Lazarus. Even the resurrection of one from the dead would not convince a man who refuses credence to Moses and the prophets (Luke 16:29–31). The attitude of heart which leads to the

rejection of the former appeal will not be changed by even the embodiment of the truth in the resurrection of the Messiah."?

9. "There is, however, another sense in which Jesus fulfilled the law and the prophets. We do not allude to the fact that He obeyed the precepts with a moral purity and exactness never before found in human beings. Though this was true, it does not seem to be the truth suggested in the Sermon on the Mount."

Why does it seem not to be true in the Sermon on the Mount? Do you agree or disagree?

10. "And now the picture is finished. But there is not on earth one whom it resembles. There is as yet none even that comprehends it. It is folded away for four hundred years."

Discuss this period of four hundred years between the Old and New Testaments. What happened? Why was God silent?

11. Discuss the way in which Manly uses the imagery of a picture to describe the Old Testament.

12. Read the following and describe the difference between Mosaic Law and rabbinical tradition: "The act of the disciples, which the Pharisees censured, in rubbing out the ears of wheat, because it was working on the Sabbath, was not a violation of the Mosaic Law. It was in contravention of the rabbinical traditions. Hence, this cannot be pleaded as an instance in which Jesus 'must allow to pass from obligation, as a part of that law, many of its special enactments, observances, and established points of view.'"

13. Discuss the marriage and divorce laxity to which this statement refers: "Prior to the giving of the Mosaic enactments, which were civil as well as moral, great laxity as to the marriage union had sprung up among the people."

14. Discuss the common "sending away" situation as practiced in this period.

15. What does Dr. Ladd mean by this statement:

"The word used by Christ with reference to the act of Moses (suffered), seems rather to place the human law-giver in some sort at that divine point of view from which such concessions are regarded as a necessary part of the divine historic discipline."?

16. Discuss the significance of this statement, as well as the fasting practices that were occurring in Jesus' time:

"The Mosaic Law commands only one fast in the year, and that with a ceremonial significance and object, on the great day of Atonement. The Saviour objects earnestly to the multiplied and merely formal observances of this kind which had been added to the 'law of Moses.'"

17. Why is this statement true?

"Revelation with inspiration would have impressed the Jew as an unheard of anomaly, in one claiming to be a divine messenger." Do you agree or disagree? Why?

18. Discuss this era of time and the people's response to it:

"The reappearance of the prophetic order is not only predicted by the Lord Jesus, but distinctly announced by Peter on the day of Pentecost as having actually occurred. This is a peculiar and marked feature of gospel times. For some hundreds of years, confessedly, the nation had been without a prophet. They lamented over the fact."

Why did they "lament"?

19. "We may . . . profitably consider the way in which Peter refers to his beloved brother Paul's writings as a part of the Scriptures. (See 2 Pet. 3:16.)"

Why does Manly say that this is a "remarkable allusion"?

20. Discuss the following statement: "In 2 Peter 3:2, there is also a clear implication that the commandment of the apostles and that of the holy prophets are equally binding."

Why is this statement true? Do you agree or disagree with it?

21. How does Manly arrive at this particular point? "No contest, however, is likely to occur on this point, that the inspiration of the New Testament is at least equal to that of the Old."

22. "Even without explicit assertions of it, whatever sanctity, whatever divinity, the writings of the Old Covenant may be proved to have, those of the New certainly share in equal degree. In fact, most persons now are disposed to rank the New far above the Old."

    If this was true in the 1880s, when Manly wrote it, do you believe it is still true today? Why or why not?

23. Do you agree with the following? Why or why not?

    "A personal utterance of God and a saying of Scripture are simply equivalent."

    What does this mean?

24. According to Manly, how is the "living voice of the divine speaker . . . recognized in the Word"?

25. Discuss "the error of the Sadducees" as introduced by Manly.

26. "One of the last acts of our Lord, before ascending to the skies, was to open the understanding of the disciples that they might 'understand the scriptures.' He says, 'thus it is written, and thus it behoved Christ to suffer.'"

    Why do these expressions "indicate the prophetic character of the ancient Scriptures, . . . [and] strongly imply their divine origin and infallible truth"?

27. Read Exodus 4:10–16 and 7:1–2. Discuss Manly's statement: "Under Moses, the true nature of the prophetic office is indicated by the analogy of the relation of Aaron to Moses."

    Why does Manly write this? Do you agree?

28. Discuss the following seven points Manly makes:

    a. "The word of prophecy," "prophecy of Scripture," "prophecy," are all expressions to denote the inspired word, the

Old Testament, and not merely the predictive portions now commonly called prophecy.

b. This word is confirmed, made more sure, by the subsequent revelations.

c. It is inferior to the gospel light, even as a lamp shining in a dark place is inferior to the sun.

d. Notwithstanding this it is well to take heed to it.

e. It is a principle of first importance that no prophecy is of private interpretation.

f. It is of the very nature of prophecy not to come by human will.

g. But men speak from God, being moved by the Holy Spirit.

29. What does Manly mean by the term "making void the Word of God"?

30. What does Manly say concerning "the living oracles"?

31. Ponder the concept of Jesus as being both David's Lord and David's Son.

32. What were some of the promises Manly mentions that were given to Old Testament writers?

33. Discuss the quotations Manly gives that "may suffice for illustrating the ample and positive manner in which inspiration is promised to the writers of the Old Testament."

34. According to Manly, what were the promises of inspiration to the New Testament writers?

35. What does Manly mean when he refers to "the Spirit of Truth"?

36. Discuss the reasoning behind the following statement:

"Why the revelation of divine truth by God in the Old Testament period should have been so slow and deliberate. Why, in like manner, it should have been made so gradually by our Lord Himself. Why it is left incomplete even at this critical moment, when He is leaving the world, and withdrawing from the disciples whom He loved, and the sinner for whom He died, may be an interesting question. But it is certainly a fact."

37. What did Manly mean by this statement? To what does he refer? Do you agree?

    "That which is imperfect is not necessarily either faulty or false."

38. Do you agree with Manly's thesis concerning prophets? He writes:

    "It is only necessary to add that these promises did not extend indefinitely. Hence the offices both of apostle and prophet came to an end, so far as we can discover, with the apostolic age. There is no proof that either had any successors in office. If like authority is claimed for any others, the claim ought to be supported by adequate, not to say similar and equal, evidence.

39. Discuss what happened on the day of Pentecost: "In addition to those personal teachings of our risen Saviour, when the day of Pentecost was fully come, the Spirit was given."

    How were the apostles changed? "The apostles, from the notable day, were entirely different men. They were endued anew, and in higher measure than ever before, with power from on high."

    What was the reason for this sudden change?

40. Manly gives ample Scripture in his "assertions of inspiration by the New Testament writers." Choose several key verses and discuss.

41. Discuss the implications of this statement: "The special feature of our doctrine of inspiration . . . is the thorough-going ascription of a divine character to those parts of the Bible which are most obviously and unmistakably human. . . There is no part of the Bible which does not show clearly the marks of human origin."

42. In your own words, try to convince someone of this remarkable statement by Manly:

    "The divine origin is as strongly and as distinctly affirmed as if there had been no human instrumentality involved. The human agency is also as clearly and unmistakably presented as if there had been no divine interposition in the case."

Chapter 9

1. Discuss the three cases to which the law of marriage appeals, as maintained by Manly.

2. "In the Old Testament dispensation a somewhat different law had prevailed as to mixed marriages."

   What was this law? Discuss its implications.

3. What is the significance of the law? "According to the Mosaic Law, such a union [mixed marriage] was not to be formed at all between Israelites and Gentiles, between Jehovah's worshippers and idolaters."

   Why not? What were the reasons behind this law?

4. What suggestions does Paul give to the unmarried? How are his suggestions different from the "commandments of the Lord"?

5. [Paul] "closes this discussion (1 Cor. 7:40) by saying, 'I think also that I have the Spirit of God.' There are some who regard this passage as expressing Paul's doubt of his own inspiration. Because Paul says he thought he had the Spirit of God, they are quite sure that he had not. They represent it as implying uncertainty in his own mind as to his divine authorization, or as to his possessing the Spirit."

   What does Manly say about this "doubt of Paul"? Does he agree or disagree? Discuss.

6. Why did Paul use the expression "slave"? What did he *not* mean by it?

7. Do you agree with this statement? Why or why not?

   "The simple end of inspiration is to secure infallibility in the communication of truth."

8. Discuss the following statement: "All that the expression implies is, that self-praise, in itself considered, is not the work

of a Christian; it is not the work to which the Spirit of Christ impels a believer. But when it is necessary to the vindication of truth or the honor of religion, it becomes a duty."

When does self-praise become a duty?

9. Read what Paul says in 2 Corinthians 12:2–3. "Whether in the body, I cannot tell; or whether out of the body, I cannot tell; God knoweth"; literally "whether in the body, I know not; or whether out of the body, I know not; God knoweth."

What does Paul mean by these statements?

10. What observation does Manly make regarding inspiration and omniscience?

11. "But we do not allege their [inspired writers] omniscience on every subject, or even on any subject. Only that all that they say is accurate, and is uttered under divine direction and authority."

Discuss what Manly means here. Do you agree?

Chapter 10

1. Discuss the following and give your opinion.

"The general fact of the existence of difficulties and obscurities in the Bible is urged as a proof that it cannot be inspired. It is assumed by some that, if it were inspired, there would be none, that everything coming from God must necessarily be perfect, in the sense of being free from all deficiency, and therefore from all obscurity as well as liability to error."

2. What does Manly mean by the following statement?

"Some obscurities arise from the eye that sees, rather than from the nature of the object seen. Better eyesight would lay many a ghost, and clearer minds would remove many difficulties."

3. In your own words, how would you express this thought? Do you agree?

"The obscurities in His Word and those in His works correspond. The same characteristics are found in both revelations—in the Bible and in the universe."

4. Discuss Manly's various "objections from the existence of difficulties."

Chapter 11

1. Explain the following words and their meanings: *firmament*; *firmamentum*; *stereoma*; and *raqia*.

2. What did Manly mean by his statement:

"It is always unsafe and unfair to say that a thing *cannot* be, merely because we do not understand *how* it was"?

3. "It is painfully common to find some commentators making out of every difference of view or statement a contradiction, when nothing of the sort is fairly implied."

Do you agree with Manly here? Why or why not? What are the examples Manly gives to uphold his opinion? Did you find them convincing?

4. What does Manly mean by this statement:

"Some alleged discrepancies arise from the different objects had in view by the different narrators, or from the different circle of readers or hearers addressed"?

5. What does Manly say has "led many devout and earnest students to array themselves against the . . . doctrine of inspiration"? Do you agree with him?

6. Do you agree with Manly when he writes:

"The fact that such discrepancies and errors have been so often and so confidently alleged, and one after another have been found to admit of a reasonable explanation, is a ground of confidence that in the future it will be as in the past"?

Chapter 12

1. "Actions deemed censurable, or laws and principles of action regarded as immoral, are found in Scripture. Therefore it is argued that it cannot be inspired."

   Do you agree or disagree with this statement? Why or why not?

2. "Some of the actions objected to are not really censurable, when properly examined," Manley maintains.

   What following argument and examples does he give in defense of this thesis? Discuss.

3. Do you agree with this assertion?

   "Some actions, which would now and ordinarily be wrong, were right under the peculiar circumstances of the case. Or they were made right by specific divine authority, modifying the general law. Instances of this kind may be found in the marriage of brothers and sisters in the beginning of the race, the extermination of the Canaanites under Joshua, the imprecations in the Psalms and Prophets by inspired men, where God's retributive interposition is denounced or implored against foul and persecuting cruelty."

4. Manly states: "There are numerous cases where, though the general character or conduct of persons is approved, no sanction is given to the various errors or the crimes into which they fell. It is sufficient to mention, without further comment, the cases of Noah, Abraham, Jacob, David, Peter. They were good men, but, as all others on earth, imperfect good men."

   Describe the cases of Noah, Abraham, Jacob, David, and Peter. Discuss Manly's statement.

5. What is the "law of retaliation" to which Manly refers?

6. What meaning does Manly's following illustration hold? "The skill of an architect may be expended as well upon the temporary scaffolding as the permanent structure, and may be seen as truly in the rough foundation as in the polished column or carved ornaments."

7. "The success of the divine moral government as a unity, and yet a progressive unity, was dependent on such a use of gradual steps and processes."

   Why is this true? Discuss.

8. Reread Gardiner's lengthy statement. Describe in your own words what he means.

9. Read Proverbs 17:8, 18:16, and 21:14. About these, Manly writes:

   "We must be allowed, however, before passing from the subject, to protest against the charge that certain of the proverbs 'show so much of shrewdness as scarcely to escape the charge of being immoral, when considered from the Christian point of view. . .' These are simply statements of what is a fact of common observation and experience, that gifts are both used effectively and abused. They do not give any commendation or advice of bribery."

   What is Manly suggesting here? Do you agree or disagree?

10. What is meant by these two statements: "moral feebleness amounting almost to cowardice," and "complaint against the divine dealing"?

11. Reread Ladd's comment. Put his thesis in your own words and discuss.

12. In what ways is this statement true?

    "The moral grandeur of the ethics of the Bible, whether taken singly as a system, or compared with any other system that has ever been presented to man, bespeaks its divine origin."

13. Manly makes use of the imagery of a vase and the sun. In your opinion, why did he choose to use these particular analogies? What point is he making when he says:

    "We may be so absorbed in finding, or even in refuting, paltry objections against the ethics of the Bible, as to fail to take those impressive and affecting views that we should of its sublime moral teachings." Do you agree? Why or why not?

14. What is the significance of this remarkable statement? Do you agree with it?

   "During an age when comparatively enlightened and cultivated nations were still groping in darkness on moral questions, the Hebrews received, and have transmitted to all succeeding ages, a code of ethics that still furnishes the foundation for all ethical teaching for humankind."

15. "Every renewal or acceleration of moral life in the world, every quickening of worn-out nationalities, or amelioration of savage tribes, may be traced directly to the influence of the Bible. The decadence which has occurred, in numerous distressing cases, in Christendom itself, is no less distinctly connected with the neglect of the Word, with departure from its plain precepts, and with holding it back systematically from the people."

   Manly believes this to be true in his day. Is it still true today? Discuss how the world has changed in the last one hundred or so years in relation to Manly's statement.

16. "The infallible test of all religious teaching is its practical result in the lives of those that receive it."

   Do you agree with this statement made by L. Abbott?

17. What was happening in Manly's day in Spain and Italy that would make him make the following statement?

   "The most invincible argument against the substitution of the Church of Rome for the authority of God's Word is sullen, stagnant, sinking Spain. And the effect of even the partial introduction of the Scriptures is to be seen in the awakening of Italy."

Chapter 13

1. Define the words "judge" and "critic" as Manly does.

2. What does Manly say about distinguishing text criticism from higher criticism? Do you agree?

3. What does Manly say regarding Hebrew vowel-points?

4. How does Manly come to this conclusion? Describe his argument that leads up to this point:

"What we affirm is, that the sacred Scriptures, . . . had the characteristics of accuracy and authority, as messages from God."

5. "The Scriptures . . . were specially protected, not only by a general providential guardianship, . . . but by several favoring circumstances of no small importance."

What are those "favoring circumstances" to which Manly refers? Discuss them.

6. Reread the argument that Manly cites by text critics Westcott and Hort. In your own words, what are they saying? Do you agree? Is the argument logical? Why is it important?

7. Would you agree with the logic and truth of the comment made by Dr. Philip Schaff? Why or why not?

8. What did Richard Bently mean when he said that even the worst of manuscripts does not pervert or set aside "one article of faith or moral precept"?

9. Have you ever thought about this possibility?

"Neither can it be justly said that there is no probability that God would supernaturally inspire the writings, unless He also miraculously preserved them from erroneous transcription."

Do you agree?

10. "A true 'higher criticism' may be just as valuable as a false or misguided attempt at it may be dangerous and delusive."

What does Manly mean by this statement?

11. What do you think of this statement?

"Some critical theories of large extent and pretension are based on cool assumptions of what is utterly devoid of proof."

Do you agree?

12. What does Manly state about the Leyden school of theologians and the Tubingen school?

13. Why does E. H. Sears call John's gospel, "the Heart of Jesus Christ"?

Chapter 14

1. What is your opinion on this statement?

   "All truth is consistent with all other truth."

2. Do you agree or disagree:

   "A thing cannot be true in theology and false in fact, or reliable in science but wrong in practice, any more than it can be both true and false at the same time, or than black can be white"?

3. What does Manly mean when he writes:

   "The Bible does not profess to teach physical science"?

4. Do you agree with Manly on this point:

   "Our interpretations of Scripture are not Scripture"? Discuss.

5. What does Manly mean with this:

   "Scientific conclusions and opinions are not always correct"? Discuss his thesis.

6. What was Manly's overall opinion of science?

7. What did Manly mean when he wrote:

   "The language of Scripture in describing physical facts is the language of common life, the language of appearances"?

8. What are "phenomenal expressions"?

9. What does Manly mean when he uses the expressions "God's Word and God's works"?

10. Put in your own words the point William E. Gladstone makes in his discussion with Mr. Huxley.

11. What does Manly suggest when he writes:

    "The absence of definitely established contradictions so far is a remarkable phenomenon"?

    Explain what he means and the treatment he gives the topic.

12. Ponder the following statement:

"Every line in [the Bible] has been subjected to a minute, jealous, microscopic scrutiny, by friend and by foe, such as no other writing has ever experienced. The fires of criticism have kindled all around it and over it, hot enough to detect and to burn out the dross, if there was any. It stands today the book in all the world most loved, most hated, most studied, most misused."

Would you agree? If this was true more than one hundred years ago, at the writing of this statement, is it still true today? In more or less degree?

13. "They that are with us as to the divine origin of the Bible are more and mightier than those that are against us."

Do you agree? Is this suggestion still true today, more than a century after Manly wrote?

Chapter 15

1. What parts of Scripture does Manly suggest some might consider insignificant details? Give examples and explain.

2. What do the details tell us about Timothy, about Paul? About the humanness of each?

3. Notice and discuss the beauty in which Manly writes about Paul in Paul's final prison days. Do Manly's touching words help you to see a different side of Paul in his latter years?

4. Reread and reflect on the powerful ending statement made by Mr. McConaughy, in the *Sunday School Times*.

Notes

Chapter 1

1. "The existence or not of an infallible standard of right and truth is a difference of kind, and not of degree, and therefore a fundamental difference. The more or the less of human error, the greater or less degree of man's fallibility, is a difference that sinks into unimportance in comparison with it." James Bannerman, *Inspiration*, 104.

2. "He comes to the Bible, and sits over its contents in the attitude of a judge who is to decide for himself what in it is true and worthy to be believed, and what in it is false and deserving to be rejected; not in the attitude of the disciple who, within the limits of the inspired record, feels himself at Jesus' feet, to receive every word that cometh out of his mouth. . . . The assurance that the Bible is the Word of God, and not simply containing it, in more or less of its human language, is one fitted to

solemnize the soul with a holy fear, and a devout submission to its declarations as the very utterances of God. The assurance, on the contrary, that the truths of revelation are mingled, in a manner unknown and indeterminate, with the defects of the record, is one which reverses the attitude, and brings man as a master to sit in judgment on the Bible as summoned to his bar, and bound to render up to him a confession of its errors, and not a declaration of its one and authoritative truth." Ibid., 107. Compare 241–42.

3. "If on simple historical testimony it can be proved that Jesus wrought miracles, uttered prophecies, and proclaimed his divinity,—if it can be shown that he was crucified to redeem sinners, that he rose again from the dead, and that he made the destiny of men to hinge on their acceptance of him as their Saviour,—then, whether the records which contain those truths be inspired or not, woe unto him who neglects so great salvation!" F. L. Patton, *Patton on Inspiration*, 23.

Chapter 2

1. "Falsehood was no part of man's original nature; and the presence of error was not essential to themselves being men, or to their writings being human writings. On the contrary, in being protected from liability to error, and exalted above the power of untruth, they were but restored in the hour of inspiration, in so far, to that condition of freedom from evil in which they were created in the beginning. . . . They were lifted up into a condition more appropriate to human nature, as it was designed and at first made to be, than any in which it would have been possible for them to have uttered or recorded error." Bannerman, *Inspiration*, 436.

2. "The doctrine of the plenary inspiration of the Bible, which regards it as all in one sense man's, and all in another sense God's, is the only view that *gives full place to the human element* in Scripture, all theories except itself more or less putting aside or impairing its perfection. Other views, such as that of an inspiration different in degree or kind as respects different truths or portions of Scripture, make the sacred volume to be, in some of

its passages or statements, no more than partly human, just as they make it in others to be no more than partly divine. Unless we are prepared to adopt the theory that the Bible is nothing but the composition of man, alone and exclusively, there is no other view except that of a plenary inspiration which conserves equally the divine and the human element in the recorded word. Ibid., 446–47.

3. Philip Schaff, *History of the Christian Church*, 1:93.

4. B. K. Peirce, *The Word of God Opened*, 23–24.

5. B. F. Westcott, *Introduction to the Study of the Gospels.*

6. Henry Alford, Prolegomena to his *Greek New Testament*, 21.

7. Edward Garbett, *God's Word Written*, 143–45.

8. E. P. Humphrey, *Second General Council of the Presbyterian Alliance*, Philadelphia, 1880.

9. J. A. Smith, *The Spirit and the Word*, 114–15.

10. Other definitions of *inspiration* are as follows: "That special divine influence upon the minds of the Scripture writers in virtue of which their productions, apart from errors of transcription, and when rightly interpreted, together constitute an infallible and sufficient rule of faith and practice." A. H. Strong, *Systematic Theology*, 95.

"Inspiration is such an influence over the writers of the Bible that all their teachings which have a religious character are trustworthy." E. A. Park.

"Inspiration is help from God to keep report of divine revelation free from error. Help to whom? No matter to whom, so the result is secured. The final result, viz. The record or report of revelation, this must be free from error. Inspiration may affect one or all of the agents employed." W. C. Wilkinson.

While Professor Ladd gives no formal definition of inspiration that I have observed, he states it as an element of the conception of sacred Scripture held by the church, that "sacred Scripture owes its origin to that specific movement of the Divine Spirit within the human spirit which forms the necessary ethical condition of receiving and appropriating the truths of redemption by all members of the body of believers." George T. Ladd, *Doctrine of Sacred Scripture*, 2:271.

"Inspiration consists in that actuating, controlling, and guiding influence of the Holy Spirit, under which God's chosen messengers spoke and wrote the original Scriptures." W. W. Gardner, *Gardner on Inspiration*, 2.

"The books of the Bible . . . were composed by men who acted under the influence of the Holy Ghost to such an extent that they were preserved from every error of fact, of doctrine, of judgment; and these so influenced in the choice of language that the very words they used were the words of God." F. L. Patton, *Patton on Inspiration*, 92.

11. "Both admit that, in a miraculous manner unknown to us, the revelation from God was conveyed to the mind of the prophet originally in a form of absolute purity and infallible truth. The point at which the divergence between the two views begins, is after the revelation was made by God, and made perfectly, and when it came to be recorded by man. According to the views of the advocates of plenary inspiration, the same supernatural power which guarded the revelation, in the act of being made to the prophet, from all incompleteness and mistake, also presided over the act by which he recorded it in the Bible; so that the result of this second step in the process, no less than of the first, was miraculously guarded from error, and the product was a record marked by infallible truth and divine authority." Bannerman, *Inspiration*, 98.

Chapter 3

1. Alexander Carson, *Works*, 5:5, 12, 21, 73, 105 respectively.

2. Ladd, *Doctrine of Sacred Scripture*, 2:259.

3. Quoted in Ibid., 2:222.

4. Ibid., 1:759.

5. Ibid., 2:275, 497.

6. Ibid., 2:178.

7. Ibid., 2:502.

8. Compare Luke 1:2; Mark 2:2; 14:14; Acts 10:36; 1 Thess. 2:13; 2 Thess. 2:15; 2 Cor. 5:19.

9. Ladd, *Doctrine of Sacred Scripture*, 2:508–12.

10. Hävernick, *Introduction*, 1:67.

11. Carson, *Works*, 5:31.
12. Thomas F. Curtis, *Human Element in the Inspiration of the Scriptures*, 88.
13. Compare Curtis on inspiration, *Human Element*, 94.
14. Frederick W. Robertson, *Life and Letters*, 1:271; 2:143–50, Sermon 1.
15. F. W. Farrar, "Preface," *History of Interpretation*, xvi.
16. Curtis, *Human Element*, 120.
17. Ibid., 311.

Chapter 4

1. Farrar, "Preface," xx.
2. Ladd, *Doctrine of Sacred Scripture*, 2:182.
3. Ibid., 2:152.
4. Ibid., 2:247.
5. "Dictation to an amanuensis is not teaching. (Compare 1 Cor. 2:13: 'Words . . . which the Holy Ghost teacheth.') He may write dictated words of wisdom, without possessing any of the wisdom from which they proceed, without receiving any instructions, and without even thinking about the import of what he writes. The Holy Scriptures were not written after this manner." John L. Dagg, article in *Alabama Baptist*.
6. See Exod. 9:19; 20:1, 19, 22; Deut. 4:33, 36; 5:4, 22.
7. The manifoldness of Scripture, in comparison with the work of a single author, is well brought out by Dean Stanley in his description of the Koran. "It is as the Old Testament might be if composed of the writings of the single prophet Isaiah, or Jeremiah; or the New Testament, if it were composed of the writings of the single Apostle Paul. It is what the Bible as a whole would be, if from its pages were excluded all individual personalities of its various writers, all differences of time and place and character. . . .The Koran represents not merely one single person, but one single stage of society. It is, with few exceptions, purely Arabian. It is what the Bible would be, if all external influences were obliterated, and it was wrapped up in a single phase of Jewish life. The Koran 'stays at home'; the Bible is the book of the world, the companion of every traveler, read

even when not beloved, necessary even when unwelcome." Dean A. P. Stanley, *History of the Eastern Church*, 372.

8. How did God communicate these things to them? If I may be pardoned for adopting the expression of a fair German friend, describing how they answer some question in Saxony, I would say, "Ich kann es ganz genau sagen: Ich weiss nicht." This means "I can tell that exactly: I do not know."

9. John Macnaught, *Macnaught on Inspiration*, 192–96.

10. An argument of the same kind as Macnaught's is suggested by Harvey Goodwin in the Hulsean Lectures for 1855, on the ground of the analogy between man's creation and the Bible. Because "God . . . breathed into his nostrils the breath of life; and man became a living soul" (Gen. 2:7), he affirms, "an *inspired* work of God this, if ever there was one" (p. 86). From which he proceeds to argue that it is unwise and dangerous to infer infallibility in the Bible, when man, also "inspired," is certainly fallible. The words employed in the original for *breath* of life and *spirit* of life are entirely different, and never confounded. And so the analogy breaks down at the very first step.

11. "Inspiration, as we have repeatedly had occasion to say, left the inspired historians under the power and regulation of the same laws and influences that guide other authors in their compositions, with the single exception of supernaturally preserving them from error. It is quite compatible, then, with the free development of the individuality of the sacred penmen as authors, and with their using for the purposes of their authorship the means and the materials and the helps which other authors use in composing their productions. It is compatible with using their own eyesight, and narrating what they saw, if spectators of the events they had to chronicle. It is compatible with searching out the facts and studying the reports of other men, and the traditions handed down, if through such means they might have perfect knowledge of the events recorded. It is compatible with adopting, by means of quotation from other authors, or reference to existing documents, the facts they had to narrate, if taught by supernatural revelation to do so, for the purposes of their composition. There is nothing in all this

inconsistent with the supernatural inspiration of God present and cooperating with them in their work; unless, indeed, it is believed that the divine and the human cooperation in all cases and under all circumstances is impossible." Bannerman, *Inspiration*, 535.

"That every word of Scripture has been inspired, does not imply that every speech or sentiment recorded there should be inspired. The letter of Claudius Lysias was not inspired, but it is inserted in the Scriptures by inspiration, and for a purpose useful for the edification of the people of God." Carson, *Works*, 83.

Chapter 6

1. B. F. Westcott, after speaking of the ordinary methods of proof of inspiration, forcibly says: "On the other hand we may examine the character and objects of the books themselves, and put together the various facts which appear to indicate in them the presence of more than human authority and wisdom, no less in the simplicity and rudeness of their general form than in the subtle harmony and marvelous connection of their various elements. And if this method of proof is less direct and definite than the other,—if it calls for calm patience, and compels thought in each inquirer,—it is also broader and more elastic, capable of infinite extensions and applications. Nor is it less powerful even while it is less cogent. To many perhaps the inward assurance which it creates is more satisfactory than the rigid deductions of direct argument. The unlimited multiplication of convergent presumptions and analogies builds up a strong and sure conviction, possessing a moral force which can never belong to a mere formal proof, even where the premises are necessary truths.

"It is in the perfection and oneness of their social teaching, so to speak, that the strongest internal proof of the plenary Inspiration of the Gospels is to be found. . . .The manner in which these questions—the foundation doctrines of a Christian community—are treated by the Evangelists is such as to exclude the idea of a mere personal intuition, for that leaves no room for those combinations in which the fullness of the Gospel lies. However far one Evangelist might have been led by the laws of his own mind, it can only be by the introduction of a higher power that four unconsciously combine to rear from different sides a harmonious and perfect fabric of Christian truth." Westcott, *Introduction to the Study of the Gospels*, 20–26.

2. Enoch Henderson, *Henderson on Inspiration*, 219.

3. "With the Evangelists, authorship could not have been the product of experience. If not the offspring of experience, authorship could not have been the result of education. If not the effect of education, authorship could not have had its birth in instinct, since instinct must emerge in the formulating intellect to become art. And at this point the ideal is inexplicable, except on the ground of a divine revelation in conjunction with a divine inspiration. Revelation applies to the facts used, inspiration to their mode of using them." Dr. A. A. Lipcomb, *Studies in the Forty Days*, 80.

4. It is a very strange misapprehension and exaggeration of the amount of stress assigned to the presumptive arguments, when Coleridge states what he considers to be the strength of the arguments in behalf of inspiration with which he had to contend, or the "motives usually assigned for maintaining and enjoining it. Such, for instance, are the arguments drawn from the anticipated loss and damage that would result from its abandonment; as that it would deprive the Christian world of its only infallible arbiter in questions of Faith and Duty; suppress the only common and inappellable tribunal; that the Bible is the only religious bond of union and ground of unity among Protestants, and the like." (Samuel Taylor Coleridge, *Confessions of an Inquiring Spirit*, "Letter IV.") Whatever weight these considerations are justly entitled to, they should have; but Mr. Coleridge surely was unfortunate, if he found these to be the *chief* arguments which upholders of the strict idea of inspiration "usually assigned for maintaining and enjoining it." They are commonly stated, it is true, but always in a brief and preliminary way. The other arguments, hereafter to be presented, are the ones usually and mainly relied on.

Chapter 7

1. Bannerman, *Inspiration*, 281.

2. Ibid., 284.

3. Ladd, *Doctrine of Sacred Scripture*, 1:17. The postulates subsequently stated by Professor Ladd are three: "1. the self-revelation of God in redemption, involving the possibility and the actuality of miracles, and of inspiration as prophecy,—the subject miracle; 2. the infallible authority of Jesus Christ upon matter included in the doctrine of salvation, . . . not necessarily including in itself the claim to infallibility on the part of Christ with respect to merely critical and historical matters; 3. the reality of those truths which underlie the persistent and universal thoughts and feelings of the Christian consciousness" (1:21). To the second of these, as unduly limited, and to the third, as vague and capable of the most varied interpretation and application, we should have to object decidedly. For us the authority of Jesus Christ is primal and final, wherever a sure word of His can be found. We see no reason for excepting "critical and historical matters," nor any practicable method of determining how far the range of such an exception is to extend. It is scarcely satisfactory to be assured that Jesus Christ spoke the truth, *except* on "critical and historical matters," even if accompanied by the assurance that these "rarely appear to have entered the horizon of his teaching." How much is criticism? How much is history? Are all matters of fact, all questions of interpretation, to be included in this range of topics on which *what he said is not to be relied on?*

And as to "Christian consciousness," it is too liable to speak with the voice of its interpreter, who he may be, just as all Swedenborg's alleged interlocutors in the spiritual world *Swedenborgianize.*

It seems to us that the learned author has himself been unduly subject to the influence of this last "postulate." The keynote to his whole treatise is a sentence near its commencement, which affirms that "any dogma as to its [the Bible's] origin and nature must be content to take simply the place which fitly belongs to it as assigned by the Christian consciousness, developing under the guidance of the Spirit who gave the Bible to the Church" (1:5; compare also 1:18). Nevertheless, he frankly admits that it is "imperative that we should acknowledge the falsity of many opinions held by the learned, and by the entire community of believers, during all the past history of the Church." He adds appropriately, that, "although some parts of this inquiry can scarcely be put into scientific form, yet they are not for this reason devoid of real and great value. The heart of the Church and of the race may be heard to beat, and its warm life recognized as present, where no exact anatomical description can be given" (1:20).

Professor Ladd says many things grandly and truly, but it appears to us that he often takes away with one hand what he has given with the other. He announces an important doctrine of fact but then follows with so many exceptions and limitations, and balances so nicely between truth and error, as scarcely to leave room for distinct or cordial conviction.

Christ's authority is indeed recognized by him as primal and absolute; but he assures us that Christ's "attitude is manifestly uncritical." Jesus "believed the Old Testament to contain certain important divinely revealed truths"; but "does not commit his opinion to its entire historical accuracy." His "reserve" as to debated questions "cannot be held to be *wholly* due to ignorance." If Jesus alludes to the history of Jonah or of the flood, this, we are told, cannot be "pleaded in favor of the historical accuracy" of these accounts, because He did not *design* to authenticate them. Doubtless His *specific design* in the allusion may have been to illustrate His teaching, rather than to authenticate those facts—which indeed was unnecessary, as none of His hearers doubted them. But does not the allusion unmistakably recognize them as *facts?*

Again we are told, "Jesus may *speak as though* he held a certain opinion upon a critical question of the Old Testament, and yet the inference may be by no means valid that he really held this opinion." The Bible, as a whole, is unquestionably divine; but it is "not infallible" in "historical views and statements," in its "narrative of miracles," or even of the "life and resurrection of

Christ." Nor can we affirm that "the logic of its argumentative passages is irreproachable, and its interpretation of its own earlier passages always defensible"; nor "that the Scripture is free from even immoral feeling impressed upon it by the human character of its origin." "Even in the New Testament we cannot deny that there exist mistaken impressions in matters of ethical and religious kind." But when the Bible has been "sifted by critical and historical research," and tested and approbated by the "Christian consciousness," it is alleged that it is the great source of information as to the person and work of Christ.

To us it seems as if, in all this, there is a great mingling of the miry clay of conjecture and error with the iron of the mighty truths which Dr. Ladd elsewhere vigorously states and advocates.

4. This peculiarity of method is very properly recognized by Professor Ladd: "There is a marked correspondence between Jesus' method of teaching and the divine method of instruction and discipline in nature and providence. We discover less effort to force the truth upon men than to stir their inquiry; little care to guard the careless against misapprehension, much care to rouse them to a true apprehension. His teaching is not a copy-lesson, but a spur to industry." Ladd, *Doctrine of Sacred Scripture*, 1:31.

Chapter 8

1. Compare Bannermann, *Inspiration*, 311–51; also excellent articles by Dr. Howard Osgood on "The Old Testament according to the Testimony of Jesus and the Apostles," in *Baptist Quarterly*, (1883): 88 f.; also Dr. Frederick Gardiner in *Sunday School Times* (May 26, 1886).

2. "Our Lord's appeal to the Old Testament is to be considered in view of these two facts. (1) He recognizes in his teaching no human authority, and (2) He does recognize absolutely the authority of his heavenly Father. Whatever recognition, then, he gives to the authority of the Old Testament, can only be on the ground of its having proceeded from his Father. Compare Matt. 7:28–29; John 8:28." Dr. F. Gardiner.

3. It is suggested by Dr. Ladd, in connection with this passage, that the Saviour accuses the Jews "of folly and sin in idolizing the written Word, while neglecting its ideal contents of truth" (Ladd, *Doctrine of Sacred Scripture*, 1:51). But does he? He commends their search of the Scriptures, blames their blindness to the truth so plainly contained in it, and censures their unauthorized additions to it by tradition; but says not a word about idolizing the written Word.

4. Ladd, *Doctrine of Sacred Scripture*, 1:36.

5. Ibid., 1:43.

6. Ibid., 1:46.

7. Matt. 9:14–17; Mark 2:18–22; Luke 5:33–39.

8. See Lev. 19:13; Deut. 24:14–15.

9. "The Scripture is here identified with God, its Author. The case, as Tholuck remarks, is different when merely something *contained* in Scripture is introduced by 'the Scripture saith'; there 'the Scripture' is merely personified. The justice of Tholuck's remark will be apparent, if we reflect that this expression could not be used of the *mere ordinary words* of any man in the historical Scriptures, Ahab, or Hezekiah—but only where the *text itself* speaks, or where *God spoke*, or, as here, some man under the inspiration of God" (Alford, *Greek New Testament*, on Rom. 9:17). It is also worthy of notice, that, while the apostle quotes ordinarily from the Septuagint, as the version familiar to the people, he in this expression (as in many other instances) departs from it, to introduce a more literal and exact translation of his own from the original Hebrew.

10. B. F. Westcott, *The Bible in the Church*, 42.

11. H. Olshausen, Comm. *in loco*.

12. Ellicott (*in loco*) discusses the passage fairly and ably, as is his wont, and says: "It is very difficult to decide. . . . Lexicography and grammar contribute little towards a decision. . . .We are thus remanded wholly to the context,"—which he regards as on the whole favoring the rendering adopted by the revisers. But he distinctly affirms that "*pasa graphe* (every Scripture) implies every individual *graphe* (Scripture) of those previously alluded to in the term *hiera grammata* (sacred writings)." If the article had

been used with *graphe*, the interpretation *all* Scripture would be undisputed. But that *graphe*, Scripture, as a proper name, may legitimately omit the article (as in John 19:37, Rom. 1:2; 16:26; 2 Pet. 1:20) is obvious;—just as in all Jerusalem (Matt. 2:3), all Israel (Rom. 11:26), all the house of Israel (Acts 2:36; 1 Sam. 7:2–3; Neh. 4:16; Jth. 8:6; Matt. 10:6; 15:24).

13. Exod. 4:10–16; 7:1–2.

14. Philo, ed. *Mangeyi*, 2:343,

15. Dr. Ladd well paraphrases the passage: "No prophecy contained in the Old Testament Scripture has its origin as a matter of merely subjective explication, as a result of the prophet's own power intuitively to discern the meaning of the subject he cogitates; and prophecy is never sent by the will of man as a cause, but is rather uttered by men who are borne along by the Holy Ghost, and therefore speak as from a divine source." Ladd, *Doctrine of Sacred Scripture*, 1:162.

16. Ibid., 2:503.

17. Bannerman, *Inspiration*, 328.

18. Ladd, *Doctrine of Sacred Scripture*, 63.

19. Dr. Lee has aptly styled these chapters "the Holy of Holies of Christ's history; that wonderful passage, from every line of which shines forth the Divinity of Him who spake, though each syllable be tinged with the sadness of a Soul which even now gazed full upon the agony in the Garden, and bore in prospect the crown of thorns,—syllables, too, which were uttered from the very shadow of the tomb." William Lee, *Lee on Inspiration*, 35.

20. Ibid., 271.

21. "In case the disciples should commit to writing these commandments, whether as embodied in words or in deeds, and whether for the purpose of discipling the nations or of instructing their converts, the promise of Christ would surely not be withdrawn." Ladd, *Doctrine of Sacred Scripture*, 1:76.

22. Broadus on Matt. 22:31.

23. Heb. 3:7; 9:8; 10:15. "In this remarkable epistle, God, or the Holy Ghost, is continually named as the speaker in the passages quoted from the Old Testament; and this not merely in

those of which it is said in the context of the Old Testament Scriptures, 'God said,' but also in those in which some human being speaks, e.g. David, as composer of a Psalm. In this the view of the author clearly expresses itself as to the Old Testament and its writers. He regarded God as the Principle that lived, and wrought, and spoke in them all by his Holy Spirit; and accordingly Holy Scripture was to him a pure work of God, although announced to the world by man." H. Olshausen, *Die Echtheit des N.T.*, 170.

24. Robert Hooker, *Ecclesiastical Polity*, Book 3:c. 10.
25. Bishop Butler, *Analogy*, Part 2:c. 7.

Chapter 9

1. Dr. Ladd, while admitting clearly that "the distinction here called for is not that between the words of an Apostle when inspired, and the words of the same Apostle when not inspired," alleges that the teachings of Jesus personally are infallible and permanent, but that the "other contents of truth" are "mixed with possible error, since they came by remoter inferences from the truth of Christ, and were given in the trustworthy yet fallible judgments of the Apostles." Accordingly, he thinks that, besides the "unequivocal declarations of the mind of Christ," and "certain wise teachings of an inspired Apostle, the acceptance of which was ethically best for those to whom he wrote," there are here "certain *erroneous opinions*, the rejection of the practical application of which was best for the same persons. Among these last may we class the opinions and preferences into which the Apostle was led by his erroneous impression as to the nearness of the Second Coming." Ladd, *Doctrine of Sacred Scripture*, 1:203, 205.

We venture humbly, notwithstanding, to agree with Paul's opinions and advice, so guardedly and yet frankly expressed, as "good by reason of the [then] present distress" (1 Cor. 7:26); and also to question whether he was in any error as to the immediate nearness of the Second Coming. He did not know when it would be. Neither did the other apostles (Acts 1:7; 1 Thess. 5: 1–2). Neither did our Lord during His earthly sojourn (Mark 13:32).

But they all taught the duty of living with constant reference to it, and in a state of cheerful expectancy of it (Matt. 24:42; 1 Cor. 1:7; Titus 2:13; 2 Pet. 3:12). And Paul earnestly admonished his Thessalonian brethren against imagining that "the day of Christ is at hand" (2 Thess. 2:1–3).

2. On 1 Corinthians 7:10, De Wette observes: "Hitherto the Apostle has spoken from his own judgment illuminated by the Holy Ghost (verse 40); so also in what follows (verses 12, 25, 40); but here (verse 10) he appeals to an expression of the Lord (Mark 10:12)." And Meyer says: "The Apostle was conscious that his individuality was under the influence of the Holy Ghost (verse 40). He therefore distinguishes, here and in verses 12 and 25, not between his own and inspired commands, but between those which proceeded from his own inspired subjectivity, and those which Christ himself maintained by his objective word."

3. Charles Hodge *in loco*.

Chapter 11

1. Broadus on Matt. 9:2–34.

Chapter 12

1. Ladd, *Doctrine of Sacred Scripture*, 1:476.
2. Frederick Gardiner, *Old and New Testament in Their Mutual Relations*, 49.
3. Ladd, *Doctrine of Sacred Scripture*, 1:466.

Chapter 13

1. Dr. Ladd affirms: "We may say in brief of the Masoretic text, punctuation as well as consonants, as does Wellhausen, 'As a type of speech, the punctuation is for us unalterable; as a commentary, inasmuch as it reproduces that construction of the sense of a given passage which has prevailed since the Christian era, it is, although not unchangeable, still at least incomparably the most valuable help to the understanding.'" Ladd, *Doctrine of Sacred Scripture*, 1:697.

2. The only two passages in the New Testament, of any considerable length, where the genuineness of the text may be disputed, are Mark 16:9–20, and John 7:53 to 8:11. The latter, probably, ought to be abandoned; the former, we think, should be retained. Scholars have ample opportunities of information on the subject in the works of Scrivener, Alford, Tregelles, Tischendorf, and Westcott and Hort. Even those slightly familiar with the topic may find enough to satisfy their doubts in the candid and accurate statements of Schaff in his *Companion to the New Testament*.

3. Westcott and Hort, *The New Testament in Greek*, 2:2.

4. Philip Schaff, *Companion to the New Testament*, 177.

5. Ezra Abbot, article in *Sunday School Times* (May 28, 1881).

6. Ladd, *Doctrine of Sacred Scripture*, 1:491.

7. Ibid., 1:497.

8. Ibid., 1:576.

9. Ibid., 1:577.

10. It is with pleasure that we refer to the able vindication of this authorship by Dr. Ladd (*Doctrine of Sacred Scripture*, 1:550–72) and to the more ample and elaborate discussions of Bishop Lightfoot and of Doctor Ezra Abbot.

Chapter 14

1. James McCash, article in *Homiletic Monthly*, (January, 1884): 234.

2. William E. Gladstone, article in *Nineteenth Century*, (January, 1886): 16.

Chapter 15

1. Gaussen, *Origin and Inspiration of the Bible*, 317–22.

2. Ibid., 313.

3. McConaughy, article in the *Sunday School Times* (1880): 551.

Appendix

Report of the Presidential Theological Study Committee

Note: The Theological Study Committee was appointed by Southern Baptist Convention President H. Edwin Young in 1992 and submitted its report in the spring of the following year. The purpose of this study group was to examine those biblical truths which are most surely held among the people of God called Southern Baptists and, on this basis, to reaffirm our common commitment to Jesus Christ, the Holy Scriptures and the evangelical heritage of the Christian church. In light of the pressing need for a positive biblical witness on basic Christian beliefs, this report is published, not as a new confession of faith, but rather as a reaffirmation of major doctrinal concerns set forth in the Baptist Faith and Message of 1963.

(Those serving on the Presidential Theological Study Committee: Timothy F. George, Co-chairman; Roy L. Honeycutt, Co-chairman; William E. Bell; J. Walter Carpenter, Jr.; Mark T. Coppenger; Stephen D. C. Corts; Carl F. H. Henry; Herschel H. Hobbs; Richard D. Land; R. Albert Mohler, Jr.; William B. Tolar; and H. Edwin Young, president of the Southern Baptist Convention.)

Part 1

In every generation, the people of God face the decision either to reaffirm "the faith which was once delivered unto the saints" (Jude 3) or to lapse into theological unbelief. Precisely such a challenge now confronts the people of God called Southern Baptists.

As we approach the 150th anniversary of the founding of the Southern Baptist Convention, we are presented with unprecedented opportunities for missionary outreach and evangelistic witness at home and abroad. We must bear a faithful gospel witness to a culture in decline; we must be the salt and light in a society which has lost its moral compass. We must also pass on to the rising generation the fundamentals of the Christian faith and a vital sense of our Baptist heritage. To meet these goals, we seek to move beyond the denominational conflict of recent years toward a new consensus rooted in theological substance and doctrinal fidelity. We pray that our effort will lead to healing and reconciliation throughout the Southern Baptist Convention and, God willing, to a renewed commitment to our founding purpose of "eliciting, combining, and directing the energies of the whole denomination in one sacred effort, for the propagation of the gospel."

Baptists are a people of firm conviction and free confession. Southern Baptists have expressed and affirmed these convictions through *The Baptist Faith and Message* confessional statements of 1925 and 1963.

This committee affirms and honors *The Baptist Faith and Message*, as overwhelmingly adopted by the 1963 Convention, embraced by millions of faithful Southern Baptists and their churches, affirmed by successive convention sessions and adopted by Southern Baptist Convention agencies, as the normative expression of Southern Baptist belief. Therefore, this committee declines to recommend any new confession or revision of that statement.

However, each generation of Southern Baptists faces unique and pressing challenges to faithfulness which demand attention and test the integrity of our conviction. This report addresses several issues of contemporary urgency in a spirit of pastoral concern and a commitment to the unity of our Baptist fellowship as well as the integrity of our doctrinal confession. These emphases are intended to illuminate articles of *The Baptist Faith and Message*, consistent with its intention and content, and are thus commended to the Convention, its agencies, its churches, and the millions of Bible-believing cooperating Southern Baptists who freely join this Convention in its sacred work. We seek to clarify our historic Baptist commitment to Holy Scripture, the doctrine of God, the person and work of Jesus Christ, the nature and mission of the church, and biblical teaching on last things. We reaffirm our commitment to these great theological tenets since they are assailed, in various ways, by subtle compromise, blatant concession, and malign negligence.

We also affirm the historic Baptist conception of the nature and function of confessional statements in our religious and denominational life. Baptists approve and circulate confessions of faith with the following understandings:

- As an expression of our religious liberty. Any group of Baptists, large or small, has the inherent right to draw up for itself and to publish to the world a confession of faith whenever it wishes. As a corollary of this principle, we reject state imposed religious creeds and attendant civil sanctions.

- As a statement of our religious convictions. We affirm the priesthood of all believers and the autonomy of each local congregation. However, doctrinal minimalism and theological revision, left unchecked, compromises a commitment to the gospel itself. Being Baptist means faith as well as freedom. Christian liberty should not become a license for the masking of unbelief.

- As a witness to our confidence in divine revelation. The sole authority for faith and practice among Baptists is the Bible, God's Holy Word. It is the supreme standard by which all creeds, conduct and religious opinions should be tried. As in the past so in the future, Baptists should hold themselves free to revise their statements of faith in the light of an unchanging Holy Scripture.

None of these principles, sacred to Baptists through the ages, is violated by voluntary, conscientious adherence to an explicit doctrinal standard. Holy living and sound doctrine are indispensable elements of true revival and genuine reconciliation among any body of Christian believers. Desiring this end with all our hearts, we commend the following report to the people of God called Southern Baptists.

Part II
Article One: Holy Scripture

Southern Baptists have affirmed repeatedly and decisively an unswerving commitment to the divine inspiration and truthfulness of Holy Scripture, the Word of God revealed in written form. We believe that what the Bible says, God says. What the Bible says happened really happened. Every miracle, every event, in every one of the 66 books of the Old and New Testaments is true and trustworthy. In 1900, James M. Frost, first president of the Baptist Sunday School Board, declared: "We accept the Scriptures as an all-sufficient and infallible rule of faith and practice, and insist upon the absolute inerrancy and sole authority of the Word of God. We recognize at this point no room for division, either of practice or belief, or even sentiment. More and more we must come to feel as the deepest and mightiest power of our conviction that a 'thus saith the Lord' is the end of all controversy."

The Baptist Faith and Message affirms this high view of Scripture by declaring that the Bible "has God for its author, salvation for its end, and truth without any mixture of error, for its matter." The chairman of the committee who drafted this statement, Herschel Hobbs, explained this phrase by reference to II Timothy 3:16 which says, "all Scripture is given by inspiration of God." He explained: "The Greek New Testament reads 'all'- without the definite article and that means every single part of the whole is God-breathed. And a God of truth does not breathe error."

Recent developments in Southern Baptist life have underscored the importance of a renewed commitment to biblical authority in every area of our denominational life.

In 1986 the presidents of the six Southern Baptist Convention seminaries issued the *Glorieta Statement* which affirmed the "infallible power and binding authority" of the Bible, declaring it to be "not errant in any area of reality." The miracles of the Old and New Testaments were described as "historical evidences of God's judgment, love and redemption."

In 1987 the Southern Baptist Convention Peace Committee called upon Southern Baptist institutions to recruit faculty and staff who clearly reflect the dominant convictions and beliefs of Southern Baptists concerning the factual character and historicity of the Bible in such matters as

- the direct creation of humankind including Adam and Eve as real persons;

- the actual authorship of biblical writings as attributed by Scripture itself;

- the supernatural character of the biblical miracles which occurred as factual events in space and time;

- the historical accuracy of biblical narratives which occurred precisely as the text of Scripture indicates.

In 1991 the Baptist Sunday School Board published the first volume of the *New American Commentary*, a projected 40-volume series of theological exposition on every book of the Bible. The commentary was intended to reflect a "commitment to the inerrancy of Scripture" and "the classic Christian tradition." *The Chicago Statement on Biblical Inerrancy* was adopted as a guideline more fully expressing for writers the intent of Article I of *The Baptist Faith and Message*.

In light of these historical commitments, we call upon all Southern Baptists:

- to foster a deep reverence and genuine love for the Word of God in personal, congregation and denomination life;

- to use the Scriptures in personal evangelistic witnessing, since they are "able to make one wise unto salvation;"

- to read the Bible faithfully and to study it systematically; and

- to encourage the translation and dissemination of the Bible throughout the world.

We commend to all Baptist educational institutions and agencies the *Report of the Peace Committee* (1987), the *Chicago Statement on Biblical Inerrancy Hermeneutics* (1982) as biblically grounded and sound guides worthy of respect in setting forth a high view of Scripture. We encourage them to cultivate a biblical world view in all disciplines of learning and to pursue a reverent, believing approach to biblical scholarship that is both exegetically honest and theologically sound. There need be no contradiction between "firm faith and free research" as long as both are exercised under the Lordship of Jesus Christ and in full confidence of the truthfulness of His Word.

Article Two: The Doctrine Of God

The God revealed in Holy Scripture is the sovereign God who created the worlds and all therein, the God who called Israel out from the nations as a witness to His name, the God who spoke from a burning bush, and the God who decisively and definitively revealed Himself through His Son, Jesus Christ, through whom He brought redemption and reconciliation.

Baptists, and all evangelical Christians, recognize the centrality of biblical theism. We honor and worship the one true God and our first act of worship is to acknowledge Him even as He has revealed Himself.

This means that we affirm God's nature as revealed in Holy Scripture. He alone has the right to define Himself, and He has done so by revealing His power and His grace, seen in His absolute holiness and love.

The biblical doctrine of God has been compromised in recent years as efforts to redefine God have rejected clear biblical teachings in the face of modern challenges. Southern Baptists cannot follow this course. As a fellowship of evangelical Christians we must recommit ourselves to the eternal truths concerning God, even as He has freely, graciously, and definitively revealed Himself. As Norvell Robertson, one of our earliest Southern Baptist theologians, wrote: "The Word of God is truth. What He says of Himself is true . . . He alone knows Himself."

Thus, we must submit ourselves to the knowledge God has imparted concerning Himself and His divine nature.

First, Baptists affirm that God is limitless in power, knowledge, wisdom, love, and holiness. He suffers no limitations upon His power or His personality. He is not constrained by any external force or internal contradiction. We reject any effort to redefine God as a limited deity.

Second, Baptists affirm that God, the Father of our Lord Jesus Christ, is none other than the God of Abraham, Isaac, and Jacob, of Sarah, and Rachel, and Ruth. God's self-revelation in Scripture is progressive, but fully consistent. He is the universal Creator and thus deserves universal recognition and worship as the one true God.

Third, Baptists affirm that God is one, and that He has revealed Himself as a Trinity of three eternally co-existent persons, Father, Son, and Holy Spirit. We acknowledge the Trinity as essential and central to our Christian confession, and we reject any attempt to minimize or compromise this aspect of God's self-disclosure.

Fourth, Baptists affirm that God has revealed Himself as the Father of the redeemed. Jesus characteristically addressed God as His Father, and instructed His disciples to do the same. We have no right to reject God's own name for Himself, not to employ impersonal or feminine names in order to placate modern sensitivities. We honor the integrity of God's name, and acknowledge His sole right to name Himself even as we affirm that no human words can exhaust the divine majesty. But God has accommodated Himself to us by naming Himself in human words.

Fifth, Baptists affirm that God is the sovereign Creator of the universe, who called all things into being by the power of His Word, and who created the worlds out of nothing. His creative acts were free and unconstrained by any other creative force.

Sixth, Baptists affirm that God is sovereign over history, nature, time, and space, and that His loving and gracious providence sustains and orders the world.

These statements, based upon Scripture and undergirded by historic Baptist confessions, force our attention to contemporary compromises which threaten the fidelity and integrity of our faith.

We call upon the Southern Baptist Convention, its churches and its institutions, to beware lest revisionist views of God such as those popularly modelled in process and feminist theologies, as well as the esoteric doctrines of the New Age movement, compromise our faithful commitment to biblical truth.

Article Three: The Person And Work Of Christ

Jesus Christ is the center and circumference of the Christian faith. The God of heaven and earth has revealed Himself supremely and definitively in the Son, and the most fundamental truth of Christianity is that "God was in Christ, reconciling the world unto Himself" (II Cor. 5:19).

Jesus Christ is the sole and sufficient Savior of the redeemed throughout the world and of all ages. He is the divine Word by which the worlds were created; He is also the unique and solitary Savior in whom alone there is redemption and forgiveness of sin. From beginning to end the Bible proclaims salvation through Jesus Christ and no other. The Church is commanded to teach and preach no other gospel.

In His incarnation—an event in historical space and time— Jesus Christ was the perfect union of the human and the divine. He was truly God and truly man, born of a virgin and without sin, remaining sinless throughout His earthly incarnation. He was crucified, died, and was buried. On the third day, He rose from the dead, the first fruits of the redeemed. He ascended to the Father and now rules as King and Judge. He will consummate the age by His physical return to earth as Lord and King.

Scripture bears faithful witness to Jesus Christ. The words and deeds of Christ set forth in the New Testament are an accurate record of what He said and did, even as the Old Testament prophetically revealed His identity and His purpose of redemption. The miracles of Jesus as revealed to us in Scripture were historical events which demonstrated Christ's identity and His power over sin, earth and Satan.

All human beings, marked by original sin and their own individual sins, are utterly helpless before God and without excuse, deserving of eternal punishment and separation from God. Nevertheless, in Jesus Christ and His cross, God revealed both the extent of our lostness and the depth of His redemptive love. All human beings—in all places and of all ages—are lost but for salvation through Jesus Christ. He is the only hope of salvation and the only Savior.

Christ's redemption was wrought by His atonement which was both penal and substitutionary. Christ died in our place, bearing in His body the penalty for our sin and purchasing our redemption by His blood.

The cross of Christ is thus the apex of God's plan of redemption, revealing God's absolute holiness and infinite love. The gospel of that cross is the only message which can and does save.

The redeemed are justified before God by grace through faith in Jesus Christ, trusting in Him alone for their salvation and acknowledging Him as Savior and Lord.

Therefore, Baptists must reject any effort to deny the true nature and identity of Jesus Christ or to minimize or to redefine His redemptive work. Baptists must reject any and all forms of universalism and bear faithful witness to salvation in Jesus Christ, and in Him alone. Furthermore, Baptists must join with all true Christians in affirming the substitutionary nature of Christ's atonement and reject calls—ancient and modern—for redefining Christ's reconciling work as merely subjective and illustrative.

Article Four: The Church

We acknowledge Jesus Christ not only as personal Savior and Lord, but also as the head, foundation, lawgiver, and Teacher of the church which is his building, body, and bride. The person who despises the church despises Christ, for "Christ . . . loved the church, and gave Himself for it" (Eph. 5:25).

In the New Testament the word "church" sometimes refers to all of the redeemed of all ages but, more often, to a local assembly of baptized believers. Until Jesus comes again the local church is a "colony of heaven" (Phil. 3:20), a "sounding board" of the gospel (I Thes. 1:8), and a fellowship through which God's people carry out the Great Commission of their Lord. The central purpose of the church is to honor and glorify God; the central task of the church is to bear witness to the gospel of Jesus Christ through evangelism and missions.

In light of this mandate, we call upon all Southern Baptists to reaffirm our commitment to these distinctive principles of our Baptist heritage.

The priesthood of all believers.

Every Christian has direct access to God through Jesus Christ, our great High Priest, the sole mediator between God and human beings. However, the priesthood of all believers is exercised within a committed community of fellow believers-priests who share a like precious faith. The priesthood of all believers should not be reduced to modern individualism, not used as a cover for theological relativism. It is a spiritual standing which leads to ministry, service, and a coherent witness in the world for which Christ died.

The autonomy of the local church.

A New Testament church is a gathered congregation of baptized believers who have entered into covenant with Christ and with one another to fulfil, according to the Scriptures, their mutual obligations. Under the Lordship of Christ, such a body is free to order its own internal life without interference from any external group. This same freedom applies to all general Baptist bodies, such as associations and state and national conventions. Historically, Baptist churches have freely cooperated in matters of common interest without compromise of beliefs. We affirm the wisdom of convictional cooperation in carrying out our witness to the world and decry all efforts to weaken our denomination and its cooperative ministries.

A free church in a free state.

Throughout our history Baptists have not wavered in our belief that God intends for a free church to function in a free state. Since God alone is Lord of the conscience, the temporal realm has no authority to coerce religious commitments. However, the doctrine of religious liberty, far from implying doctrinal laxity or unconcern, guarantees the ability of every congregation and general Baptist body to determine (on the basis of the Word of God) its own doctrinal and disciplinary parameters.

We declare our fervent commitment to these distinctive convictions of the Baptist tradition. We also call for a renewed emphasis on the faithful proclamation of God's Word, believers' baptism by immersion, and the celebration of the Lord's Supper as central elements of corporate worship.

Article Five: Last Things

With all true Christians everywhere, Baptists confess that "Christ has died, Christ is risen, Christ will come again." The God who has acted in the past, and is acting even now, will continue to act bringing to final consummation His eternal purpose in Jesus Christ. Our faith rests in the confidence that the future is in His hands.

While detailed interpretations of the end times should not be made a test of fellowship among Southern Baptists, we affirm with confidence the clear teaching of Holy Scripture on these essential doctrinal truths:

The return of Jesus Christ in glory.

Christians await with certainty and expectancy the "blessed hope" of the outward, literal, visible and personal return of Jesus Christ to consummate history in victory and judgment. As E. Y. Mullins put it, "He will come again in person, the same Jesus who ascended from the Mount of Olives."

The resurrection of the body.

In His glorious resurrection, Jesus Christ broke the bonds of death, establishing His authority over it, and one day He will assert that authority on our behalf and raise us. The righteous dead will be raised unto life everlasting. The unrighteous dead will be cast into hell which is the second death (Rev. 20:14-15).

Eternal punishment and eternal bliss.

Following the resurrection and judgment, the redeemed shall be forever with the Lord in heaven, a place of light and glory beyond description, and the lost shall be forever with the devil in hell, a place of utter darkness and inexpressible anguish. Nowhere does the Bible teach the annihilation of the soul or a temporary purgatory for those who die without hope in Christ.

The second coming of Christ is the blessed, comforting, and purifying hope of the church. We call upon all Southern Baptists to claim this precious promise in every area of our life and witness, and thus "to live holy and godly lives as we look forward to the day of God and speed its coming" (II Peter 3:11).

The Chicago Statement On Biblical Inerrancy

(The International Conference on Biblical Inerrancy (ICBI), Chicago, October 1978.)

A Short Statement

1. God, who is Himself Truth and speaks truth only, has inspired Holy Scripture in order thereby to reveal Himself to lost mankind through Jesus Christ as Creator and Lord, Redeemer and Judge. Holy Scripture is God's witness to Himself.

2. Holy Scripture, being God's own Word, written by men prepared and superintended by His Spirit, is of infallible divine authority in all matters upon which it touches; it is to be believed, as God's instruction, in all that it affirms; obeyed, as God's command, in all that it requires; embraced, as God's pledge, in all that it promises.

3. The Holy Spirit, Scripture's divine Author, both authenticates it to us by His inward witness and opens our minds to understand its meaning.

4. Being wholly and verbally God-given, Scripture is without error or fault in all its teaching, no less in what it states about God's acts in creation, about the events of world history, and about its own literary origins under God, than in its witness to God's saving grace in individual lives.

5. The authority of Scripture is inescapably impaired if this total divine inerrancy is in any way limited or disregarded, or made relative to a view of truth contrary to the Bible's own; and such lapses being serious loss to both the individual and the Church.

Articles Of Affirmation And Denial

Article I

We affirm that the Holy Scriptures are to be received as the authoritative Word of God.

We deny that the Scriptures receive their authority from the Church, tradition, or any other human source.

Article II

We affirm that the Scriptures are the supreme written norm by which God binds the conscience, and that the authority of the Church is subordinate to that of Scripture.

We deny that Church creeds, councils, or declarations have authority greater than or equal to the authority of the Bible.

Article III

We affirm that the written Word in its entirety is revelation given by God.

We deny that the Bible is merely a witness to revelation, or only becomes revelation in encounter, or depends on the responses of men for its validity.

Article IV

We affirm that God who made mankind in His image has used language as a means of revelation.

We deny that human language is so limited by our creatureliness that it is rendered inadequate as a vehicle for divine revelation. We further deny that the corruption of human culture and language through sin has thwarted God's work of inspiration.

Article V

We affirm that God's revelation in the Holy Scriptures was progressive.

We deny that later revelation, which may fulfill earlier revelation, never corrects or contradicts it. We further deny that any normative revelation has been given since the completion of the New Testament writings.

Article VI

We affirm that the whole of Scripture and all its parts, down to the very words of the original, were given by divine inspiration.

We deny that the inspiration of Scripture can rightly be affirmed of the whole without the parts, or of some parts but not the whole.

Article VII

We affirm that inspiration was the work in which God by His Spirit, through human writers, gave us His Word. The origin of Scripture is divine. The mode of divine inspiration remains largely a mystery to us.

We deny that inspiration can be reduced to human insight, or to heightened states of consciousness of any kind.

Article VII

We affirm that God in His Work of inspiration utilized the distinctive personalities and literary styles of the writers whom he had chosen and prepared.

We deny that God, in causing these writers to use the very words that He chose, overrode their personalities.

Article IX

We affirm that inspiration, though not conferring omniscience, guaranteed true and trustworthy utterance on all matters of which the biblical authors were moved to speak and write.

We deny that the finitude or fallenness of these writers, by necessity or otherwise, introduced distortion or falsehood into God's Word.

Article X

We affirm that inspiration, strictly speaking, applies only to the autographic text of Scripture, which in the providence of God can be ascertained from available manuscripts with great accuracy. We further affirm that copies and translations of

Scriptures are the Word of God to the extent that they faithfully represent the original.

We deny that any essential element of the Christian faith is affected by the absence of the autographs. We further deny that this absence renders the assertion of biblical inerrancy invalid or irrelevant.

Article XI

We affirm that Scripture, having been given by divine inspiration, is infallible, so that, far from misleading us, it is true and reliable in all the matters it addresses.

We deny that it is possible for the Bible to be at the same time infallible and errant in its assertions. Infallibility and inerrancy may be distinguished, but not separated.

Article XII

We affirm that Scripture in its entirely is inerrant, being free from all falsehood, fraud, or deceit.

We deny that biblical infallibility and inerrancy are limited to spiritual, religious, or redemptive themes, exclusive of assertions in the fields of history and science. We further deny that scientific hypotheses about earth history may properly be used to overturn the teaching of Scripture on creation and the flood.

Article XIII

We affirm the propriety of using inerrancy as a theological term with reference to the complete truthfulness of Scripture.

We deny that it is proper to evaluate Scripture according to standards of truth and error that are alien to its usage or purpose. We further deny that inerrancy is negated by biblical phenomena such as a lack of modern technical precision, irregularities of grammar or spelling, observational descriptions of nature, the reporting of falsehoods, the use of hyperbole and round numbers, the topical arrangement of material, variant selections of material in parallel accounts, or the use of free citations.

Article XIV

We affirm the unity and internal consistency of Scripture.

We deny that alleged errors and discrepancies that have not yet been resolved vitiate the truth claims of the Bible.

Article XV

We affirm that the doctrine of inerrancy is grounded in the teaching of the Bible about inspiration.

We deny that Jesus' teaching about Scripture may be dismissed by appeals to accommodation or to any natural limitation of His humanity.

Article XVI

We affirm that the doctrine of inerrancy has been integral to the Church's faith throughout its history.

We deny that inerrancy is a doctrine invented by Scholastic Protestantism, or is a reactionary position postulated in response to negative higher criticism.

Article XVII

We affirm that the Holy Spirit bears witness to the Scriptures, assuring believers of the truthfulness of God's written Word.

We deny that this witness of the Holy Spirit operates in isolation from or against Scripture.

Article XVIII

We affirm that the text of Scripture is to be interpreted by grammatico-historical exegesis, taking into account of its literary forms and devices, and that Scripture is to interpret Scripture.

We deny the legitimacy of any treatment of the text or quest for sources lying behind it that leads to relativizing, dchistoriciz-ing, or discounting its teaching, or rejecting its claims to authorship.

Article XIX

We affirm that a confession of the full authority, infallibility, and inerrancy of Scripture is vital to a sound understanding of the whole of the Christian faith. We further affirm that such confession should lead to increasing conformity to the image of Christ.

We deny that such confession is necessary for salvation. However, we further deny that inerrancy can be rejected without grave consequences, both to the individual and to the Church.

The Chicago Statement On Biblical Hermeneutics

(The International Conference on Biblical Inerrancy (ICBI), Chicago, November 1982)

Articles Of Affirmation And Denial

Article I

We affirm that the normative authority of Holy Scripture is the authority of God Himself, and is attested by Jesus Christ, the Lord of the Church.

We deny the legitimacy of separating the authority of Christ from the authority of Scripture, or of opposing one to the other.

Article II

We affirm that as Christ is God and Man in one Person, so Scripture is, indivisibly, God's Word in human language.

We deny that the humble, human form of Scripture entails errancy any more than the humanity of Christ, even in His humiliation, entails sin.

Article III

We affirm that the Person and work of Jesus Christ are the central focus of the entire Bible.

We deny that any method of interpretation which rejects or obscures the Christ-centeredness of Scripture is correct.

Article IV

We affirm that the Holy Spirit who inspired Scripture acts through it today to work faith in its message.

We deny that the Holy Spirit every teaches to any one anything which is contrary to the teaching of Scripture.

Article V

We affirm that the Holy Spirit enables believers to appropriate and apply Scripture to their lives.

We deny that the natural man is able to discern spiritually the message apart from the Holy Spirit.

Article VI

We affirm that the Bible expresses God's truth in propositional statements, and we declare that biblical truth is both objective and absolute. We further affirm that a statement is true if it represents matters as they actually are, but is an error if it misrepresents the facts.

We deny that, while Scripture is able to make one wise unto salvation, biblical truth should be defined in terms of this function. We further deny that error should be defined as that which willfully deceives.

Article VII

We affirm that the meaning expressed in each biblical text is single, definite, and fixed.

We deny that the recognition of this single meaning eliminates the variety of its application.

Article VIII

We affirm that the Bible contains teachings and mandates which apply to all cultural and situational contexts and other mandates which the Bible itself shows apply only to particular situations.

We deny that the distinction between the universal and particular mandates of Scripture can be determined by cultural and situational factors. We further deny that universal mandates may ever be treated as culturally or situationally relative.

Article IX

We affirm that the term hermeneutics, which historically signified the rules of exegesis, may properly be extended to cover all that is involved in the process of perceiving what the biblical revelation means and how it bears on our lives.

We deny that the message of Scripture derives from, or is dictated by, the interpreter's understanding. Thus we deny that the "horizons" of the biblical writer and the interpreter may rightly "fuse" in such a way that what the text communicates to the interpreter is not ultimately controlled by the expressed meaning of the Scripture.

Article X

We affirm that Scripture communicates God's truth to us through a wide variety of literary forms.

We deny that any of the limits of human language render Scripture inadequate to convey God's message.

Article XI

We affirm that translations of the text of Scripture can communicate knowledge of God across all temporal and cultural boundaries.

We deny that the meaning of biblical texts is so tied to the culture out of which they came that understanding of the same meaning in other cultures is impossible.

Article XII

We affirm that in the task of translating the Bible and teaching it in the context of each culture, only those functional equivalents which are faithful to the content of biblical teaching should be employed.

We deny the legitimacy of methods which either are insensitive to the demands of cross-cultural communication or distort biblical meaning in the process.

Article XIII

We affirm that awareness of the literary categories, formal and stylistic, of the various parts of Scripture is essential for proper exegesis, and hence we value genre criticism as one of the many disciplines of biblical study.

We deny that generic categories which negate historicity may rightly be imposed on biblical narratives which present themselves as factual.

Article XIV

We affirm that the biblical record of events, discourses and sayings, though presented in a variety of appropriate literary forms, corresponds to historical fact.

We deny that any event, discourse, or saying reported in Scripture was invented by the biblical writers or by the traditions they incorporated.

Article XV

We affirm the necessity of interpreting the Bible according to its literal, or normal, sense. The literal sense is the grammatical-historical sense, that is, the meaning which the writer expressed. Interpretation according to the literal sense will take account of all figures of speech and literary forms found in the test.

We deny the legitimacy of any approach to Scripture that attributes to it meaning which the literal sense does not support.

Article XVI

We affirm that legitimate critical techniques should be used in determining the canonical text and its meaning.

We deny the legitimacy of allowing any method of biblical criticism to question the truth or integrity of the writer's expressed meaning, or of any other scriptural teaching.

Article XVII

We affirm the unity, harmony, and consistency of Scripture and declare that it is its own best interpreter.

We deny that Scripture may be interpreted in such a way as to suggest that one passage corrects or militates against another. We deny that later writers of Scripture misinterpreted earlier passages of Scripture when quoting from or referring to them.

Article XVIII

We affirm that the Bible's own interpretation of itself is always correct, never deviating from, but rather elucidating, the single meaning of the inspired text. The single meaning of a prophet's words includes, but is not restricted to, the understanding of those words by the prophet and necessarily involves the intention of God evidenced in the fulfillment of those words.

We deny that the writers of Scripture always understood the full implications of their own words.

Article XIX

We affirm that any preunderstandings which the interpreter brings to Scripture should be in harmony with scriptural teaching and subject to correction by it.

We deny that Scripture should be required to fit alien preunderstandings, inconsistent with itself, such as naturalism, evolutionism, scientism, secular humanism, and relativism.

Article XX

We affirm that since God is the author of all truth, all truths, biblical and extrabiblical, are consistent and cohere, and that the Bible speaks truth when it touches on matters pertaining to nature, history, or anything less. We further affirm that in some cases extrabiblical dates have value for clarifying what Scripture teaches, and for prompting correction of faulty interpretations.

We deny that extrabiblical views ever disprove the teaching of Scripture or hold priority over it.

Article XXI

We affirm the harmony of special with general revelation and therefore of biblical teaching with the facts of nature.

We deny that any genuine scientific facts are inconsistent with the true meaning of any passage of Scripture.

Article XXII

We affirm that Genesis 1-11 is factual, as is the rest of the book.

We deny that the teachings of Genesis 1-11 are mythical and that scientific hypotheses about earth history or the origin of humanity may be invoked to overthrow what Scripture teaches about creation.

Article XXIII

We affirm the clarity of Scripture and specifically of its message about salvation from sin.

We deny that all passages of Scripture are equally clear or have equal bearing on the message of redemption.

Article XIV

We affirm that a person is not dependent for understanding of Scripture on the expertise of biblical scholars.

We deny that a person should ignore the fruits of the technical study of Scripture by biblical scholars.

Article XV

We affirm that the only type of preaching which sufficiently conveys the divine revelation and its proper application to life is that which faithfully expounds the text of Scripture as the Word of God.

We deny that the preacher has any message from God apart from the text of Scripture.

Index

U

Universal inspiration
        50, 52
Uriah 74

V

Voetius 57
Voltaire 194

W

Weiss 155
Wellhausen 157
Westcott, B. F. 34, 71,
        106, 157, 174
Wilson, Daniel 47–48
Woods, Leonard 48

Z

Zophar 72
Zumpt 154

Scripture Index